Patterns of Censorship
Around the World

Patterns of

CENSORSHIP

Around the World

edited by
ILAN PELEG

Westview Press
BOULDER • SAN FRANCISCO • OXFORD

Copyright © 1993 by Westview Press, Inc.

Published in 1993 in the United States of America by Westview Press, Inc., 5500 Central Avenue, Boulder, Colorado 80301-2877, and in the United Kingdom by Westview Press, 36 Lonsdale Road, Summertown, Oxford OX2 7EW

Library of Congress Cataloging-in-Publication Data
Patterns of censorship around the world / edited by Ilan Peleg.
       p. cm.
    Includes index.
    ISBN 0-8133-1185-3
    1. Censorship.   2. World Politics—1945– .   I. Peleg, Ilan, 1944– .
Z657.P28   1993
363.3'1—dc20
                                                                    92-32778
                                                                    CIP

Printed and bound in the United States of America

The paper used in this publication meets the requirements
of the American National Standard for Permanence of Paper
for Printed Library Materials Z39.48-1984.

10 9 8 7 6 5 4 3 2 1

To my wife, Sima,
for everything

Contents

PART 4
LIBERAL DEMOCRATIC SYSTEMS

PART 5
CONCLUSION

Preface

This volume addresses an important aspect in the political life of most societies today: limitations on freedom of expression and the existence of censorship. As a topic for research, study, and reflection—particularly in its comparative dimension—freedom of expression is a somewhat neglected area. The vast majority of studies in this field focus either on a specific aspect of freedom of expression or on a specific country. The current volume, however, assumes that there is much to be gained by studying freedom of expression and censorship practices broadly and comparatively. In a world grown small, global perspective is possible and beneficial, particularly when it is applied to an issue of great relevance for all societies.

As is probably the case with other books, the origins of this volume are to be found not in a purely intellectual endeavor but in an intensely personal experience. Over the past few years, in the process of doing my usual academic work, I twice encountered situations in which I was told that I would not be able to publish what I had written because of the *content* of the material. Although neither of these situations caused serious damage to my career, let alone my reputation, in both cases I felt violated—deprived of the fundamental right (and, to me, the obligation) to express my views freely and openly.

These personal encounters with censorship generated my interest in the topic reflected in this book. It is my conviction—shared by the other contributors—that freedom of expression is one of the most fundamental of all freedoms. Without freedom of expression, it seems, many other rights and freedoms are meaningless. Thus, how could the right of participation in the political life of one's country be meaningfully achieved unless one is free to receive the information and analysis pertinent for such participation?

In addition to the chapter contributors, I would like to thank a number of individuals for making this volume possible. Brian Walsh was an efficient, conscientious, and resourceful research assistant. Ruth Panovec proved once again to be diligent, effective, and patient in typing a complex manuscript. She was assisted by Rose Miller. Lafayette's Committee on Advanced Study and Research gave me the grants necessary for the timely completion of this work.

Ilan Peleg
Lafayette College
Easton, Pennsylvania

PART ONE

Introduction

1

Censorship in Global and Comparative Perspective: An Analytical Framework

Ilan Peleg

There is an interesting paradox in regard to freedom of expression. On the one hand, the right to free expression of one's opinions or ideas is one of the most universally recognized human rights in the contemporary world. On the other hand, this right is one of the most commonly violated ones; thus, the number of political systems denying people the right of free expression is much larger than the number of political systems respecting this right.

The task of this introductory chapter is to offer a preliminary, analytical approach for the systematic study of this paradox and for the inquiry of other dimensions of censorship and freedom of expression in today's world. Although the chapter refers to many incidents of censorship, these are included not in an attempt to study empirically the phenomenon of free expression but as examples of the type of issues that should be explored in an effort to understand the conditions of free expression in the contemporary world.

A series of important dimensions should be included in a study of censorship and free expression, especially when such study is conducted within a global and comparative framework: (1) the *international legal context* of censorship and freedom of expression, (2) the *methods* used to prevent free expression, and (3) the *objectives* of censorship. These are among some of the most interesting facets of the issue. In addition to specifics, however, one must identify a general approach to the topic at hand. This chapter offers such an approach, which sees censorship primarily as an instrument of power. It seems that censorship could best be studied by identifying regime types as environments for the development of limitations on free expression. Finally, the chapter offers some generalizations about censorship, but these should be understood as merely tentative and suggestive in nature.

Definition and Legal Context

Censorship can be defined in a variety of ways. Yet if one looks at this phenomenon in the contemporary world from a political perspective, the one adopted here, censorship could be defined as *the systematic control of the content of communication by a government through various means.*[1] There are a few important elements in this definition of censorship:

1. Censorship involves a systematic effort to control ideas and their communication to others: The intensity and comprehensiveness of this effort vary from one regime type to another, but censorship is always a behavioral pattern, not merely a separate incident.
2. Those who promote censorship, normally governments, do so because of the specific content of the ideas they are trying to control (although in some extreme cases all independent ideas, all creativity, and all individuality are suppressed).[2]
3. The methods and means used to control the "production" of ideas and their dissemination are many and extremely varied: legal, economic, physical, and so on. Also, these vary significantly from one regime to another.

Michael Scammell, an internationally recognized expert on censorship, views censorship as a political tool and limitations of freedom of expression as "an instrument to assist in the attainment, preservation or continuance of someone's power." For Scammell, censorship is merely "the extension of physical power into the realm of the mind and the spirit." He contributes to the comparative study of censorship when he states that "the more centralized the physical power and the more total its claims, the more intolerant, wide-ranging and complete the censorship will tend to be."[3]

The reality of censorship as a political tool used frequently and systematically by numerous governments is very different from the legal status of free expression in today's world, either in terms of the domestic law governing different societies or in terms of international law, including its human rights provisions. The international norms governing freedom of expression are very clear. Article 19 of the Universal Declaration of Human Rights (UDHR) states that "Everyone has the right to freedom of opinion and expression; this right includes freedom to hold opinions without interference and to seek, receive and impart information and ideas through any media regardless of frontiers."[4] Although the 1948 document is a declaration and not a binding treaty, it is widely regarded as having achieved the status of customary international law. As such, all governments of the world ought to be bound by the UDHR, including its unambiguous position on freedom of expression.

Numerous additional documents reiterate the UDHR's position on freedom of expression:

1. The International Covenant on Civil and Political Rights (ICCPR), also in Article 19, guarantees freedom of expression in all forms and media,

subject to certain restrictions relating to the rights and reputations of others (slander), protection of national security or public order, and considerations of public health or morals.[5]

2. A few regional (continental) documents also emphasize the "right to receive information" (African Charter on Human and People's Rights, Article 9), "freedom of thought and expression" (American Convention on Human Rights, Article 13),[6] and the right to hold opinions and to receive and impart information and ideas "without interference by public authority: (European Convention on Human Rights, Article 10).[7]

3. The Helsinki Final Act (1975) has sections dealing with improving the dissemination of information of all kinds and the working conditions of journalists.

Despite the inclusion of far-reaching, solid commitments to free expression in so many international documents and in numerous national constitutions, the reality of freedom of expression does not match the legal theory. Journalists and artists of all kinds have been a particular target of repression, sometimes as a class; they have been imprisoned, tortured, and even killed, and their works have been banned. It is interesting to note that censorship is by no means a new phenomenon: Every era has its Ovids, Dantes, and Solzhenitsyns.

Furthermore, various aspects of freedom of expression are often violated. Two such aspects are particularly noteworthy: (1) the right to express one's views and give information by all means and through any media and (2) the right to receive information, which is essential for the protection of other human rights and especially political rights. The right of expression and the right to receive information are closely linked and are, in fact, often violated together.

Censorship and Regime Types

If one wants to analyze censorship as a political instrument, one could do so effectively within the comprehensive framework of regime types. Limitations of freedom of expression are rarely imposed haphazardly: They are an outgrowth of patterns of social behavior, institutions, and political philosophies (that is, of regimes).

There are many meaningful ways to differentiate between and among regimes: one-party versus bi- or multiparty systems; military versus civilian regimes; unitary versus federal systems; monarchies versus republican states; fundamentalist/religious versus secular orders; developing versus developed countries, and so forth. Yet it seems (hypothetically) that for the purpose of dealing with the objectives and methods of censorship in the contemporary world, as well as of understanding the general role censorship plays in various countries today, it would be useful to adopt a rather traditional differentiation among totalitarian, authoritarian, and liberal democratic regimes. As true of all terminologies and classifications, this approach is not free of problems, but its usefulness seems to justify its employment in the analysis of freedom of expression within a comparative framework.

Totalitarian Regimes

There is no general agreement on what exactly totalitarianism, a twentieth-century term, means. Carl J. Friedrich and Zbigniew K. Brzezinski see it as a "syndrome" of six features.[8] Some of these features are extremely relevant for censorship: an official ideology, party control over all aspects of societal life (including mass communications), police terror, and the like. In short, a totalitarian regime is one that has an almost complete monopoly of power in the service of an ideology and a leader (or a small group of leaders). The totality of the control and the regime's penetration into all aspects of life give this regime type its name and general character.

Totalitarian regimes exhibit a tendency to monopolize under governmental control all means of effective mass communication, such as press, radio, and motion pictures.[9] Artistic control, and even more so control over journalists, tends to be systematic, comprehensive, organized from above, and rigidly imposed. In all totalitarian regimes, there is a "commitment to a single, positively formulated substantive goal,"[10] and all means are used to achieve this goal, including censorship and the suppression of all organizations or individuals not dedicated to the substantive goals of the regime.

Authoritarian Regimes

Some of the definitional problems plaguing "totalitarianism" also plague "authoritarianism." Nevertheless, for purposes of this study, a distinction between the two is useful. A authoritarian polity is one dominated by one individual or a small group, but the regime has not been successful (or maybe even interested) in controlling all aspects of life within the society. In authoritarian regimes, power is used exclusively, extensively, and arbitrarily by the rulers because (as in the case of totalitarianism) there is no division of power or a system of checks and balances (which characterize liberal democracy). Authoritarianism resembles totalitarianism in substantially restricting and even eliminating most or all civil liberties.[11] However, an authoritarian regime generally does not try to implement a revolutionary program, does not try to force through a new system of values in society, and does not try to implement a well-conceived, comprehensive ideology (e.g., Marxism-Leninism, national socialism, or fascism).

It could be useful to hypothesize that the approach of authoritarian regimes toward censorship tends to be different from that of totalitarian regimes. Although censorship is frequently used in both types of regimes, in an authoritarian order it is employed less comprehensively and enforced less systematically. Although terror and violence are also used in authoritarian society—sometimes even more than in a totalitarian society (which, having institutionalized censorship, does not frequently have to resort to violence)— they are deployed erratically and inconsistently. Moreover, in an authoritarian country, censorship is normally applied against explicit political acts or writing; in a totalitarian environment, the sanctions are applied in a much broader context, against any and all deviations from the prescribed order and the sacred truth of the regime.

Maybe the fundamental difference (as it relates to censorship) between a totalitarian and an authoritarian regime is that a totalitarian state is always associated with some sort of ideological superstructure:

> This ideology or political philosophy is presented in a more or less systematic and coherent manner explaining historical, social and political phenomena in the form of primitive theses and meaningless, universal, eternal "absolute truths." They are usually undeniable truisms connected in a chain of assertions which are presented . . . as a key to the kingdom of happiness . . . [and] as the answer to all the knotty questions posed by all other . . . philosophies.[12]

Since authoritarian regimes (for example, Pinochet's Chile, Marcos's Philippines, or Assad's Syria) do not have such limitless claim on truth, their policy on censorship tends to be less comprehensive, systematic, and sophisticated.

Liberal Democracy

One analyst described contemporary liberalism as a system that values the "free expression of individual personality" and subscribes to the "belief in men's ability to make that expression valuable to themselves and to society" and the "upholding of those institutions and policies that protect and foster both free expression and confidence in that freedom."[13] If this is the definition of liberalism and of liberal democracy, then censorship in such a system should exhibit operational patterns entirely different from those of either a totalitarian or authoritarian system. This distinction could lead to the hypothesis that in a liberal democracy, censorship and limitations on free expression are the exception, whereas they are the rule in the other two regime types. Moreover, many observers believe that although in liberal democratic systems, free expression is limited for very specific and primarily nonpolitical targets (e.g., slander, pornography), in the other two forms of government, censorship is applied in a much broader fashion and often in a manner that is thoroughly political. Finally, many also believe that in liberal democracy, limitations on free expression can be used within the confines of the law, but in the other systems, their application is considerably more arbitrary and often contradict the existing legal norms.

As will be clear from some of the chapters in this book, not everyone believes liberal democracy has really solved the issue of censorship.[14] Even the American system of free expression, which is libertarian to the extreme, is now under serious challenge.[15] The idea that the political debate in the United States is "largely an intramural contest between different wings of liberalism" is by no means universally accepted.[16]

Objectives of Censorship in Regime Types

The objectives in imposing limitation on freedom of expression vary significantly among the different regime types. Although similarities are not uncommon (after all, the function of censorship is often identical—to maintain power), differences seem to be more pronounced.

In a totalitarian polity the overarching goal of censorship is to eliminate all opposition not only to the rulers but also to the regime and to its political and social philosophy. It goes without saying that in a totalitarian environment, direct opposition to the regime is severely punished.[17] Yet censorship in a totaltiarian state is imposed not only on the expression of political challenge but on any description or analysis of reality that does not coincide with the beliefs the rulers want to promote. Werner Kastor-Volkmer wrote about Monika Mason's novels that they "cannot be published in East Germany, where she lives, not because she attacks socialism, but because her work, which presents the human individual, amid the impersonal machinery of modern lie, is too negative."[18] A totalitarian regime has no tolerance for direct attacks on its heads or its institutions and no tolerance for any description of societal reality that is not rosy and cheerful or, at least, generally positive.

Totalitarianism, as a comprehensive approach to politics, is extremely history-conscious. It seeks to use history as an instrument of the state: It promotes the manipulation of history books, and it imposes severe limitations on the publication of material that does not agree with government's historical interpretation. In the former USSR under Mikhail Gorbachev, there was a ongoing effort to free the society from seven decades of the control and manipulation of history. In the past, numerous individuals were severely penalized for deviating from the official Soviet version of history.[19]

In addition to these general goals of censorship in totalitarian countries, there are some more specific ones as well. For example, totalitarian regimes often suppress ethnic and nationalistic feelings by censoring or banning books suspected of encouraging such feelings.[20] Similarly, religion has often been a target for special treatment.[21] Thus, the totalitarian regime actively seeks to destroy all alternative sources of identity and loyalty.

In authoritarian countries, the objectives of censorship are usually considerably narrower than in totalitarian states. Since many of these regimes lack genuine legitimacy, they concentrate on crushing direct political dissent; at the same time, they focus much less on a more general, societal critique within the system. In Kuwait, for example, censorship is imposed (Printing and Publishing Law, 1961) on material considered an "incitement to hatred or overthrow of the system of government."[22] In Chile, a volume edited by Moy de Toha and Isabel Letelier, *Allende: Uncompromising Democrat*, was seized by government order in November 1986.[23]

In authoritarian societies, censorship is often imposed on any criticisms of the ruler{s}: In Iraq, insulting the president (or the authorities) is an offense punishable by death,[24] and in Morocco's Constitution (Article 23), any criticism of the king is forbidden.[25] The censorship is often imposed on rather specific positions. Thus, the Nobel Prize–winning author Najib Mahfūz (an

Egyptian) had many of his works banned throughout the Middle East because he supported the Camp David Accords.[26]

Moreover, authoritarian regimes tend to use censorship as a tool to conceal their own questionable deeds or illegal actions. Thus, the Taiwanese police seized all copies of a book by Hung Chih-liang in which he exposed a fabricated trial designed to destroy opposition leader Huang Hsin-chich and seven others.[27] Similarly, the Chilean secret police confiscated books dealing with the investigation of the attempt on Augusto Pinochet's life.[28]

Many authoritarian regimes, especially in traditional societies, focus their censorship efforts on curbing material considered blasphemous (a campaign reaching a peak with the publication of Salman Rushdie's *Satanic Verses*) or indecent. Often the focus is, as in totalitarian regimes, on quelling material of ethnic or nationalistic character.

Liberal democracies seem to have censorship objectives that are narrower than those of either totalitarian or authoritarian regimes. On rare occasions, there is censorship in the interest of maintaining the democratic regime. Thus, the Federal Republic of Germany banned the book *Das Info: Briefe Gefangenen aus der RAF aus der diskussion,* explaining that it was "written in the interests of a still existing terrorist organization [Red Army faction]."[29] Public order is also used sometimes to justify a limitation on books. France's Interior Ministry has banned the book *Euskadi gidan* (Basque country at war) because it considers it a threat to public order.

In some democracies, there are unwritten rules of censorship (and self-censorship) that prevent the media from discussing certain topics. In Japan, for example, the media would not criticize the royal family, would not condemn the exploitation of certain people (the Burakumin outcast, the native Ainu people, the Koreans, and the Okinawans), and would not expose the relationships between gangsters and politicians.[30]

Like other societies, liberal democracies are willing to censor material that is sensitive from the point of view of national security,[31] widely considered indecent or obscene,[32] or deemed defamatory material.[33] Some liberal democracies display particular intolerance toward material considered unusually dangerous to children or threatening to racial or ethnic harmony.[34]

Methods of Censorship in Regime Types

Regimes vary not only in the objectives they pursue through censorship but also in the methods they employ in achieving these objectives.

Totalitarianism routinely uses tough policies, which occasionally include violence against authors. (In contrast, liberal democracies, in the rare situations in which they use censorship, prefer to ban a specific work.) In numerous cases under totalitarianism, authors lose their right or opportunity to publish: If an author falls out of the government's grace, he or she may never publish again; though physical violence is not frequently used. Examples of long-term banning abound: Marek Nowakowslki in Poland,[35] Vaclav Havel in Czechoslovakia,[36] Mihajlo Mihajlov in Yugoslavia.[37]

Author banning in a totalitarian country may take many forms: banning an author's entire body of work,[38] expelling an author from the country or from the writers union,[39] refusing the author permission to reenter the country, forcing an author to flee the country, and so forth.[40]

Book banning is also quite common in totalitarian regimes. These regimes prefer completely to restrict printing and distribution before publication (whereas other systems, such as liberal democracies, may ban a book after publication). As recently as December 12, 1988, a Belgrade court banned Vojislav Seselj's *A Plea for a Democratic Constitution* on the grounds that it would be harmful to Yugoslavia's reputation.[41] Totalitarian regimes have often banned not only specific manuscripts but also oppressed groups of artists considered dangerous. For example, on March 23, 1983, the Hungarian police raided the homes of six dissident intellectuals deemed to be cosympathizers and confiscated a large quantity of books and manuscripts.[42]

Totalitarian governments have at their disposal a wide variety of economic means for silencing opponents, and these options have been used extensively. Expelling an author from the writers union could very well mean that the person will never again publish in the society where the government is in full control of the economy in general and the publishing business in particular. Thus, the Romanian poet Dorin Tudorin was dismissed as editor of the country's literary magazine *Lucafarul* and banned from publishing.[43] Totalitarian regimes can also control publication by restricting the supply of paper and newsprint.[44]

Possibly the most commonly used punishment by totalitarian governments is the imprisonment of writers. Communist countries have used this method for silencing authors rather routinely; examples include the former USSR,[45] Romania,[46] and China.[47] Other methods for warning writers or stopping them completely include intimidation through threat, terror, and interrogations;[48] Czech playwright (later President) Vaclav Havel was put under round-the-clock police surveillance.[49] Some authors are banned from traveling abroad as a punishment and as a method designed to prevent them from garnering international publicity.[50] Others have been stripped of their citizenship. As a general method of controlling information and expression, totalitarian regimes have even imposed restrictions on access to libraries and imposed strict limitations on the possession and use of typewriters and copy machines.

Authoritarian regimes use some of the methods used by totalitarian regimes but in different degrees. Because authoritarian regimes allocate fewer resources to censorship than do totalitarian regimes and their efforts in this field are generally less comprehensive, they often tend to ban authors rather than books. It is easier to ban suspected authors completely than to examine each individual work. In postrevolutionary Iran, no fewer than 4,350 writers have been on an official blacklist.[51] In Indonesia, the well-known novelist Toer has been banned for nearly a decade.[52]

Since authoritarian regimes often use violence against their opponents, writers have a tendency to flee and to seek exile in places where they can write freely. About 300–400 Iranian authors fled the country after Khomeini's takeover.[53] Kenya's foremost writer, Ngugi wa Thiong'o, has been forced to live in exile since mid-1982,[54] as has the poet Frank Chipasula of Malawi.[55]

Banning, burning, and confiscation of books are also quite common in authoritarian states, but the books attacked tend to be highly political and perceived as direct challenges to the ruler{s} in power. For example, in Chile, books about the life and murder of President Salvador Allende were banned,[56] and other books considered subversive meet a similar fate—in 1986, 14,000 copies of Colombian novelist Gabriel Garcia Marquez's *Miguel Littin's Undercover Adventure in Chile* were burned on their arrival at the port of Valparaiso.[57] In Taiwan, the original manuscript of the memoirs of Lei Chen (a prominent political leader and dissident who has become disenchanted with Taiwan's one-party system) was burned in April 1988 at a military prison.[58] In Turkey, the authorities have cracked down on booksellers from time to time and confiscated thousands of books.[59] And in Paraguay, copies of a book by the journalist Alcibiades Gonzalez Delvalle, *Mi voto por el pueblo* (My vote for the people), which had been published in Argentina, were confiscated at the Paraguayan border in October 1984.[60]

Obviously, authoritarian regimes have also gone quite beyond banning specific books and authors: Some have resorted to murder as a means for silencing writers. Interestingly, totalitarian regimes have used killings less frequently than authoritarian ones, possibly because they have found more gentle but more comprehensive methods to establish effective censorship. The Iranian Writers Association in Exile, which is based in Paris, documented the death of thirty-nine of its members, some executed after quick trial and others without any legal proceedings. The assassinations included many publishers and editors killed mostly in London and Paris.[61] Within this context, Iran's threats on the life of Salman Rushdie are not too difficult to comprehend.

Iraq has also adopted a severe censorship policy that can entail executions. Under the Iraqi penal code, a death penalty can be given to anyone insulting the president of the republic "or those who are acting on his behalf."[62] Raad Mushatat reported in *Index on Censorship* that in the Iraqi army, one is allowed to read only government newspapers and magazines: "If they find any other literature on you, even harmless material such as Tolstoy or Walt Whitman, you can be accused of circulating anti-state literature and executed."[63]

In numerous authoritarian countries, writers are not executed following a trial—they simply disappear. International PEN's Writers in Prison Committee reported for years on the disappearance of writers,[64] as have *Index on Censorship*[65] and Amnesty International. Less dramatic means of punishing authors include imprisonment, intimidation (through threats and interrogations), torture during arrest, travel restrictions, and an assortment of economic sanctions (e.g., dismissals from work, limitations on paper supply to publishers).

In terms of the methods of censorship employed by liberal democracies, it is important to note that these types of regimes use limitations on expression much more sparingly than other types, and mostly within the confines of a law that endorses, as a matter of principle, freedom of expression with only minimal exceptions.

In general, liberal democracies tend to ban a book and not an author. If there is a ban on a book, which is a rare event, it does not apply to other books by the same author. Books are banned only for very serious reasons (from the perspective of the particular society): Red Army–faction terrorism in Germany, obscene material in Ireland, and the like.

Imprisonment of writers, editors, or publishers in democracies is rare but not unheard of. Ernest Zundel, a Canadian publisher, was sent to prison for nine months for publishing an overtly anti-Semitic book.[66] Yet in this case, as occurs in most other liberal democracies, the government implemented its censorship through the court system. Thus, the British government conducted a full-fledged judicial battle to stop the publication of *Spycatcher*,[67] and the U.S. government did the same in regard to books by Frank Snepp.[68] According to the British and American governments, these books endangered national security.

Conclusion

The preceding description of censorship in the various regime types should be viewed only as general hypotheses regarding existing conditions—not as a final picture of what the status of free expression is or an explanation for it. The regime types should be understood as the environments that determine the form and intensity of censorship in a particular society. Alternatively, it is legitimate to hypothesize that both the overall regime type and the existing censorship pattern are merely reflections of conditions determined by a third factor: the dominant culture of the society.

At this preliminary stage, it is clear that censorship can be understood politically and that it varies significantly from one society to another in terms of its objectives and methods. In a totalitarian society, censorship is often based on the rulers' belief that absolute truth is on their side. Prepublication censorship dominates and is managed by a web of state agencies that zealously watch over the artistic and journalistic communities. The existing censorship laws are strict, and violations lead to heavy penalties. In a totalitarian state, rights are clearly above the individual's rights—and nowhere is that clearer than in the area of free expression.

Censorship in authoritarian regimes seems to be an inherent characteristic of the political system. Yet the objectives and the modes of control are somewhat different than in totalitarianism, in that the objectives are significantly less comprehensive and the methods are less consistent, although not necessarily less harsh.

In liberal democracies, limitations on the freedom of expression tend to be different from those in either totalitarian or authoritarian regimes. The reasons for imposing censorship are generally well defined and relatively narrow: As a rule, the restrictions do not prevent lively political debate on public policy issues. Nevertheless, in liberal democracies (especially of the American type), censorship is frequently initiated by private citizens or organizations rather than the government, and it would be a mistake to assume that censorship does not exist.

These generalizations are offered here as mere hypotheses; the remaining chapters in the book examine their applicability in the real world. These chapters deal with a series of case studies of totalitarian, authoritarian, and liberal democratic governments. They should enhance our understanding of censorship and free expression.

Notes

I would like to thank Brian Walsh for his invaluable assistance in the research resulting in this chapter. Thanks are also due to the Committee on Advanced Study and Research of Lafayette College.

1. Michael Scammell, "Censorship and Its History—A Personal View," in Kevin Boyle, ed., *Article 19: Information, Freedom, and Censorship (World Report 1988)* (New York: Times Books, 1988), p. 10 (cited hereafter as *Article 19*).

2. Zhdanovism under Stalin had this character, and in Kampuchea under the Khmer Rouge this seemed to be the policy.

3. Scammell, "Censorship," p. 5.

4. For the text of the UDHR, see *The International Bill of Human Rights* (Glen Ellen, CA: Entwhistle, 1981), pp. 3–12.

5. For the text of the ICCPR, see *ibid.*, pp. 31–64.

6. *Ibid.*, p. 86.

7. *Ibid.*, p. 73. Also, the International Convention on the Elimination of All Forms of Racial Discrimination, especially Article 5(d)(viii), deals with the right of expression.

8. Carl J. Friedrich and Zbigniew K. Brzezinski, *Totalitarian Dictatorship and Autocracy* (Cambridge, MA: Harvard University Press, 1956).

9. American Academy of Arts and Sciences, Carl J. Friedrich, ed., *Totalitarianism* (Cambridge, MA: Harvard University Press, 1954).

10. Herbert T. Spiro. "Totalitarianism," in *International Encyclopedia of the Social Sciences* (New York: Macmillan, 1933), Vol. 16, p. 108.

11. Otto Stammer, "Dictatorship," in *ibid.*, Vol. 4, p. 161.

12. Mieczyslav Maneli, *Freedom and Tolerance* (New York: Octagon, 1984), p. 296.

13. David G. Smith, "Liberalism," in *International Encyclopedia of the Social Sciences,* Vol. 9, p. 276.

14. See for example, Chapter 12.

15. See, for example, Chapter 10.

16. Terrence Ball and Richard Dagger, "The 'L-Word': A Short History of Liberalism," *Political Science Teacher,* Vol. 3, no. 1, Winter 1990, p. 5.

17. Professor Nicolae Stoia, whose book *Adevarul* was critical of President Nicolae Ceaușescu's regime in Romania, disappeared after his arrest in 1984. *Index on Censorship,* January 1988, Vol. 17, no. 1, p. 39 (cited hereafter as *Index*).

18. *Index,* April 1987, Vol. 16, no. 4, p. 9.

19. For example, Yuri Badyzo, who wrote a 1,400-page account of cultural conditions in the Ukraine (International PEN Writers in Prison Committee, July 1988 report, p. 41); or Mikhail Zhikharyev, whose samizdat book *The Great Swindle* exposed the corruption of local authorities (*Violations of the Helsinki Accords*: USSR, November 1988, pp. 37–38).

20. In the former USSR, nationalistic feelings in the Baltic republics were a target for censorship for many years (e.g., Mart Niklus in Estonia, see *Index,*

January 1988, Vol. 17, no. 1, p. 28); and Albanian writers have been targeted in Yugoslavia (*Index*, July-August 1987, Vol. 16, no. 7, p. 40), etc.

21. *Index*, April 1985, Vol. 14, no. 2, p. 57.

22. *Article 19*, pp. 271–272; for censorship of the poetry of Abdulle Raze Taraweh in Somalia, see *Index*, February 1987, Vol. 16, no. 2, p. 3.

23. *Index*, February 1987, Vol. 16, no. 2, p. 23.

24. *Article 19*, p. 258.

25. *Ibid.*, p. 276.

26. *Index*, January 1989, Vol. 18, no. 1, p. 14.

27. *Index*, January 1986, Vol. 15, no. 1, p. 35.

28. *Index*, March 1987, Vol. 16, no. 3, p. 37.

29. *Index*, January 1988, Vol. 17, no. 1, p. 37.

30. Recently a book coauthored by David Kaplan and entitled *Yakuza: The Explosive Account of Japan's Criminal Underworld* was refused publication by Japan's publishing houses even though it was published in six other languages. The book deals with the link between politicians and gangsters in Japan.

31. In both the United States and the United Kingdom, former members of the security forces may not publish their memoirs at will. See *Index*, June 1980, Vol. 9, no. 3, p. 70 re Phillip Agee's books; also *Index*, November-December 1987, Vol. 17, no. 7, p. 7. Some democracies use prepublication censorship when national security is at issue.

32. *Article 19*, p. 71, re Canada. For Ireland's tough policy on sexual morality, see *ibid.*, p. 194, or *Article 19 Bulletin*, Issue 1, August-September 1987, p. 2.

33. *Article 19*, p. 69 (Canada), pp. 178–179 (Denmark), and pp. 282–283 (Australia); *Index*, August 1988, Vol. 17, no. 7, p. 34 (France), are only some examples.

34. In Canada, publisher Ernest Zundel was sentenced to nine months' imprisonment for publishing anti-Semitic material (*Index*, June-July 1988, Vol. 17, no. 6, p. 35), and Arthur Butz's book *Hoax of the Twentieth Century* has been banned from being imported. West Germany also has a similar policy.

35. *Index*, October 1986, Vol. 15, no. 9, p. 15.

36. *Index*, November-December 1986, Vol. 15, no. 10, p. 19.

37. *Index*, Spring 1972, Vol. 1, no. 1, p. 91.

38. Vaclav Havel, Boris Pasternak, Aleksandr Solzhenitsyn, and other well-known literary figures received such a treatment.

39. For the USSR, see *Index*, September-October 1979, Vol. 8, no. 4, p. 71, or *Index*, Autumn 1973, Vol. 2, no. 3, p. ix; for Hungary, see *Violations of the Helsinki Accords: Hungary*, p. 17 (the case of Gaspar Nagy, who was expelled from the Union of Writers for writing a poem that mentioned the execution of Imre Nagy in 1956).

40. Igor Pomerantsev had to flee the USSR under KGB pressure for "spreading anti-Soviet propaganda." See *Index*, March 1986, Vol. 15, no. 3, pp. 13–14.

41. *Index*, February 1989, Vol. 18, no. 2, p. 41.

42. *Index*, August 1983, Vol. 12, no. 4, p. 41.

43. *Violation of the Helsinki Accords: Romania*, p. 16.

44. *Article 19, Freedom of Information and Expression in Romania* (London, 1987), p. 18; *Index*, August 1985, Vol. 14, no. 4, p. 2.

45. *Index*, January 1988, Vol. 17, no. 1, p. 28, re Mart Niklus, the Estonian writer.

46. *Ibid.*, p. 39, re Nicelae Stoia.

47. *Index*, November-December 1988, Vol. 17, no. 10, p. 26.

48. See the case of the Czech writer Bohmil Hrabal in *Index*, January 1988, Vol. 17, no. 1, p. 15; or that of Filip Tabacaruc, a Romanian Baptist, in *Index*, May 1988, Vol. 17, no. 5, p. 129.

49. *Index*, February 1987, Vol. 16, no. 2, p. 37.

50. U.S. Helsinki Watch Committee, *Yugoslavia: Freedom to Conform* (New York, 1982), p. 16; *Index*, October 1986, Vol. 15, no. 9, p. 50, re the Polish poet Luther Herbst; *Index*, January-February 1978, Vol. 7, no. 1, p. 68, re Hungarian writer Miklos Haraszti.

51. *Index*, May-June 1989, Vol. 18, no. 5, p. 7.

52. International PEN Writers in Prison Committee, July 1988 report, pp. 12–13.

53. *Article 19*, pp. 253–254, 259.

54. *Ibid.*, p. 35.

55. *Index*, February 1988, Vol. 17, no. 2, p. 22.

56. *Index*, February 1987, Vol. 16, no. 2.

57. *Article 19*, p. 76; *Index*, March 1987, Vol. 16, no. 3, p. 37.

58. *Index*, October 1988, Vol. 17, no. 9, pp. 40–41.

59. *Index*, September 1987, Vol. 16, no. 8, p. 36.

60. *Index*, January 1985, Vol. 14, no. 1, p. 63.

61. *Article 19*, pp. 253–255.

62. *Ibid.*, p. 258.

63. *Index*, February 1986, Vol. 15, no. 2, p. 29.

64. See, for example, International PEN Writers in Prison Committee, July 1988 report on Ethiopia and El Salvador, pp. 10–11.

65. Many disappearances in Argentina were reported. See, e.g., *Index*, October 1981, Vol. 10, no. 5, p. 43.

66. *Index*, June-July 1988, Vol. 17, no. 6, p. 35.

67. *Article 19*, p. 234, on the legal proceedings in Australia; *Index*, February 1988, Vol. 17, no. 2, p. 34, on the legal proceedings in New Zealand.

68. *Index*, July-August 1979, Vol. 8, no. 4, p. 70.

2

Censorship and Language Taboos: The Supreme Court's Flying Circus

Scot A. Duvall

Within our society, language is the primary way in which persons interact with one another.[1] In serving as a mechanism for communication, language enables us to conceive and express our thoughts.[2] Accordingly, the language we use helps shape both our thought and our society.[3] In essence, language "serves . . . as a guide to social reality."[4] If we are to maximize our potential for freedom in American society, we need to recognize the important role language plays in communicating our emotions and beliefs and in exercising our political autonomy. When interpreting the First Amendment, the United States Supreme Court generally has failed to recognize that persons use differing styles of language to convey different messages or to target such messages to a specific group of individuals. Persons can also use similar styles with differing motives. Instead, the Court has conceived a rhetoric-ideology of "freedom of speech" that exalts mainstream methods of communication but enervates less conventional techniques of expression.[5] As a result, the Court in its opinions tends directly to disparage persons outside the political mainstream and to suppress speech by or meant for such persons.[6]

The Role of Language Taboos in Communication

Euphemisms enable us to communicate about unpleasant or unflattering things without sounding too blunt or too scientific.[7] The British comedy troupe Monty Python provides us with an instructive example of the use (and misuse) of euphemisms. The "Chemist Sketch" on *Monty Python's Flying Circus* involved a pharmacist using euphemisms while dispensing prescriptions:[8]

> A number of men and women are sitting around in an area by the counter where there is a large sign saying "Dispensing Department." A cheerful chemist appears at the counter.
>
> *Chemist:* Right. I've got some of your prescriptions here. Er, who's got the pox? (*Nobody reacts*). . . . Come on, who's got the pox . . . come on . . . (*A*

man timidly puts his hand up) . . . there you go. (*Throws bottle to the man with his hand up*) Who's got the boil on the bum . . . boil on the botty? (*Throws bottle to the only man standing up*) Who's got the chest rash? (*Woman with a large bosom puts up hand*) Have to get a bigger bottle. Who's got wind? (*Throws bottle to a man sitting on his own*) Catch.

Caption: THE CHEMIST SKETCH—AN APOLOGY

Voice-over: The BBC would like to apologize for the poor quality of the writing in that sketch. It is not BBC policy to get easy laughs with words like bum, knickers, botty or wee-wees. (*Laughs off camera*) Ssssh!

(*Cut to a man standing by a screen with a clicker*)

BBC Man: These are the words that are not to be used again on this programme. (*He clicks the clicker. On screen appear the following slides:*

B*M
B*TTY
P*X
KN*CKERS
W**-W**
SEMPRINI

A girl comes into shot.)

Girl: Semprini!?

BBC Man: (*Pointing*) Out!!

(*Cut back to the chemist's shop. The chemist appears again.*)

Chemist: Right, who's got a boil on his Semprini, then?

(*A policeman appears and bundles him off.*)

Note that most of the words "not to be used again" contained asterisks to avoid printing the entire word. This is known as "bowdlerizing," a term named after Thomas Bowdler, who in 1818 edited the plays of William Shakespeare so that families could read his works together at home.[9] The effect of bowdlerizing is not only to convey the "taboo" word[10] but to convey that the *actual* word (if spelled out completely) is somehow unspeakable (or unprintable). Hence, the complete spelling of "Semprini" in the list of words is instructive. Because the audience had not yet heard the word used on the program, it was necessary to spell out the entire word to let them know exactly what word was taboo. But in doing so, the hypothetical BBC is forced to be hypocritical, breaking the taboo while establishing it. Bowdlerizing seems to be nothing but a cheap way to avoid looking like a hypocrite, enabling us to inform others of the taboo while honoring the taboo at the same time.

The "Chemist Sketch" takes a jab at censorship—the Pythons demonstrate that if it is taken to extremes, government can go too far in regulating the words we hear.[11] Furthermore, the sketch highlights the silly results that occur if we declare words taboo solely because they sound funny or, worse, because they produce a laugh. As already mentioned, that is the purpose of euphemisms—to enable us to communicate about unpleasant things without being *too* disturbing. However, the sketch also demonstrates that resorting to euphemisms may be no more desirable than using a neutral or even a coarse-sounding word. Some euphemisms (such as "botty," "wee-wee," or "pee-pee") are so soft or cute-sounding that we are uncomfortable using them in ordinary discourse. In light of this observation, it is appropriate to consider the important role that coarse-sounding language plays in our communication with others.

In contrast to euphemisms, which tend to be respectful, refined, and softened words, cacophemisms tend to be blunt and coarse words that enable people to express disrespect for societal norms.[12] Cacophemisms generally communicate in the same way that obscenities do—they shock the unprepared listener.[13] Using a cacophemism can make other persons anxious or uneasy because use of the cacophemism violates taboos against speaking certain sounds or writing certain words.[14] As such, cacophemisms are an important, if not exclusive, means to convey certain ideas. Cacophemisms tend not to express positive attitudes but negative or self-serving ones.[15] By using cacophemisms, communicators call attention to themselves and express disrespect toward certain societal norms or the subject being communicated.[16] Hence, the cacophemistic communicator can convey feelings such as "deep expression, counter-evocation, suppression of pain and conquest of fear, [and] the disowning of assumed pieties."[17] Yet the use of such cacophemisms does not necessarily require some negative impact upon the listener. Indeed, some persons use cacophemisms as a shortcut means of communication. If a person's philosophy is to tell it like it is, cacophemisms can effectively communicate to the listener that the communicator is a "straight shooter."[18]

George Carlin has provided us with an instructive example of employing cacophemisms to communicate a message. In his "Filthy Words" monologue, Carlin discusses words that were taboo for broadcast:[19]

> I was thinking one night about the words you couldn't say on the public . . . airwaves. . . . The original seven words were shit, piss, fuck, cunt, cocksucker, motherfucker, and tits. Those are the ones that will curve your spine, grow hair on your hands and (laughter), maybe even bring us, God help us, peace without honor (laughter). . . . ***The big one, the word fuck [—]that's the one that hangs them up the most. . . . It's a great word, fuck, nice word, easy word, cute word, kind of. Easy word to say. One syllable, short u. Fuck. . . . Kind of a proud word, too. Who are you? I am FUCK, FUCK OF THE MOUNTAIN. (laughter) . . . It leads a double life, the word fuck. First of all, it means, sometimes, most of the time, fuck. What does it mean? It means to make love. . . . Right? And it also means the beginning of life, it's the act that begins life, so there's the word hanging around with words like love, and life, and yet on the other hand, it's also a word that we really use to hurt each other with, man. It's a heavy. . . . It would be nice to change the motives that we already have and substitute the word fuck for the word kill, wherever we could, and some of those movie cliches would change a little bit. Madfuckers still on the loose. Stop me before I fuck again. Fuck the ump, fuck the ump, fuck the ump. Easy on the clutch Bill, you'll fuck that engine again. . . . ***I found three more words that had to be put on the list of words you could never

say on television, and they were fart, turd and twat, those three. (laughter) . . . Fart, . . . it's harmless. It's like tits, it's a cutie word, no problem. Turd, you can't say but who wants to, you know? . . . Twat is an interesting word because it's the only one I know of, the only slang word applying to : . . . a part of the sexual anatomy that doesn't have another meaning to it. Like, ah, snatch, box and pussy all have other meanings, man. Even in a Walt Disney movie, you can say, We're going to snatch that pussy and put him in a box and bring him on the airplane. . . . Everybody loves it.

Carlin's monologue[20] is the ultimate in cacophemism: He not only expresses disrespect for societal norms but also disrespect for societal norms *about language.* Carlin also brings to light a common characteristic of most cacophemisms—they are blunt-sounding. But we do not respond negatively to names like "Mack," "Mark," "Mike," "Nick," "Rick," or "Dick"—if we did not already know that "fuck" was one of those words that are taboo, and we met someone called "Fuck," we probably would not know the difference. Moreover, Carlin indicates that some cacophemisms, such as "fart," "turd," and "twat," might be tabooed merely because they *sound* embarrassing, as in the case of the euphemisms "botty," "wee-wee," and the nonsense word "Semprini." Accordingly, some words with dual meanings, which might be taboo given the "right" context, pose no problem because they just do not sound embarrassing.

In contrast to cacophemisms, which tend to express attitudes of disrespect for societal norms or the subject being communicated, disphemisms (which tend to be pejorative and derogatory words) generally indicate the communicator's contempt, dislike, or prejudice for a particular person, group, or thing.[21] It is important to note that Carlin admits to the dual role of a cacophemism like "fuck" as a means to express contempt for someone when used in the context of an argument; all that is needed is to add the pronoun "you." In this sense, "fuck" operates as a disphemism. The *Monty Python* sketch "Prejudice" provides an example of disphemisms. The sketch takes the form of a television program in which bigotry is pervasive. The host does not hold back one bit. Early on, we can discern the contempt he has for different ethnic groups:[22]

Braddon: Good evening and welcome to another edition of 'Prejudice'—the show that gives you a chance to have a go at Wops, Krauts, Nigs, Eyeties, Gippos, Bubbles, Froggies, Chinks, Yidds, Jocks, Polacks, Paddies and Dagoes. (Fake applause)

Superimposed caption: ALL FACTS VERIFIED BY THE RHODESIAN POLICE

Braddon: ***Well now, the result of last week's competition when we asked you to find a derogatory term for the Belgians. Well, the response was enormous and we took quite a long time sorting out the winners. There were some very clever entries. Mrs. Hatred of Leicester said "Let's not call them anything, let's just ignore them" . . . and a Mr. St. John of Huntingdon said he couldn't think of anything more derogatory than Belgians. . . . But in the end we settled on three choices: number three . . . the Sprouts . . . sent in by Mrs. Vicious of Hastings . . . very nice; number two . . . the Phlegms . . . from Mrs. Childmolester of Worthing; but the winner was

undoubtedly from Mrs. No-Supper-For-You from Norwood in Lancashire
. . . Miserable Fat Belgian Bastards.

To be sure, the host's long list of ethnic groups is *intended* to communicate
the prejudice that the host and the audience have for them. Yet the sketch is
humorous. The long succession of insulting characterizations *sounds* funny.
The "Prejudice" sketch is a clear example of how the overuse of disphemistic
terms can evoke genuine laughter. The Pythons enable us to see how silly such
characterizations really are.[23]

The "Prejudice" sketch also demonstrates how the human imagination
(almost endlessly) can conceive derogatory terms. Take, for example, the clever
entry "the Sprouts." That term obviously is a play on "brussels sprouts"—a
vegetable children typically abhor—and the fact that Brussels is the capital of
Belgium. Nevertheless, if the term catches on within the culture, the term
would evolve into a bona fide epithet. The term "Kraut," derogatory when
describing Germans, most likely was derived from sauerkraut, a traditional food
of the German-speaking peoples. Hence, the "Prejudice" sketch demonstrates
our potential to come up with new disphemisms.

The winning entry, "Miserable Fat Belgian Bastards," is the most effective
epithet—we can tell that it is deliberately insulting and not at all clever. The
phrase is immediately effective as an epithet. We know exactly how the
communicator feels about Belgians. Whether Belgians actually tend to be fat or
to be miserable, or tend toward illegitimacy in childbirth is wholly beside the
point. Hence, "Miserable Fat Belgian Bastards" gets first place, hands-down. ☛

Thrashing a Few Cases: The Supreme Court's Flying Circus

FCC v. Pacifica Foundation

Around 2 P.M. on October 30, 1973, a New York radio station owned by
Pacifica Foundation broadcast the George Carlin "Filthy Words" monologue as
part of a program about contemporary society's attitude toward language.[24] A
man and his young son heard portions of the twelve-minute monologue,[25] and
the man complained a few weeks later to the FCC.[26] In February 1975, the
FCC did not impose a formal sanction against Pacifica, but noted that Pacifica
could have been subject to administrative sanctions.[27] Accordingly, the FCC
reserved the right to sanction Pacifica at a later date.[28] Moreover, the FCC
characterized the language used by Carlin as "patently offensive" and determined
that such speech should be regulated by principles similar to those of nuisance
law,[29] principles that would justify requiring such material to be broadcast at
other times of the day.[30] The FCC concluded that the language as broadcast was
"indecent" and prohibited by federal statute.[31]

The United States Supreme Court reviewed the FCC's ruling that the Carlin
monologue was indecent.[32] Noting that "indecent" merely refers to
"nonconformance with accepted standards of morality,"[33] the Court
distinguished that term from "obscene" and determined that no "prurient appeal"
was necessary for speech to be "indecent" under the terms of the statute.[34]

Hence, the Court agreed with the FCC that the language broadcast was indecent.[35] Moreover, the Court noted that the broadcasting of patently offensive references to excretory and sexual organs and activities "surely lies at the periphery of First Amendment concern."[36]

The Court then determined that the FCC's action in holding that Pacifica violated the federal statute was constitutional.[37] The Court justified the FCC's control of patently offensive and indecent content on two grounds: First, because the broadcast of such material confronts citizens not only in public but also in their homes, regulation was appropriate to protect "the individual's right to be left alone."[38] Second, because broadcasting is "uniquely accessible to children" regardless of any ability to read, the Pacifica broadcast could "[enlarge] a child's vocabulary in an instant."[39] The Court noted that the government's interest in the well-being of its youth and in supporting parental authority at home justified the FCC's regulation of otherwise protected expression.[40]

The *Pacifica* court seems to believe that the use of such words as old as "cunt" and "piss" are somehow unworthy of First Amendment protection.[41] Similarly, the Court ignores that a cacophemism like "fuck" has emotive meaning. There is no other way to express "fuck" but to say or write "fuck."[42] Indeed, that is why the word is taboo; the word has an inherent emotional charge to it. The Court's avowed interest in "social order and morality" converts to an interest in "form over substance"—a concept that is anathema to individual expression.

Further, the *Pacifica* court seems to be interested in protecting children from hearing sexually oriented language. This concern demonstrates a fundamental misunderstanding of how children tend to develop and use such language:

> There is a widespread belief . . . that children enjoy scatological and sexual humor of both the verbal and nonverbal varieties. . . . Depending on a society's attitudes, children's curiosity regarding body waste and sex may be repressed, encouraged, or satisfied in a casual way. The prevalence of scatological and sexual humor among children in any society may be closely related to that society's attitudes and to the resulting child-rearing practices.[43]

Adolescents are known to engage in scatological insults and to use taboo words.[44] Moreover, before children master the niceties of the English language, they create their own language, incomprehensible to adults.[45] The Court's concern about enlarging the vocabulary of children, who generally already know and use such words, is unwarranted.[46] Arguably, it is the parents who should determine their children's exposure to "filthy words."[47]

Bethel School District v. *Fraser*

On April 26, 1983, Matthew Fraser nominated a fellow student for elective office at their high school in Pierce County, Washington, during a school assembly.[48] Fraser's clever speech employed sexual double entendre:

> I know a man who is firm—he's firm in his pants, he's firm in his shirt, his character is firm—but most . . . of all, his belief in you, the students of

Bethel, is firm. Jeff Kuhlman is a man who takes his point and pounds it in. If necessary, he'll take an issue and nail it to the wall. He doesn't attack things in spurts—he drives hard, pushing and pushing until finally—he succeeds. Jeff is a man who will go to the very end—even the climax, for each and every one of you. So vote for Jeff for A.S.B. vice-president—he'll never come between you and your best our high school can be.[49]

The following morning, the assistant principal called Fraser into her office and told him that the school considered Fraser's speech a violation of Bethel's disciplinary rule prohibiting the use of certain language.[50] After Fraser admitted his deliberate use of sexual innuendo, he was suspended from school for three days and his name was removed from the list of candidates to speak at the school's graduation ceremonies.[51] Fraser appealed the disciplinary action, but to no avail.[52] Fraser served two days of his suspension and was allowed to return to school in the third day.[53]

Fraser sued in federal district court, alleging a violation of his First Amendment rights and seeking injunctive relief and monetary damages under 42 U.S.C. § 1983, the federal civil rights statute.[54] Fraser recovered $278 in damages and $12,750 in litigation costs and attorney's fees.[55] Moreover, Fraser's school district was enjoined from preventing Fraser from speaking at the commencement ceremonies.[56] While the case continued through the federal courts on appeal, Fraser was elected graduation speaker by a write-in vote of his classmates and delivered a speech at graduation.[57]

The U.S. Supreme Court accepted the case and determined that the school district "acted entirely within its permissible authority."[58] The Court determined that Fraser's First Amendment appeal was unfounded:

> The undoubted freedom to advocate unpopular and controversial views in schools and classrooms must be balanced against the society's countervailing interest in teaching students the boundaries of socially appropriate behavior. ***The pervasive sexual innuendo in Fraser's speech was plainly offensive to both teachers and students—indeed to any mature person. By glorifying male sexuality, and in its verbal content, the speech was acutely insulting to teenage girl students. . . . The speech could well be seriously damaging to its less mature audience, many of whom were only 14 years old and on the threshold of awareness of human sexuality.[59]

Indeed, Chief Justice Warren Burger exercised his prerogative to pass judgment not only on Fraser's style of speech but on Fraser himself—calling the student "this confused boy."[60] The Court also drew a line between children and adults regarding the First Amendment's guarantee of freedom of speech.[61]

Fraser is an extension of the Court's approach in *Pacifica*. In both cases, the Court asserts its interest in safeguarding the presumptively virgin ears and minds of America's youth.[62] However, *Fraser* presents two differences. First, Fraser did not use any of the seven "filthy" words from Carlin's *Pacifica* monologue. Second, unlike Carlin, Fraser was a minor communicating to his contemporaries. However, the end result is the same: The Court disparages Fraser and his speech in a manner similar to its treatment of Carlin and his speech in *Pacifica*. The irony is that the *Fraser* context involved a school-sponsored program in self-government. Fraser was making a speech for an essentially political reason, to help his colleague get elected. Moreover, Fraser attempted to use language in an unorthodox manner for maximum political effect. He obviously understood what would appeal to his audience, and they no doubt understood him.

Nevertheless, under *Fraser*, minors have no First Amendment rights; indeed, they have no right to engage in dialogue that affects their political affairs. Although the students of Bethel finally managed to assert their will by electing Fraser as the commencement speaker, the Court would have denied them that choice as well had the issue not been moot. The message the Court sends to minors is no different from the message sent to Carlin and culturally progressive radio stations: If you are outside the political mainstream and your speech violates mainstream taboos, your speech is not worthy of First Amendment protection.

Hustler Magazine v. *Falwell*

There is no better or clearer example of an expression of insolence than the November 1983 *Hustler* Campari ad parody featuring an unwilling Rev. Jerry Falwell. Campari liquor used an advertising campaign in which various celebrities would be interviewed about their "first time" drinking Campari. *Hustler* printed a parody of a Campari liquor advertisement featuring Jerry Falwell as the "celebrity." Falwell, too, allegedly describes his "first time"—an incestuous encounter with his mother in an outhouse that also involved their excessive consumption of Campari. The ad parody contained a disclaimer at the bottom of the page in small print: "AD PARODY—NOT TO BE TAKEN SERIOUSLY."[63]

At his deposition, Larry Flynt, the publisher of *Hustler* magazine,[64] admitted that when he approved the parody for publication, he intended to "assassinate" Falwell's integrity.[65] Falwell's lawyer asked, "Do you realize, Mr. Flynt, that you can injure people by inflicting mental suffering and disturbance on them that will cause pain that is as great or greater than physical suffering?"[66] Flynt replied, "You're goddamn fucking right. And you're all going to be on your knees before we finish here."[67]

Even without the benefit of Flynt's testimony, there is little doubt exactly what Flynt intended. Though perhaps no one would ever take seriously the characterization of Falwell as having participated in the specific acts portrayed in the ad parody, one could take seriously the implication that Falwell is an alcoholic and immoral. Accordingly, one also could conclude that Falwell is hypocritical—because he is a preacher and founder of the Moral Majority.[68] One also would assume Flynt intended that Falwell would interpret the ad parody as a communicative assault—Flynt's testimony makes it indisputable. Hence, the ad parody is a fine example of a person's employment of language taboos in a way that cuts across subcultural lines. Accordingly, there should be at least a cultural consensus on what was being communicated—Flynt's utter contempt for Falwell.

Jerry Falwell talks about his first time.*

FALWELL: My first time was in an outhouse outside Lynchburg, Virginia.

INTERVIEWER: Wasn't it a little cramped?

FALWELL: Not after I kicked the goat out.

INTERVIEWER: I see. You must tell me all about it.

FALWELL: I never *really* expected to make it with Mom, but then after she showed all the other guys in town such a good time, I figured, "What the hell!"

INTERVIEWER: But your mom? Isn't that a bit odd?

FALWELL: I don't think so. Looks don't mean that much to me in a woman.

INTERVIEWER: Go on.

FALWELL: Well, we were drunk off our God-fearing asses on Campari, ginger ale and soda—that's called a Fire and Brimstone—at the time. And Mom looked better than a Baptist whore with a $100 donation.

INTERVIEWER: Campari in the crapper with Mom . . . how interesting. Well, how was it?

FALWELL: The Campari was great, but Mom passed out before I could come.

INTERVIEWER: Did you ever try it again?

FALWELL: Sure . . .

lots of times. But not in the outhouse. Between Mom and the shit, the flies were too much to bear.

INTERVIEWER: We meant the Campari.

FALWELL: Oh, yeah. I always get sloshed before I go out to the pulpit. You don't think I could lay down all that bullshit *sober*, do you?

© 1983 – Imported by Campari U.S.A. New York, NY 48°proof Spirit Aperitif (Liqueur)

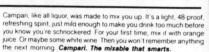

CAMPARI® **You'll never forget your first time.**

*AD PARODY—NOT TO BE TAKEN SERIOUSLY

Hence, it seems that language taboos are not always relative to class. Being able to tell the difference may make all the difference when government steps in to regulate our use of words. We can argue that to ensure citizens within subcultures can communicate with each other effectively, government should avoid the temptation to censor their language; however, when a person's use of language crosses subcultural lines and purposefully hurts another citizen, the case for government regulation becomes stronger. The problem is in determining when a person's use of language does not have political value such that government's regulation might be legitimate. If a principled line cannot be drawn, then the government's interest in regulation must give way to the need of its citizens to communicate effectively with each other.

Soon after the November 1983 issue of *Hustler* hit the newsstands, Falwell sued in federal court on three grounds: libel, invasion of privacy, and intentional infliction of emotional distress.[69] The district court sent Falwell's claims for libel and emotional distress to the jury.[70] The jury rejected Flynt's libel claim noting specifically that the ad parody could not "reasonably be understood as describing actual facts about [Falwell] or actual events in which [he] participated."[71] However, the jury found for Falwell on the emotional distress claim and awarded $100,000 compensatory damages, and $50,000 punitive damages from both *Hustler* and Flynt.[72] The United States Supreme Court ultimately decided to hear the case on appeal.[73]

In a unanimous decision, the Court vacated the jury's damage award for Falwell's emotional distress claim.[74] The Court characterized the Campari ad parody as speech that was patently offensive and was intended to inflict emotional injury but that could not have been reasonably interpreted as stating actual facts about Falwell.[75] Struggling to classify Flynt's ad parody, the Court determined that "the sort of expression involved in *[Falwell]* does not seem to us to be governed by" such "exceptions" to general First Amendment principles as the *Pacifica* doctrine.[76]

Although admitting that Flynt's caricature of Falwell was "at best a distant cousin of . . . political cartoons, and a rather poor relation at that," the Court stated that it could not lay down a principled standard to separate one from the other.[77] The Court reasoned that the standard of "outrageousness" required under most states' emotional distress torts, if applied to political and social discourse, would enable jurors to punish a speaker because of their tastes or views or because of their dislike for the speaker's particular expression.[78] Indeed, the Court claimed, the fact that the speaker's opinion is offensive is all the more reason for according the speech constitutional protection.[79]

The Court stressed the role of the First Amendment in fostering criticism of public officials or figures, who are involved in resolution of important public questions or who shape events in areas of societal concern.[80] Further, the Court noted that whether expression is protected does not depend on the less-than-admirable motives of the speaker—what matters is whether the utterance was "honestly believed."[81] Indeed, Justice Rehnquist practically suggests that Falwell deserved the criticism inherent in Flynt's parody: "[T]he candidate who vaunts his spotless record and sterling integrity cannot convincingly cry 'Foul!' when an opponent or industrious reporter attempts to demonstrate the contrary."[82]

The Justices in *Falwell* seemed most concerned about the result a different holding might have for political cartoonists and satirists. The court noted the intent of political cartoonists and their works—"often calculated to injure the feelings of the subject of the portrayal[;] . . . often not reasoned or evenhanded, but slashing and one-sided"[83]—and pointed to the example of Thomas Nast's series of cartoons depicting William M. "Boss" Tweed and his corrupt associates, which "continuously [went] beyond the bounds of good taste and conventional manners."[84]

At first glance, *Falwell* seems to be a departure from the Court's approach in *Pacifica* and *Fraser*. Here, the speech is offensive, gross, and repugnant, but it is protected. *Pacifica* is now couched in terms of "an exception" to general First Amendment principles. The Campari ad parody even exploited incest, a tabooed activity, rather than the mere words that were the subject of *Pacifica* and *Fraser*—yet the Court dispensed the cloak of First Amendment protection. Moreover the protected speech in *Falwell* cut viciously across the subcultural divide between Flynt the smut-peddler and Falwell the Holy Roller, whereas in *Pacifica* and *Fraser*, the unprotected speech was aimed harmlessly toward members of a similar subculture who would understand and not be offended by the speech. Could it be that the Court has changed its taboo-reverent approach to free speech? Maybe so. Nevertheless, the political results for the persons involved are similar to those entailed in *Pacifica* and *Fraser*.

Falwell, the First Amendment "loser," if you will, was still disparaged in the Court's opinion. And as for Flynt—who has never had the reputation for saying anything kind about the Supreme Court, who has through his publications expressed the same contempt for the nine Justices as he did for Falwell, and who has reveled in his ability to make money from "unprotected expression"—the Court elevated his Campari ad parody to a level of protection coequal with conventional political cartoonists. Despite the harmful character of the speech, the Court afforded First Amendment protection to speech about a person outside the political mainstream. Although Flynt also is outside that mainstream, the Court protected his speech only to ensure that conventional methods of expressing political dissent, such as editorial cartooning, would be protected.

Moreover, the Court in *Falwell* legitimated speech that was not as worthy of protection as the speech in *Fraser* and *Pacifica*. The speech in *Falwell* was not of the type that only some subcultures could fully appreciate and understand; overall, the Campari ad parody employed mainstream language in a mainstream format. Indeed, Flynt's ad parody seemed well outside the Court's jurisprudence of "political speech." It was a defamatory, relentless attack on a man's character. If ever the Court could legitimately draw a principled line, *Falwell* was the place to do it. Instead, fearful of endangering "legitimate" political expression, the Court begrudgingly protected Flynt's assault-in-print.

Conclusion

Censorship is a practical and political means to satisfy the "ideological and practical needs of communities or, as some would say, of their rulers."[85] Though censorship typically identified with modern dictatorships such as Nazi Germany and Franco's Spain,[86] democracies are not immune to the temptation to suppress particular ideas by attacking "their originators or principal exponents."[87] In cases involving nonconventional language, the U.S. Supreme Court tends to disparage both the speech and the speaker, so long as conventional modes of expression are not threatened. Moreover, the Court tends to resolve free-speech cases in ways that persecute those persons whose views are outside the political mainstream.

Notes

1. Larry A. Samovar and Richard E. Porter, "Approaching Intercultural Communication," in Larry A. Samovar and Richard E. Porter, *Intercultural Communication: A Reader* (Belmont, CA: Wadsworth, 1988), p. 27.

2. See *id.* ("Language influences perceptions and transmits and helps pattern thoughts").

3. Stuart Chase, *Power of Words* (New York: Harcourt, Brace, 1954), p. 109.

4. Porter and Samovar, *supra* note 1, p. 27.

5. See generally David Kairys, "Freedom of Speech," in David Kairys, *The Politics of Law* (New York: Pantheon, 1982), p. 167 (discussing the development and use of "free speech" in the United States).

6. It is important to mention that I claim only that the Court "tends" to do these things, not that the Court necessarily "intends" to do these things.

7. Joel Feinberg, *The Moral Limits of the Criminal Law: Offense to Others* (New York: Oxford University Press, 1985), p. 254. Euphemisms assumed an important role in primitive societies. For example, the Alfoors of Halmahera (an island to the west of New Guinea) spoke of smallpox as a "king" to hide the ugliness of the disease. Sir James George Frazer, *Aftermath: A Supplement to* The Golden Bough (New York: Macmillan, 1937) p. 285. Frazer noted that this was an appropriate image because the disease "visit[ed] district after district, village after village, like a prince making royal progress." *Id.*

8. The excerpt of "Chemist Sketch" is taken from *The Complete Monty Python's Flying Circus: All the Words,* Vol. 1 (New York: Pantheon, 1989) (hereafter *Flying Circus*), pp. 230–231. Reprinted with permission; © Python Productions Limited 1989.

9. E. D. Hirsch, Joseph F. Kett, and James S. Trefil, *The Dictionary of Cultural Literacy* (Boston: Houghton Mifflin, 1988), p. 142.

10. When I refer to words that are "taboo," I mean only that the words are generally regarded as vulgar or impolite by most members of American society. See, e.g., John C. Condon and Fathi S. Yousef, *An Introduction to Intercultural Communication* (Indianapolis: Bobbs-Merrill, 1975), p. 261. It is important to note that I use the word "taboo" in a different sense from most others who have written about taboos. The most frequent sources of taboos are bodily functions, sex, and death. *Id.,* p. 142. Taboos have been associated primarily with primitive races. See Sigmund Freud, *Totem and Taboo* (New York: New Republic, 1927) (A. A. Brill trans.), pp. 30–31. Freud's theories of totemism built upon the works

of Frazer's *The Golden Bough*. According to Frazer, taboos imposed on language and speech generally required that persons avoid mentioning personal names because they were acquainted with the body, and the names of gods and spirits because "the mere utterance of them may work wonders and disturb the course of nature." John B. Vickery, *The Literary Impact of* The Golden Bough (Princeton: Princeton University Press, 1973), p. 48, quoting Sir James George Frazier, The Golden Bough: *Taboo and the Perils of the Soul* (London: Macmillan, 1911), p. 384.

11. The Pythons' fears regarding the British Broadcasting Corporation's potential for television censorship became reality in America on the CBS television network. On *The Smothers Brothers Comedy Hour,* CBS censors deleted an ostensibly political part of Joan Baez's dedication of a song to her husband, a convicted draft resister. The network broadcast "he is going to prison for three years." The censors deleted the sentence that followed: "The reason is that he resisted selective service and the draft and militarism in general." Obviously, this cast a different light on Baez's husband than she intended. See David H. Tribe, *Questions of Censorship* (New York: St. Martin's, 1973), p. 203.

More ironically, the Pythons waged a battle against the ABC television network as a result of ABC's censorship of the Pythons' material prior to broadcast in October 1975. See *Gilliam v. American Broadcasting Companies, Inc.,* 538 F.2d 14 (2d Cir. 1976). The Pythons' lawsuit resulted from ABC's failure to run three episodes of *Monty Python's Flying Circus* as they originally aired on the BBC. *Id.* at 18. ABC deleted a total of twenty-four minutes of the original ninety minutes of Python material. *Id.* ABC claimed that the editing was necessary to include commercials and to delete "offensive or obscene matter." *Id.* ABC took such action despite the fact that no prior U.S. broadcast of *Monty Python* (on both public and commercial television stations) had been edited. *Id.* at 23.

The *Gilliam* court noted that some deletions, such as "hell" and "damn," especially given the late-night television slot of 11:30 P.M. to 1:00 A.M., "seem[ed] inexplicable given today's standard television fare." *Id.* at 23 and n.8. ABC also bleeped perhaps the Pythons' most famous euphemism—"naughty bits"—thus making the Pythons' humor appear crude rather than witty. Robert Hewison, *Monty Python: The Case Against* (New York: Grove, 1981), p. 44. Other expressions deleted included "good lord," "good god," "oh my god," "bastards," "intercourse," "pert thighs," and "erogenous zone." *Id.,* p. 48. The result of such deletions was, in the words of Python member Terry Jones, to "[leave] in things which (with the cuts they'd made) were weak, pointless, and unfunny." *Id.,* p. 45.

Accordingly, the Pythons obtained a preliminary injunction under the Lanham Act on grounds of ABC's "distortion" of the episodes that impaired the integrity of the Pythons' work. *Gilliam,* 538 F.2d at 26–27. Ultimately, the parties settled out of court: The Pythons received $35,000 toward their court costs, assurance that all programs would be shown in their entirety, and the exclusive rights to distribute their work beginning in 1981. Hewison, *supra,* p. 56.

12. Feinberg, *supra* note 7, pp. 252–253.

13. See *id.,* p. 249 (discussing the effect of "obscene" words on unprepared listeners); *id.,* p. 252 (noting that obscenities are a subclass of cacophemisms).

14. *Id.,* p. 249.

15. "Fuck" is perhaps the alltime favorite cacophemism. See Jay E. Daily, *The Anatomy of Censorship* (New York: M. Dekker, 1973), p. 8 (noting that "fuck" is the choice word of graffiti in the English-speaking countries).

16. Feinberg, *supra* note 7, pp. 249–250.

17. *Id.*, p. 250.

18. *Id.*, p. 251.

19. George Carlin very likely had television in mind when he recorded the "Filthy Words" monologue. Little did he know that a radio station's broadcast would grab the attention of the FCC and the U.S. Supreme Court in *Federal Communications Commission v. Pacifica Foundation*, 438 U.S. 726 (1978). The monologue's entire text is appended to the Court's opinion. *Id.* at 751.

20. The preceding excerpt of "Filthy Words" in the text is taken from *Pacifica*, 438 U.S. at 751, 753–755.

21. Feinberg, *supra* note 7, p. 253–254.

22. The excerpt of "Prejudice" that follows in the text is taken from *Flying Circus, supra* note 8, vol. 2, p. 208. Reprinted with permission; © Python Productions Limited 1989.

23. A cynic might respond as follows to my claim that the Pythons' "Prejudice" sketch is humorous: "The Pythons merely condone the use of racial and ethnic epithets in ordinary discourse." Indeed, any group can use ethnic humor to "malign, downgrade and ridicule other group(s)" as a way to assert self-perceived superiority. See Mahadev L. Apte, *Humor and Laughter: An Anthropological Approach* (Ithaca, NY: Cornell University Press, 1985), p. 144 (discussing ethnic humor). But this misses the point: The hurtful aspect of the epithets, at least for the duration of the sketch, have been effectively disarmed. For once, we can laugh *at* the bigot and at ourselves—hold him or her in contempt without laughter, and let ourselves "off the hook" for a while—for who has not at one time or another used such an epithet? See *id.*, p. 145.

24. *Federal Communications Commission v. Pacifica Foundation*, 438 U.S. 726, 729–730 (1978).

25. *Pacifica*, 438 U.S. at 729–730.

26. *Id.* at 730.

27. *Id.*

28. *Id.*

29. *Id.* at 731.

30. *Id.*

31. *Id.* at 732. The FCC noted that the concept "indecent" was "intimately connected with the exposure of children to language that describes . . . sexual or excretory activities and organs at times of the day when there is a reasonable risk that children may be in the audience." *Id.* (quoting 56 F.C.C.2d 94, 98). Noting that the words were broadcast in the early afternoon, a time when children were "undoubtedly" in the audience, and that the "offensive" words were continually repeated, the FCC determined that the language as broadcast violated 18 U.S.C. § 1464 (1976). *Id.* (quoting 56 F.C.C.2d at 99). 18 U.S.C. § 1464 (1976) provides: "Whoever utters any obscene, indecent, or profane language by means of radio communication shall be fined not more than $10,000 or imprisoned not more than two years, or both." *Id.* at 731 n.3.

32. *Pacifica*, 438 U.S. at 738–739.

33. Id. at 740 and n.14 (quoting Webster's Third New International Dictionary (1966)).

34. Id. at 740–741.

35. Id. at 741.

36. Id. at 743.

37. Id. at 750–751.

38. Id. at 748. The Court noted that because audiences constantly tune in and out,

prior warnings cannot completely protect the listener from unexpected program content. *Id.*

39. *Id.*

40. *Id.* at 749.

41. "Cunt" is derived from the Latin *cunnus* which, ironically, is a *masculine* noun of the second declension. Daily, *supra* note 15, pp. 6–7. "Piss" is derived from the Old French *pissier;* the word is not taboo in French. *Id.*, p. 8.

42. See *id.*, p. 9 (discussing taboo words).

43. Apte, *supra* note 23, p. 92.

44. See *id.*, p. 96 (discussing adolescent use of scatological and taboo language).

45. See *id.*, p. 85 (discussing children's language development).

46. See *id.*, p. 96 (discussing adolescent use of scatological and taboo language).

47. Justice Brennan makes a similar argument in his dissenting opinion in *Pacifica,* 438 U.S. at 770.

48. *Bethel School District v. Fraser,* 478 U.S. 675, 677 (1986). Students were required to attend the assembly, or to report to the study hall if they elected not to attend. *Id.* Hence, the assembly was not mandatory in the strictest sense. Roughly 600 students attended the assembly. *Id.* at 681.

49. *Id.* at 687 (Brennan, J., concurring).

50. *Id.* at 678. The disciplinary rule that Fraser allegedly violated provided: "Conduct which materially and substantially interferes with the educational process is prohibited, including the use of obscene, profane language or gestures." *Id.*

51. *Id.*

52. The grievance procedure's hearing officer determined that Fraser's speech was "indecent, lewd, and offensive." *Id.* at 678–679. The examiner determined that the speech fell within the disciplinary rule's meaning of "obscene." *Id.* at 679.

53. *Id.*

54. *Id.*

55. *Id.* Fraser's award of $278 was based on the loss of two days' schooling. *Id.* at 686 n.*.

56. *Id.* at 679.

57. *Id.* The United States Court of Appeals for the Ninth Circuit affirmed the judgment of the district court, explicitly rejecting the school district's argument that Fraser's speech was disruptive to the educational process. *Id.* The Ninth Circuit also rejected any interest the school district asserted to protect an essentially captive audience of minors from "lewd and indecent language." *Id.* The court noted the risk that giving the school district "unbridled discretion" to determine "decent" discourse would "increase the risk of cementing white, middle-class standards for determining what is acceptable and proper speech and behavior in [the] public schools." *Id.*

58. *Id.* at 685.

59. *Id.* at 681, 683.

60. *Id.* at 683. Apparently the Chief Justice has some institutional right to deride those who bring to the Court their cases and their interpretation of the proper bounds of the First Amendment. Two years later, Chief Justice William Rehnquist engaged in an arguably personal attack on the Rev. Jerry Falwell in his opinion for a unanimous Court in *Hustler Magazine v. Falwell.* See *infra* note 83 and accompanying text (discussing *Falwell*).

61. See *id.* at 682 ("[T]he constitutional rights of students in public school are not automatically coextensive with the rights of adults.").

62. This paternalistic view of youth is not without precedent. Mark Twain's works *The Adventures of Tom Sawyer* and *The Adventures of Huckleberry Finn, Tom*

Sawyer's Comrade, were banned from the children's room of the Brooklyn Public Library because they did not correspond with adults' views of "childish innocence and docility" and because they depicted a black-white friendship. Tribe, *supra* note 11, p. 34.

63. The Campari ad parody in the text is reproduced from Rodney A. Smolla, *Jerry Falwell v. Larry Flynt* (New York: St. Martin's, 1988), p. 313.

64. See *id.,* p. 3. In 1983, the year *Hustler* published the Campari ad parody, *Hustler's* circulation approximated 2.5 million copies per month throughout the United States. *Id.,* p. 38.

65. *Id.* p. 60.

66. *Id.* p. 62.

67. *Id.*

68. See *Hustler Magazine v. Falwell,* 108 S. Ct. 876, 882 n.5.

69. *Id.* at 878.

70. *Id.*

71. *Id.*

72. *Id.* To recover in an action for intentional infliction of emotional distress under Virginia law, Falwell was required to show, among other things, that Flynt's conduct "offend[ed] generally accepted standards of decency or morality." *Id.* at 879 n.3.

73. The United States Court of Appeals for the Fourth Circuit affirmed the jury's judgment, rejecting the idea that the "actual malice" standard of *New York Times Co. v. Sullivan,* 376 U.S. 254 (1964), is a prerequisite to recovery for emotional distress. *Id.* at 878 (citing *Falwell v. Flynt,* 797 F.2d 1270 (4th Cir. 1986)). The Fourth Circuit determined that because the requisite level of culpability in the actual malice standard was "knowing . . . or reckless conduct," and because Virginia law required as an element of the tort that conduct be "intentional or reckless," the state-law standard satisfied the requirements in *Sullivan. Id.* at 878–879. Hence, the Fourth Circuit discounted the *Sullivan* requirement that the statement be false and ignored the issue of whether the ad parody was factual or expressed opinion. The Fourth Court *en banc* denied petition for rehearing. *Id.* at 879. The Supreme Court granted certiorari. *Id.*

74. To assure adequate "breathing space" under the First Amendment, the *Falwell* Court grafted the *Sullivan* "actual malice" standard (previously applicable in libel cases involving public figures) to the intentional infliction of emotional distress tort. *Falwell,* 108 S. Ct. at 882. The Court determined that because Falwell was a "public figure" for purposes of First Amendment law, and because the jury's finding indicated that the ad parody "was not reasonably believable," both the libel claim and Falwell's claim for emotional distress damages must fail. *Id.* at 882–883. Though perhaps a laudable decision on First Amendment grounds, the decision was doctrinally unsound given the different purposes of the libel and emotional distress torts. See generally Scot A. Duvall, "Intentional Infliction of Emotional Distress and Libel Law: 'A Tale of Two Torts' and the Need for Reform After Hustler" (unpublished manuscript on file with Dean Randall P. Bezanson, Washington and Lee School of Law, Lexington, VA, 1990).

75. *Falwell,* 108 S. Ct. at 879.

76. *Id.* at 882. The Court later described the Campari ad parody as "a caricature." *Id.* at 883.

77. *Id.* at 881. The Court used a lexical definition for "caricature": "the deliberately distorted picturing or imitating of a person, literary style, etc., by exaggerating *features or mannerisms* for satirical effect." *Id.* (quoting *Webster's New*

Unabridged Twentieth Century Dictionary of the English Language, p. 275 (2d ed. 1979)) (emphasis added). Because the Campari ad parody was a slashing attack, exaggerating Falwell's character rather than his features or mannerisms, the Court's definition of "caricature" is an inapt characterization of Flynt's avowed attempt to assassinate Falwell's integrity.

78. *Id.* at 880, 882.

79. *Id.* at 882 (citing *Federal Communications Commission v. Pacifica Foundation,* 438 U.S. 726, 745–746 (1978)). It is rather ironic that the Court would use language contained in *Pacifica* to uphold speech that it considered "doubtless gross and repugnant in the eyes of most." *Falwell,* 108 S. Ct. at 879.

80. *Id.* at 879.

81. *Id.* at 880–881 (citing *Garrison v. Louisiana,* 379 U.S. 64, 73 (1964)).

82. *Id.* at 880 (quoting *Monitor Patriot Co. v. Roy,* 401 U.S. 265, 274 (1971)).

83. *Id.* at 881.

84. *Id.* (quoting Charles Press, *The Political Cartoon* (Rutherford, NJ: Fairleigh Dickinson Press, 1981), p. 251).

85. Tribe, *supra* note 11, p. 47. See also Daily, *supra* note 15, p. 283 ("[W]herever there is a group enjoying an elitist status and special privilege, there is a center of conservatism that is endangered whenever it discovers an open challenge to the authority and status of the group").

86. See Tribe, *supra* note 11, p. 31 (discussing censorship).

87. *Id.,* p. 277.

PART TWO

Totalitarian Systems

3

Soviet Censorship's "True Colors": A Chameleon Adapting to Glasnost

Vladimir Wozniuk

One word of truth outweighs the world.
—Old Russian Proverb

As the title of this chapter suggests, the system of Soviet censorship during the presidency of Mikhail Gorbachev was in flux, trying to adapt to the environment created by his glasnost policy much as a chameleon might change color to protect itself from predators. Under Gorbachev, basic constitutional principles regarding individual freedoms were not accepted unequivocally by the Communist Party of the Soviet Union (CPSU) or tested by a judicial system that was short on precedent and continued to question the relevance of "rule of law" as we understand this term in the West. This all indicated that the rules of the game, including those regarding censorship, were still fluctuating as a "new stage" began in the attempt to build a "civil society" in the USSR.[1]

This struggle to create a civil society continued even after the aborted coup in August 1991, which catapulted Boris Yeltsin into power and led to the quick and unexpected dissolution of the Soviet Union itself. Democratic politicians in Russia and other nations of the caretaker Commonwealth of Independent States organization continued to struggle to overcome the legacy of a long and painful cultural tradition of censorship. This chapter discusses this heritage in an attempt to outline the parameters of the difficult task facing politicians attempting to dismantle a censorship regime as pervasive as the one that existed in the Soviet Union.

Truth and Censorship

For decades, Soviet society was driven by the Leninist vision that a society engineered on the basis of "scientific" principles would eventuate in the

This chapter was completed prior to the dissolution of the USSR.

perfection of "new Soviet individuals" living together in harmony in a social utopia where justice would govern human relations. At every stage in the construction of this utopia, the leadership of the CPSU itself would determine the character of truth. In the words of Sanislaw Baranczak, "In totalitarian thinking, there is no objective truth and no objective reality; only those facts and objects exist which are allowed to exist by the ruling power."[2] Soviet censorship had always reflected this contradictory and paradoxical teleology: If necessary, representation of reality must be intentionally distorted, ostensibly in order to serve the cause of socialist justice.

However, this Orwellian definition of truth was never universally accepted in Soviet society. The Russian words for the concept of "truth," *pravda* and *istina,* do not lend themselves easily to such distortion. Unshackled and unintimidated even by threat of renewed repression, every segment of Soviet society under Gorbachev struggled to realize truth in all aspects of individual and communal life. At the same time, the party's definition was rejected outright, even as opponents to democratization in the Communist bureaucracy, the *nomenklatura,* tried to force the genie of glasnost unleashed by Gorbachev back into its bottle and under party control in the name of preserving order and avoiding chaos.

Under Gorbachev, Soviet politicians were still in the early stages of learning the art of reasonable compromise. The dichotomous relationship of glasnost (openness) and perestroika (restructuring) in Soviet reality must be seen in the context of this learning process, in which some balance of demands for both justice and order was deemed critical. The CPSU promoted restructuring through controlled and limited reforms only as a last resort to preserve order; its incentive was the very survival of the Stalinist system of bureaucratic privilege that preserved order at the expense of justice for so long.

Glasnost, however, quickly resulted in crusades for truth and justice at all levels of Soviet politics and society and contributed to increasing disorder in Soviet society. Glasnost was opposed by the party bureaucracy from the very beginning because, by definition, openness has no limits and therefore is less possible to control.

Dostoevsky's Grand inquisitor assessed the human condition this way: "Nothing is more seductive for man than his freedom of conscience, but nothing is a greater cause of suffering." This observation could be extended to the dichotomous relationship between glasnost and perestroika in Soviet politics under Gorbachev. Freedom of expression is a precious thing—but it does not fill the belly. Dreams of truth and justice can quickly be reduced to the level of a cruel joke in the face of economic deprivation and increasing chaos.

Official Censorship and Soviet Political Culture

The Imperial Legacy

Because "censorship is as old as articulate public opinion in Russia,"[3] it is a key facet of Russian and Soviet political culture. Lenin and his successors built and improved upon a well-established system of tested methods and mechanisms of censorship, the strengths and weaknesses of which the Bolsheviks knew only too well from their own dealings with the tsarist censors and secret police from the late nineteenth century until 1917. One important lesson Lenin and his associates learned from the tsarist state was the usefulness of an effective censorship regime to the governing power in controlling the processes of reform.

A common element shared by both tsarist and Soviet censorship regimes is that both operated directly as a function of individual leaders' attempts to transform Russian society. As imperial Russian and Soviet leaders took the lead from above to reform society, censorship tended to tighten or loosen according to an individual leader's notions about which social changes were beneficial and which were harmful to Russian society.

Not only in Soviet political culture but also in its Russian imperial predecessor has the theme of creating a new individual played a key role. Peter's "perestroika" of Russia included the Europeanization of backward Russian peasant society. Catherine the Great, before reacting to the excesses of the French Revolution, had as a central objective in her educational and cultural policies a kind of perestroika as well, the goal of which was also the remolding of Russians on the European model: "The objective of the new teaching methods was to produce a new kind of man: the enlightened subject of the Russian Empire, a man (or woman) equipped to play an active and useful role in the development of the country's economy as well as its culture."[4] This agenda included the need to control the information Russians were exposed to.

It was under Peter that the state first gave priority to the dissemination of information in order to assist in the modernization of backward Russian society. But it was also under Peter that formal licensure of the press became necessary under the aegis of a Department of Morals. Later, Catherine's commitment to Age of Reason thought could not survive the threat of an expansionary revolutionary France; it was under her rule that all private publishing was prohibited and "an all embracing system of censorship [was] set in place for the whole Empire."[5] In 1826, Nicholas I, using the pretext of the Decembrist uprising, tightened the screws by instituting a Censorship Code under which all publications needed clearance from a censorship committee.[6]

This is not to say that popular pressure from below played no role in the fortunes of the Russian imperial and, later, Soviet censorship regimes. After the reforms of the 1860s, imperial censorship became increasingly ineffective and even contributed to a general liberalization of strictures, so that opposition groups actually gained strength from tsarist policy. The Bolsheviks could by 1912 regularly publish *Pravda,* the party organ, even though censorship still existed.[7] And although the provisional government in 1917 abolished censorship by dismantling the Central Administration for Press Affairs, it later could reimpose only a weak regime of censorship during the turbulent "July Days."[8]

Lenin's Legacy

The principle of free access to information was expunged by Lenin himself in 1917, in direct contravention of what he stated in his early decree on the press: "As soon as the new system is firmly established, all administrative influences on the press will be ended, it will enjoy complete freedom within the limits of responsibility to the court, according to the broadest and the most progressive law relating to the particular case."[9] Yet Lenin's first action on the issue of freedom of the press two days after the Bolsheviks' success was to close down opposition presses, which Lenin considered "no less dangerous than bombs and machine-guns."[10]

Although some Bolsheviks might have been surprised and even outraged by this action, there was little evidence that Lenin had ever considered freedom of expression and the press to be an integral component of any socialist state that would emerge in Russia. Even a brief review of his early writings on the subject, including *What Is to Be Done?* (1903) and "Party Organization and Party Literature" (1905), reveals an unambiguous perspective on the press and all literature as servants of the class struggle: "Publishing and distributing centers, book-shops and . . . libraries . . . must all come under party control."[11] Lenin also cited the necessity to "digest" what he called "inconsistent elements" within the party, at the same time condemning "talk about absolute freedom" in publishing as "sheer hypocrisy."[12]

The process of nationalization of the press, which had begun October 27, 1917, with a "temporary" decree to close opposition presses, was completed only after the conclusion of the civil war.[13] It was then that formal mechanisms of preliminary censorship were constructed. On November 12, 1921, the Bolshevik government issued a "Decree on Private Publishers," which required that permission be obtained from GOSIZDAT (State Publishing Agency) before a work could be published.[14] The censorship regime was given more concrete form and substance in 1922 with the creation of the Main Administration for Literature and Publishing (GLAVLIT), which subsequently became the bureaucratic foundation for the entire system of censorship in the Soviet Union until its dissolution.[15] Under Stalin, GLAVLIT became a powerful instrument of control that operated by several thousand censors using the infamous "Talmud," or list of subjects banned from publication by Soviet authorities.

Although the strictures of the censorship regime alternately increased and diminished in intensity under Stalin's successors, the fundamental principles that governed it remained unquestioned and unchallenged until Gorbachev assumed the top party post in 1985.

Enter Gorbachev

With reform of the stagnating Soviet economy the most urgent task before him, Gorbachev needed to improvise. He decided to allow limited democratization through promoting more openness (glasnost) in order to achieve restructuring (perestroika), without which the Soviet economy would continue to deteriorate and threaten domestic order and national security.

Without making direct reference to freedom of expression or the press, Gorbachev suggested that "stagnation" in the media and the economy were two sides of the same coin. At a Central Committee plenum soon after his appointment as CPSU General Secretary, he described the role of the media as "profoundly to analyze events and phenomena, to raise serious problems and propose ways of solving them"[16]—which of course suggested that something obstructed the media in fulfilling this task. Gorbachev began to place his associates in key editorial positions in the media, a process that continued for many months.[17]

At the watershed Twenty-seventh Party Congress in early 1986, Gorbachev criticized the lack of accurate representation of reality by writers, including journalists.[18] The attack on censorship rules, however, remained indirect: "Truth is discovered not through declarations and instruction. It is born in . . . debate and verified in action."[19] Subsequently, with economic reform as the preeminent goal, his inner circle of advisers began to condemn regularly dogmatism and "varnishing of reality" within the party as obstacles to the desperately needed reforms.[20]

It is important to note, however that all this criticism was limited to a narrowly defined context. When asked about the limits of glasnost and reform, the newly appointed head of Novosti News Agency, Valentin Falin, summed it up this way: "The principles of Marxism-Leninism are the only sacred thing. Everything else can be discussed."[21] The new party leadership wanted to accelerate reform by proclaiming "results" as a new litmus test for "correctness" of policy, but the limits of glasnost were clear—fundamental ideological principles were nonnegotiable. Indeed, the amendments to the Soviet Constitution approved on December 1, 1988, which gave birth to entirely new political institutions, carefully avoided any direct implication that dismantling the Marxist-Leninist system was possible and said nothing specific or new about censorship. The apparatus of censorship remained for the most part intact, as evidenced by the human effort devoted to the mechanical task of preliminary censorship, estimated as recently as 1989 to have been approximately 2,000 Soviet censors, although the exact figure remained a state secret.[22]

The Law on Press Freedom

An intense struggle ensued through 1989 and the first months of 1990 over the passage of a new press law to redress this deficiency. Perhaps the most graphic reminder that ending censorship would prove one of the most difficult reforms to implement occurred during the May Day celebrations of 1990.[23] In order to prevent the May Day protests from being aired during the traditional Red Square celebration, live broadcast coverage to the country was abruptly preempted, and only sanitized news clips were later shown, the first such occurrence in Soviet history.

During the debate over the liberal draft law, which was signed into law by President Gorbachev on June 12, 1990, an indication of the hostility of the deep-rooted conservative opposition to such an enterprise was given in the newspaper *Literaturnaia Rossiia:*

> The authors of this draft are devils who are ready to smash into smithereens our own home, which is ungainly but is still ours. They are ready to transform

the sacred places of the Fatherland into fashionable taverns, and temples into pagan sacrificial altars. National treasures are to be bartered in a bazaar.[24]

As the French are fond of saying, "The more things change, the more they remain the same."

The landmark law "On the Press and Other Means of Mass Information," although adopted June 12, 1990, first appeared in print in the by-then-liberal government newspaper *Izvestiia* only on June 20; it was not even mentioned during this time by *Pravda,* the more conservative party organ.[25] Although this lack of mention could be explained by the fact that *Pravda* was not a government paper and had no responsibility to publish laws, it is perhaps more likely that the party bureaucracy simply did not approve—indeed, conservative drafts of the law had been rejected by the Congress of People's Deputies in favor of the more liberal version.

The fact that printing presses and the availability of paper were controlled by the state suggests another mechanism of press control—the economic lever. The Gorbachev regime was not above punishing its opponents in the media by controlling their supply of paper. Similar paper shortages faced Russian opposition groups in the early post–October Revolution period. This strategy affected their ability to vie effectively with the Bolsheviks for power, but it also hindered the governmental authority's ability to disseminate its information.[26]

Sections 5 and 7 of the new press law were quite specific about the rights of journalists and citizens. However, it did not abolish the censorship apparatus, nor did it technically obviate the need for censors, who were supposed to be guarding against state secrets being revealed in the media. Although censorship of the press was directly forbidden, and political interference in media was also barred, there was no clear indication of how the laws would be enforced. The twin facts that Soviet political culture had suffered from a lack of respect for "rule of law" and that there was a dearth of legal precedent regarding freedom of the press seriously affected prospects of effective enforcement.

Old ways die hard. The practical situation changed very little after the adoption of the new press law. The technical reality of freedom of the press continued to be overshadowed by the selective imposition of censorship whenever it suited the government and party apparatus. The now-familiar examples of unaired and preempted television programs and interviews with opposition groups, as well as threatened dismissals of journalists by GOSTELRADIO, the State Television and Radio Agency that still controlled most of the airwaves, brought to question the regime's commitment to the rule of law.[27]

Suggestions by Gorbachev himself in January 1991 that the liberal law on press freedom be suspended "for a few months" indicated that the forces of democratization, which he himself unleashed by promoting glasnost, were on the defensive, but not yet in full retreat.[28] As criticism of Gorbachev mounted in early 1991, a popular TV program "Vzgliad" (View) was taken off the air "temporarily," and journalists were intimidated. Nevertheless, criticism of the Gorbachev regime and its policies from both the Left and the Right continued unabated through the first months of 1991.

Self-Censorship

Besides formal mechanisms of control, such as GLAVLIT and the daunting reality of socialist ownership of the "means of production" (paper and printing presses), the Soviet system of censorship continued to promote the idea of self-censorship as a patriotic virtue, which, if respected, would result in making the job of the censor much easier. Self-censorship can be referred to as "subordinating conscience" to the requirements of the state either out of genuine feelings of loyalty or outright fear.[29] Although it is clear that the effectiveness of inculcating self-censorship as a political value deteriorated greatly under glasnost, the ideological principles that undergird it continued to be propagated by opponents of glasnost as basic elements of loyalty either to the Soviet state or to the Russian nation.

The three ideological principles of self-censorship that functioned as pillars of the entire structure of state censorship from the 1930s on were *klassovost'* (class-mindedness), *partiinost'* (party-mindedness), and *narodnost'* (nation- or people-mindedness).[30] Taken together, these three principles long constituted the core of the old ideological orthodoxy regarding self-censorship, and the party *nomenklatura* continued to defend them, in the "Rules of the CPSU" and elsewhere, as touchstones of loyalty to the regime, even in the face of the nearly complete collapse of Marxism-Leninism's credibility in Soviet society.

Although these principles have often been associated with Soviet aesthetics and the movement of socialist realism in the arts, they transcend a narrow definition of the arts and get to the heart of the central issue for Communists in evaluating the quality of all literature and journalism: whether public discourse contributes to the building of Soviet socialism among the masses or not.[31]

The party-dominated Union of Soviet Writers, although changed under glasnost, was used as both a formal and an informal censorship mechanism from the 1930s on. The union assisted in promoting these principles among its membership, thereby making ideological conformity easier for GLAVLIT to monitor. Membership in the union, and with it economic livelihood, sometimes was revoked or withheld, action that thereby denied someone the necessary prerequisite to qualify as a "professional" writer.[32] The Union of Soviet Journalists, created in 1959, fulfilled similar functions. The Committee for State Security (KGB) also participated in the maintenance of self-censorship through fear. Among the "dirty tricks" used to keep people in line or to punish opponents of the Soviet system was the KGB's concoction of personal attacks against people, which it achieved by regularly enlisting the assistance of "an obedient newspaper," even under Gorbachev.[33]

Until glasnost, the three principles of *klassovost'*, *partiinost'*, and *narodnost'* prescribed what were acceptable and unacceptable political attitudes in Soviet public discourse. A Soviet censor in 1989 admitted to a Western newspaper that even under glasnost, categories of censorship listed in the "Talmud" included works and information about and by political enemies and emigres, the slander of Soviet leaders, and anti-Soviet fabrications. A small excerpt serves to illustrate the extent of continuity between pre- and post-Gorbachev censorship mentality: "Slander is the deliberate distortion of facts. Whenever it is said that

Gorbachev is just putting old wine into new bottles, that restructuring is one of the possible ways of saving Stalinism in a somewhat modernized form, that is slander. Are we always objective? I do not think so."[34] And in response to the question of whether GLAVLIT would ever be disbanded, a candid estimation of the importance of self-censorship was offered: "Yes, when editors themselves are able to judge what they can and cannot publish. At present we still have work enough, but that will not last forever."[35]

Inadvertently perhaps, the words of the censor reveal the extent of dependence of formal control mechanisms on self-censorship: Only if and when self-censorship could be perfected would the need for the formal mechanisms of censorship have been removed. Yet under glasnost, these and other ideological principles were widely disparaged. The liberal media and even some Communist Party members scorned and attacked at every opportunity these "worn-out slogans."

The principle of *klassovost'* was dealt a mortal blow in 1988 during the "Andreeva affair," when the conservative opposition to glasnost, led by Yegor Ligachev, launched an attack against suggestions by liberal reformers that the idea of "class struggle," central to Marxism-Leninism, was no longer useful as a tool of analysis.[36] The debate quickly fell out of the public eye, and glasnost picked up steam. Liberal media views briefly seemed to attain ascendancy after this affair.

Adherence to the principle of *partiinost'* had come to mean the unqualified and unequivocal support of the party, which glasnost now undermined. In 1988, the history of the party began to undergo reinterpretation as past "blank spots" were filled daily with "truthful" corrections and admissions of party officials of serious errors. Leading the way were momentous events such as the official rehabilitation of Nikolai Bukharin and other "enemies of the people" who had perished in the great purges of the 1930s, as well as blunt confessions that the invasion of Afghanistan had been a mistake.[37] Such implicit criticisms of past party policy suggested that *partiinost'* too was now moribund.

The fight by the party *nomenklatura* to preserve the ideological principles undergirding self-censorship had been only partially successful, and this success was limited to the principle of *narodnost'*. Perhaps this was because the party was supported by conservative nationalist groups such as Pamyat [Remembrance], which saw the need to maintain Russia's imperial system by preserving *narodnost'*, which they interpreted as Russia's historical right to dominate its neighbors.

Recantations of "errors" and corrections of "blank spots" were important in and of themselves, but the reality of Soviet censorship produced troubling results even when used for "good" purposes. For example, a 1988 letter to *Izvestiia* referred to librarians who were

> summoned to a special seminar and, after being told that these were the instructions from higher authorities, were ordered to remove from our collections the works of Brezhnev . . . Chernenko and a number of other writers, as well as all the political and economic literature published prior to March 1985, as material that is . . . no longer relevant. It was recommended

that we remove the materials of the 22nd through the 26th Party Congresses from our shelves and tell readers . . . that they are being used.[38]

This example suggests that the chameleon of Soviet censorship continued to search for new colors to suit its environment—in essence, it attempted to substitute a new orthodoxy for the old. Indeed, without a definition of "correctness" in political thinking, the censorship regime would cease to exist.

Censorship and the Lithuanian Crackdown

Censorship was identified by CPSU loyalists as vital to national security just before, during, and after the storming and occupation of Vilnius radio and television headquarters in mid-January 1991.[39] This blunt reminder given by the CPSU *nomenklatura* to the separatist Lithuanian leaders suggested that the party would not continue to allow control of the media to slip away without a fight.

Lithuania became a test case of the Gorbachev regime's commitment to the idea of a free press; it also was a sign that Gorbachev's policy of glasnost was in serious trouble. The Soviet crackdown followed the classic Marxist-Leninist pattern, witnessed previously during the Hungarian Revolution (1956), the Prague Spring (1968), Afghanistan (1979), and the Polish Solidarity crisis (1980–1981). In each of these cases, suppression of the opposition movement to Communist rule was closely tied to what came to be known as the (Leonid) Brezhnev Doctrine, which explicitly declared the "limited sovereignty of socialist states" in a world where the class struggle had not yet been resolved.[40] In each of these cases, coordinated Soviet media campaigns of misinformation, disinformation, and rumor served as a prelude to a military crackdown, preparing the Soviet population and world public opinion for that eventuality.

In late December 1990, Soviet KGB chief Vladimir Kryuchkov identified "foreign anti-Soviet centers" as responsible for assisting internal disgruntled elements in trying to dismantle the Soviet Union.[41] Some two weeks later, and just before the Lithuanian crackdown, Soviet Marshal Dmitri Yazov characterized the government as a "bourgeois dictatorship," and Boris Pugo, the new head of Soviet security forces, referred to the "anti-Soviet propaganda" of the Lithuanian regime, harking back not only to previous Soviet interventions in Eastern Europe to "save socialism" but also to Article 6 of the Soviet Constitution, which retained for the CPSU authority as the "leading and guiding force" in Soviet society to "determine the general perspectives of the development of society and the course of the home and foreign policy of the USSR . . . [in] their struggle for the victory of communism."[42]

On January 10, 1991, Gorbachev issued an ominous warning to the Lithuanian government, which Lithuanian authorities quickly deemed an ultimatum. He accused Vilnius of violating the Soviet Constitution and described the situation as an "acute aggravation" of the situation that had grave potential for helping the restoration of the "bourgeois order."[43] Tass and other conservative official media portrayed the crisis using classic Leninist terms, referring to a "crisis of power" in Lithuania intensifying and a "critically explosive situation" developing.[44]

The Vilnius authorities responded to charges that the Lithuanian government was acting unconstitutionally by making reference to the illegal annexation of Lithuania by the USSR in 1940 and rejecting all accusations of acting unlawfully. Soviet media reported that the Lithuanian working class demanded Soviet authorities invoke direct presidential rule in Lithuania, under emergency powers granted to Gorbachev by the Congress of People's Deputies in 1990, to stop "political blackmail and psychological terror against those committed to Soviet territorial integrity."[45]

Ironically, to justify Soviet troops storming the Vilnius media headquarters, Tass described the attack as necessary "to return property to the legitimate owner—the Communist Party Central Committee."[46] This charge had some substance, for a major debate had ensued in the Congress of People's Deputies the previous year over how to dispossess the CPSU of at least some of its massive holdings.

Constitutionally, ownership of the "means of production" was to remain socialist, yet nothing in the Soviet Constitution's economic articles referred to the party in any way. The irony lay in the fact that the party in this case claimed "private" ownership (the party was not after all a government institution), but the party bureaucracy obstructed at every step a whole set of reform initiatives that had "privatization" at their heart, including the decollectivization of agriculture and outright private ownership of land.

Intervention in Lithuania was justified under the old orthodoxy of censorship, in which "slander" and "anti-Soviet propaganda" were routine accusations made against opponents of the regime. Tass continued the pattern: "Since anti-Soviet broadcasts were constantly conducted through the channels of national television and radio and hostile remarks against the leadership of the USSR were voiced, the leadership of the National Salvation Committee decided to bring state television and radio under control."[47] Finally, Tass also censored the numbers of people killed and wounded, underreporting to its audience significantly.[48]

Other events suggested that a broader coordinated effort aimed at limiting free-press activity might be under way. It was reported that top officials for the USSR State Committee for Television and Radio decided to block the liberal Interfax News Agency's activities by impounding its equipment.[49] At the same time, *Izvestiia* referred to the "increasingly ominous tone" that "the campaign to discredit journalists" launched in late 1990 had taken on, including "undisguised pressure on journalists, the destruction of pressruns, and the banning of television programs."[50] The murder of a regional newspaper editor prompted the government newspaper to accuse unnamed parties of "overt terror tactics against glasnost," suggesting that the new press law had a long way to go before it would be fully assimilated into Soviet political culture.[51]

Ominous developments in early 1991, including Gorbachev's threat to suspend the new press law "temporarily" under the emergency powers the Congress of People's Deputies granted him, reminded many observers of Lenin's actions in 1917 and after. Events subsequent to the Lithuanian crackdown did little to ease fears about the party's intention to tighten its control of information dissemination. These measures all raised serious questions about any Soviet progress toward achieving a "civil society."

The unresolved situation continued throughout spring and summer 1991, even as more and more voices around Gorbachev, including those of Boris Yeltsin, president of the Russian Republic, and Eduard Shevardnadze, former Soviet foreign minister, warned of an impending attempt to overthrow the regime. Indeed, those leading the opposition to glasnost and perestroika decided that half measures were not enough and that the ground for a Brezhnev-style intervention had been sufficiently prepared. The August 19, 1991, coup attempt was first and foremost an attempt to restore party-led Communist orthodoxy and conformity to Soviet media, without control of which party authority was eroding.

Conclusion

The CPSU's *nomenklatura* refused to give up is struggle to maintain control of the media under Gorbachev. Soviet censorship weakened, but was still a mechanism of control in the struggle between radical reformers and conservatives. Like a chameleon adapting to its surroundings, the Soviet censorship system changed its colors—responding both to pressures from above to allow more glasnost for the sake of perestroika, and to pressures from below by radical reformers who took advantage of glasnost to press for more sweeping changes. The system became somewhat less fear-inspiring, and it is true that in a formal sense, more freedom of the press existed under Gorbachev than at any time since 1917.

Chameleons might change colors, but that fact does not alter their reptilian nature. The strong government propensity for control of the press in Russian and Soviet political culture did not disappear under Gorbachev or after. Even after his resignation as head of the Communist Party on August 24, 1991, and the subsequent discrediting of the coup leaders and banning of the party, a strong minority voice continued to maintain the old values of the hammer and sickle and still seeks to control the media and, through it, the society at large. One hopes that democratic forces have sufficient time to strengthen to repel any possible future attempts to hegemonize public debate and political authority in the newly emerging political structures in the former Soviet Union.

Notes

1. This is the evaluation of Giulietto Chiesa, the Moscow correspondent for *L'Unita,* the Italian Communist Party's organ, after his return from covering the Twenty-eighth CPSU Congress in August 1990 in "The Twenty-eighth Party Congress: A New Stage Begins," Meeting Report, Vol. 7, No. 18, Kennan Institute for Advanced Russian Studies.

2. Stanislaw Baranczak, *Breathing Under Water and Other East European Essays* (Cambridge, MA: Harvard University Press, 1990).

3. Peter Kenez, "The Origins of the Soviet Press," Kennan Institute for Advanced Russian Studies No. 121 (1980), p. 2.

4. Marc Raeff, *Understanding Imperial Russia* (New York: Columbia University Press, 1980), pp. 105–106.

5. V. J. Boss, "Areopagitica and Freedom of the Press," *East European Quarterly*, Vol. 24, No. 2 (June 1990), p. 136.

6. Ibid.

7. See Kenez, "Origins of the Soviet Press," pp. 3ff.

8. Ibid.

9. Cited by Mikhail Fedotov, "The More Freedom, the More Responsibility: Will Censorship and Glasnost Get Along?" *Moscow News*, October 23, 1988.

10. Vasilii Seliunin, "Istoki" [*Sources*], *Noviy Mir*, No. 5, May 1988, p. 168; also cited in Boss, "Areopagitica," p. 142.

11. See "Partiinaya organizatsia i partiinaya literatura," *Novaya Zhizn'*, November 13, 1905, in V. I. Lenin, *Polnoe sobranie sochinenii*, 5th ed. (Moscow: Gosudarstvennoe izdatel'stvo politicheskoi literatury, 1960), pp. 99–105.

12. Ibid.

13. Kenez, "Origins of the Soviet Press," pp. 21ff.

14. See Fedotov, "The More Freedom."

15. This was a government agency, not a party institution, and was attached to the Soviet Council of Ministers. It became known as the Main Administration for the Protection of State Secrets in the Press.

16. "O sozyve ocherednogo 27 s'ezda KPSS i zadachakh, sviazannykh s ego podgotovkoi i provedeniem" [On the convening of the 27th CPSU Congress and the problems connected with its preparation and realization], *Pravda*, April 24, 1985, pp. 1–2.

17. See Vladimir Wozniuk, "The Propaganda Campaign for a New Orthodoxy in Soviet Social Science," *Political Communication and Persuasion*, Vol. 6, No. 4, esp. pp. 251–252.

18. Ibid., p. 251.

19. M. S. Gorbachev, "Doklad Tsk KPSS 27-omu s'ezdu KPSS" [Report of the CC to the CPSU 27th Congress], *Pravda*, February 26, 1986, esp. pp. 9–10.

20. See, for example, Ivan Frolov's comments on Moscow Television on October 2, 1986, as transcribed in *Foreign Broadcast Information Service (FBIS/SOV)*, October 7, 1986, p. R5.

21. *Kurier* (Vienna), October 30, 1986, p. 5, as cited in *FBIS/SOV*, October 31, 1986, p. R2.

22. See "A Soviet Censor, Uncensored," *New York Times*, February 13, 1989, p. 13. This originally appeared in NRC Handelsblad and was first published in Enlgish by *FIBS/SOV*, January 11, 1989.

23. See "Bidding Farewell to the Past," *Moscow News*, No. 19 (1990), p. 6.

24. Cited in Yuri M. Baturin, "Glasnost Struggles: An Insider's Account," Meeting Report, Kennan Institute for Advanced Russian Studies, Vol. 7, No. 17, 1990. Baturin, who helped draft the new law on the press, was at that time senior researcher at the Institute of State and Law of the USSR Academy of Sciences.

25. The thirty-nine articles that compose the law went into effect August 1, 1990. See "O pechati i drugikh sredstvakh massovoi informatsii" [On the press and other means of mass information], *Izvestiia*, June 20, 1990, p. 3.

26. Kenez, "Origins of the Soviet Press," pp. 32, 36.

27. The editors of *Argumenty i fakty* and *Noviy mir*, Vladislav A. Starkov and Sergei Zalygin, thorns in the side of the Gorbachev regime, were dismissed by the

government, but refused to leave. See Francis X. Clines, "Soviets Approve Law to Provide Press Freedoms," *New York Times*, June 13, 1990, pp. A1, A19. Also see Mark Neuzil, "Soviet Press Talk Turkey, and Fish," *Christian Science Monitor*, November 2, 1990, p. 14.

28. See the text of the press law in *Izvestiia*, June 20, 1990, p. 3. Also see Francis X. Clines, "Soviets Approve Law to Provide Press Freedoms," *New York Times*, June 13, 1990, pp. A1, A19. Gorbachev's suggestion was in response to severe Soviet media criticism of the Lithuanian crisis after radio and television headquarters had been stormed and occupied by Soviet troops on January 13, 1991.

29. See Dmitri N. Shalin, "Ethics of Survival," *Christian Science Monitor*, December 4, 1990, p. 10.

30. *Klassovost':* Class character or -mindedness, arising out of heightened class consciousness. *Narodnost':* nationality; national character; peopleness; the orientation of art and literature to mass needs and perceptions. *Partiinost':* party-mindedness; party spirit; placing party interests above all else. Roy D. Laird and Betty A. Laird, *A Soviet Lexicon* (Lexington, MA: Lexington Books, 1988) pp. 69, 78, 85.

31. Ibid., pp. 101–102. *Partiinost'* in particular has been applied in a broad way, even to science. The Lysenko affair of the 1950s comes to mind in this regard.

32. The Nobel laureates Alexandr Solzhenitsyn and Josip Brodsky are both cases in point. See for example, "The Trial of Joseph Brodsky," *Ogonyek*, December 1988, as translated in Jonathan Eisen, ed., *The Glasnost Reader* (New York: New American Library, 1990), pp. 60–77.

33. See *Newsweek*, August 6, 1990, p. 26.

34. The GLAVLIT censor identified himself as Vladimir A. Solodin. See "A Soviet Censor," p. 13.

35. Ibid.

36. See *Sovetskaia Rossiia*, March 13, 1988, p. 3.

37. See "V komissii Politburo Tsk KPSS" [In the commission of the Politburo of the CC CPSU], *Pravda*, February 6, 1988, p. 1; "Kto zhe oshibalsya?" [Who was it that erred?], *Literaturnaia gazeta*, March 16, 1988, p. 10, cited in *Current Digest of the Soviet Press*, Vol. 40, No. 11 (1988), p. 13; and "O belykh piatnakh" [On blank spots], *Pravda*, March 12, 1988, pp. 1, 4.

38. "Novye belye pyatna" [New blank spots], *Izvestiia*, August 17, 1988, p. 6.

39. The necessity of suppressing the Lithuanian independence movement by occupying the radio and TV headquarters was explicitly affirmed. See Daniel Sneider, "Soviets Present Own Version of Baltic Events," *Christian Science Monitor*, January 15, 1991, p. 7.

40. For analysis of this pattern of Soviet behavior, see Vladimir Wozniuk, "Gorbachev, Reform, and the Brezhnev Doctrine," *Comparative Strategy*, Vol. 7, No. 3, pp. 213–225.

41. See "Chetvertyi S'yezd Narodnykh Deputatov" [The Fourth Congress of People's Deputies], *Izvestiia*, December 24, 1990, pp. 2–8.

42. See the Soviet Constitution, as amended December 1, 1988.

43. See "Verkhovnomy Sovety LSSR" [To the Supreme Soviet of Lithuania], *Pravda*, January 10, 1991, p. 1.

44. See "Vstrechi s prestaviteliami obshchestvennosti LSSR" [Meetings with community representatives of Lithuania], *Izvestiia*, January 10, 1991, p. 1; and "Krizis vlasti v Litve" [Crisis of power in Lithuania], *Izvestiia*, January 11, 1991, p. 2.

45. See "Rezoliutsia uchastnikov v protesticheskom s'ezde v gorode Vilniusa"

[Resolution of the participants in a protest rally in the city of Vilnius], *Pravda,* January 12, 1991, p. 2.

46. See "Litva, 11 Yanvar" [Lithuania, 11 January], *Izvestiia,* January 12, 1991, p. 1.

47. Cited by Sneider, "Soviets Present Own Version," p. 7.

48. Ibid.

49. See "Zayavlenie agentstva 'Interfaks'" [Statement by the Interfax Agency], *Izvestiia,* January 12, 1991, p. 2. A conservative newspaper responded to the Interfax claim by implying that this was a plot to discredit the Soviet Union by foreign newspapers, Interfax being either a dupe or agent in this cabal. See *Sovetskaia Rossiia,* January 12, 1991, p. 5.

50. "Ubit redaktor oblastnoi gazety" [Editor of province newspaper killed], *Izvestiia,* January 12, 1991, p. 1.

51. Ibid.

4

The Dual Nature of Censorship in Hungary, 1945–1991

Gábor Mihályi

Those who have been active participants of the Hungarian political and cultural life as state employees or as artists know from their own experiences in what ways and with what methods free expression and artistic aspirations were hampered and suppressed by successive totalitarian governments, although the existence of censorship in Hungary was never formally acknowledged.[1] One of the most severe transgressions about censorship was to reveal its very existence. Decrees and departmental orders were usually kept secret and were passed on by telephone so that they could always be denied. This situation explains why only those who published their writings in the clandestine samizdat papers or in the West were able to speak openly about Hungarian censorship.[2]

Although much has been written (even in the legal press) about specific cases—about novels, poems, plays, and films withheld for years from the public—most of the time the commentary has not been focused or detailed. To cite many of the single cases of censorship would mean little to anyone unacquainted with Hungarian literature and unfamiliar with the persons concerned. Therefore, this chapter deals only with the description of the very complicated mechanism of Hungarian censorship and mentions specific cases only to illustrate the methods of this censorship.

The Beginning of Repression

The Hungarian elections of November 1945, after World War II, demonstrated the deep division within the country. In the first free and secret elections—excluding from the vote only those condemned for war crimes—the Left won only 42 percent of the votes, but the Smallholders Party alone won 57 percent. Since the professed programs of the different parties—even of the Communist Party—diverged only very slightly from each other, citizens cast their votes according to the presumed intentions of the parties. Those who mistrusted the new order, especially in the small towns and among the conservative peasantry, voted for the Smallholders Party, thus giving it an absolute majority.

Since Hungary was in the Soviet sphere of influence, the Smallholders Party was prevented from forming a one-party government. Although it got the post of prime minister, the Left gained control of the key ministries. A Communist politician (Imre Nagy) became the minister of interior.

Although in a real democracy the rules of the game prohibit the establishment of censorship, in postwar Hungary only the so-called democratic parties were authorized to publish newspapers.[3] The papers were ordered to refrain from publishing material that could hurt the interests of the Soviet Union or the Western Allied forces. In practice, it meant nothing could be written that might be in opposition to the official Soviet propaganda line. From the beginning, the chief editors assumed the role of censors.

The newspapers could not report about the inner party struggles that were fought behind closed doors. The journalists could not voice doubts about court cases in which evidence was often based on the forced confession of defendants.[4] The Hungarian press did not report in 1945 the arrest and disappearance of Pál Demény, the leader of an independent communist party that did not follow the orders from Moscow.[5]

Even the social-democratic press remained silent when in 1947 Sára Karig, a well-know member of the party, was deported to Siberia by the KGB. Although Karig had evidence regarding the electoral fraud committed by the Hungarian Communist Party, even journalists dared not protest when they learned she would be deported. Hungary's borders were already closed, and no one could leave the country without Soviet permission.

To increase their income, most of the parties had their own publishing house, though for some years the most important of these remained in private hands. After 1945, many books prohibited in the former era were published, especially the works of well-known antifascist writers like Thomas Mann, Bertolt Brecht, John Steinbeck and others. At last Marxist literature (the works of Marx, Engels, Lenin, and Stalin) could also be printed. That meant a new sort of freedom, and few noticed that no work could appear if it doubted the assertions of orthodox Marxism. The writings of Kautsky, Bernstein, and Trotsky were not published in a Hungarian translation, not to mention those of George Orwell and Arthur Koestler (who, as a Hungarian, was well known in Hungarian intellectual circles).

The new order had no difficulties with the theaters. The best known figures of Hungarian theatrical art belonged to the Left, and most of them joined the Communist Party. Tamás Major, an excellent actor and the newly appointed director of the Hungarian national Theater, was a zealous Communist. Even the owners of the private theaters supported the new democracy, especially because they could hope that they too would be sponsored by the state.[6]

Because the film studios and the movie houses were also in the hands of the parties, the new Hungarian cinema had to adjust to the new political requirements. Nevertheless, the heavily subsidized film industry was able to produce some masterpieces, like *Somewhere in Europe*, directed by Géza Radványi.

The new regime, established in 1945, eliminated or purged many people associated with the old order. Those who were held responsible for the tragic fate of the country during the war were put on trial, condemned to death, and executed. Others left the country. Conservative high-ranking officials lost their posts. The democratic parties (as they called themselves) set up screening committees that condemned journalists, writers, artists, and university professors judged to be adherents of the previous regime. They lost their jobs and were prohibited from continuing their work.

The ideological purge was not confined to individuals: libraries and bookstores had to be cleared of fascist literature. Long lists of books were condemned to be sent to papermills; newspapers were carefully supervised.[7]

To understand the success of the Communist Party in quickly establishing the new order, one should know that the leaders of the party (Mátyás Rákosi, the party secretary; Ernö Gerö, charged with the reorganization of the media industry; and Jozsef Révai, in charge of cultural affairs) were all very strong personalities and well versed in orthodox Marxism. The ideals of socialism attracted many people, especially the young. Thus, in 1949, when the Communist Party managed to defeat all the other parties and became the sole possessor of state power, it could count on the support of the greater part of the intelligentsia.

Hungarian Stalinism

It took only one year from 1948 to 1949, to impose the Soviet system in Hungary and to construct the new totalitarian order. Nationalization was consistently carried through, and even small shops were confiscated. Craftspeople were forced to join pseudo-cooperatives, where they became, in fact, wage earners. Only in the villages did the party have to restrain itself, and it proceeded slowly with collectivization, since it had to rely on the peasants to produce the food needed to feed the cities. The party recalled well that in 1919, during the short-lived Hungarian Soviet Republic, forced collectivization produced disastrous effects when hunger faced people in the cities. The possession of private property also meant some sort of limited independence, a little freedom.

Stalinism brought terror and fear to Hungary. To be accused of bourgeois mentality was enough to cost people their jobs. Many intellectuals were forced to purify themselves of their sins by joining the ranks of the working class. The secret police constantly looked for agents of imperialism—and because those agents had to be found, many innocent people were sent to concentration camps, some of them were condemned to death and executed, and others were imprisoned for long periods.

The result of this process was total conformity. No one dared challenge the official line. The indoctrination started every morning at the workplace, where everyone was obliged to attend the half-hour readings of the party newspaper *Szabad Nép* (Free people). In such a situation, everyone behaved and spoke in identical terms, and it became impossible to distinguish between real and false believers. Suspicion became widespread. Naturally, these conditions obviated any need for a special office of censorship. The editors in chief were personally responsible for every word that appeared in their newspaper, but contributors and assistant editors also could be held responsible, even for a misprint (if it had a political aspect disagreeable to the party).

Editors received their instructions from above. "Above" meant the government, especially the Office of Information (under the direct control of the prime minister) but also the Central Committee of the party and the different departments of the party headquarters. There was a well-coordinated hierarchy of departments to instruct and control the dailies, weeklies, and monthlies regardless of their subject matter (politics, culture, science, literature).

It was not enough for editors to know what ought not be printed; it was even more important to know what should be written. The editor had to understand the party language and follow it. In this language, every word meant something different, and nothing could be changed without specific instructions from above. The telephone was used to transmit the instructions, which had to be carried out very strictly. Usually, no written instructions followed; thus, it was always possible to deny the existence of the instructions if something went wrong.

Editors had to be familiar with all the changes in the party line and had to assure that their papers conformed to all these changes. Nevertheless, on occasion, there were no detailed instructions from above, especially in matters such as criticism and literature, theater and film. Critics and editors had to guess what sort of view was expected—this was part of the system. When critics erred, they were warned and forced to exercise self-criticism, which gave them the chance to prove their loyalty to the party.[8]

The book publishing houses—all state owned—were put under the control of the Ministry of Culture. Naturally, only reliable comrades were engaged as editors and readers. Modeled on the Soviet system, the publishing houses were specialized. One of them published only Hungarian belles lettres; another (Europe Publishing House) dealt only with foreign literature; and a third, *Müvelt Nép* (Educated people) and later renamed *Gondolat* (Thought), got the task of publishing only cultural literature. Soviet literature had its own publisher too, called curiously the New Hungarian Publishing House. Naturally, there was also a special publisher (Kossuth Publishing House) that issued Marxist-Leninist literature and the publications of the party.

All publishers were obliged to present a "year's plan," the list of books they wanted to bring out in the next year. This plan had to be sent to the literary department of the Cultural Ministry,[9] which sent it, accompanied by its own remarks, to another department in the party center. In all cultural matters, Mátyás Rákosi, the first secretary of the Party, and József Révai, responsible for all cultural matters in the Politburo, made all decisions and interfered even in the smallest details.

The well-known Hungarian novelist Tibor Déry (1894–1977) had not yet finished his planned trilogy *Felelet* (Answer) when Révai ordered the writer to make sure that his "positive hero," a nice young worker, joined the party. But the award-winning Déry, though an avowed Communist, refused this interference in his work. Révai initiated a party scandal, and critics were forced to condemn the bourgeois mentality of Déry. The writer remained adamant, but decided to abandon his novel.

All manuscripts of Hungarian writers had to be read and approved not only by the readers on the staff of the publishing house but also by specially selected readers. These were well-known critics and specialists who, as members of the establishment, had close personal relations with the top hierarchy and whose status could protect the publishers against later disapproval from above. In general, the manuscripts were thoroughly checked—the pretense being to help the author eliminate factual errors, stylistic lapses, grammatical faults, and misprints. Although most of these interventions helped improve the quality of the text, the main task of the reader was to control the *content* of the book and judge whether it was in accordance with the general line of the party. To avoid the appearance of functioning as a censor, the reader had to use indirect methods, such as suggesting that the plot of the novel and the behavior of some of the characters might be considered untruthful, too pessimistic, and in contradiction with the bright future or the perspectives promoted by the party.

During this era of Stalinism, Hungarian writers were asked to comply with the requirements of social realism and the so-called theory of revolutionary romanticism. It was expected that a novel or a play should have a positive hero: a worker, a peasant, or a party secretary leading a victorious battle against the class enemies, who were never allowed to defend their positions. Writers were urged to report about the present, the day-to-day reality of the socialist society. But in a classless socialist society, there were no enemy classes anymore, only powerless remnants of them. Thus, as it became increasingly difficult to invent real enemies in a novel dealing with the present, some of the more zealous critics invented the theory of a novel or drama devoid of conflicts. In these works, only good and even better people should—using the method of criticism and self-criticism—discuss how to better themselves and be even more resolute soldiers of the new order.

Most of the best Hungarian writers could not follow this line of Zhdanovian theories (grounded in the writings of Andrei Zhdanov) and quickly discovered that their writings were not published. Only some of the Communist writers—all convinced followers of the party—tried to comply, but after a time, even they revolted, discovering they were unable to lie even if the party asked them to do that. Tibor Déry was not the only writer to get into conflict with the party; so too did István Örkény, who became later (in the 1960s) one of the best-known Hungarian playwrights, the master of absurd drama.[10]

The publishing houses did not have to worry about the distribution and sale of their books. That became the task of the National Book Distributing Company. Because publishing was heavily subsidized and the profit motive eliminated, books could be sold for a very low price. Although books had wide circulation, works of value and of real interest were sold out quickly. And because the libraries were also heavily subsidized, they bought even those books nobody wanted to read, such as the party literature and the collected speeches of the leaders of the party.

The nationalization of the theaters gave a big advantage to everyone working in the theater industry. All of the existing theaters were provided with a permanent company, which guaranteed the actors' livelihood. Naturally, actors could get in trouble too if they scolded the regime openly, but most transgressions could be forgotten if they would apologize. Serious consequences could follow if an actor quarreled with a superior; in most cases, the actor was transferred to another theater, from a better place to a worse one. Yet few actors were really interested in politics—most wanted primarily to get a good role.

The totally subsidized theaters, restricted as they were in what they could produce, could not satisfy the entire public, yet from the beginning the party demanded that the theaters should play before sold-out houses. The only thing that really counted was the percentage of sold tickets. Nobody cared how the tickets were sold or even whether the ticket buyers actually came to the theater. Thus, cultural propagandists, themselves employees in factories, offices, and schools, were charged with the recruitment of the public to guarantee box-office hits. Because they got a percentage of the revenue, they did their best to sell tickets without regard to the methods used. One of the tricks used was political blackmail. People had to attend plays considered politically important. One of the pledges made by the so-called "socialist brigades" was to go in a group to the theater. There were "full-house campaigns" when a factory, an agricultural cooperative, or a school had to buy all the tickets of a performance. A frequent occurrence, especially in the regional theaters, was for all tickets to be sold out but the theater in fact half empty.

The regime feared the theaters, since in the darkness, people felt less danger in applauding sentences uttered on the stage. Therefore, control of the theaters was severe. Although formally some of the theaters were (and still are) under direct state control, others belonged to the municipalities or the counties. In fact, all decisions—the nomination of theater directors, the choice of the plays produced, and so on—had to be approved by the Theater Department of the Ministry of Culture which itself was controlled by one of the deputy ministers and the party center. Before 1956, all important decisions were taken by József Révai and after that by György Aczél. With about twenty theater companies in the country, it was not difficult to know what was going on in these institutions.

The theater directors were charged with the implementation of the cultural policy of the party. The directors had to be, first of all, politically reliable persons, but because it was not always possible to find talented artists who were politically trustworthy, the artistic director had to accept as a superior an outsider the party trusted, often a party official.

The situation was not the same in Budapest as in the provinces. Since some of the young directors were staunch Communists, there was no problem in finding talented artists to head the theaters in Budapest. The best actors worked also in the capital. The countryside, however, got second-rate theater, actors, and directors.

A theater director could always earn high marks with the party by presenting new Hungarian plays, especially if they dealt with contemporary matters. The party viewed it as a point of honor to support the presentation of new

Hungarian drama, perceiving these plays as tools of socialist education. Nevertheless, the presentation of new Hungarian plays was always a shaky affair. If it was a socialist realist play, it had to be based on lies and was bad; if it told the truth, it could be good, but then it was not a socialist realistic play.

Young playwrights had to pass a tortuous way until their plays reached the stage of one of the regional theaters. Every theater employed dramatic advisers who were convinced they were paid to work with the author on the text; it was presumed these advisers were well-trained professionals who had to instruct the author. Then came the director, charged with staging the play, who continued to adapt the text. This process was considered good teamwork.[11]

The film industry was similarly controlled, with the disastrous result being the production of complete trash. The theaters always could stage classics and thus avoid external interventions, but not so with films. Some of the best film directors, like Géza Radványi, left the country. This system was perfected during the regime of Janos Kádár. Control of the film industry was through a trust called Mafilm, which financed and supervised the film studios. Each studio was led by a film director nominated by the Ministry of Culture; naturally, appointees had to be considered sufficiently trustworthy to follow the guidelines of the party. Nevertheless, the studio director had to organize an artistic council to assist him in his work. Its main duty was to screen the scripts and adapt them to the prescriptions of the day. Once the script was accepted, it had to be approved by the Filmigazgatóság (the directorial board of films), which was led by a director who had to be a loyal party member. Shooting could start only after the script was accepted. When the film was ready, it was reviewed once more—and often banned.

Art also suffered severe restrictions. Only social realism was tolerated. Tough battles were fought in the field of architecture. Music fared better, as the artists were defended and protected by the highly respected composer Zoltán Kodály. Nevertheless, modern music was considered decadent. Even Béla Bartók came under attack for a while.

During Stalin's lifetime, this system of oppression worked faultlessly. Control was so total that no opposition was possible: There was no reasonable choice—one had to conform. Resistance seemed hopeless and nobody resisted.

The Fiasco of the System

After the death of Stalin, the system started to break up, though the process of disintegration lasted for thirty years. During his lifetime, Stalin was able to maintain the myth that the new socialist order was perfection itself, that it brought prosperity and happiness to the people of the Soviet Union. The myth of Stalin—the myth of the beloved and cherished leader—was destroyed by the revelations of Nikita Khrushchev in his famous "secret speech" at the Twentieth Congress of the Soviet Communist Party in the mid-1950s. Telling the truth about the unlawful acts, the fake trials, and the mass murders that cost the lives of millions of people began the process that in the end destroyed all belief in communism.

In Hungary, Imre Nagy became prime minister in 1953. Rákosi, the first secretary of the Party, had to admit at least some of the unlawful acts committed and some of his responsibility. The Communist intellectuals, especially the writers, who until that time supported Rákosi, discovered they were cheated. Siding with Nagy, they started to demand radical changes and the punishment of those responsible for the crimes committed.

But the leadership of the party, its bureaucracy, and the secret police quickly discovered how much they could lose if they gave up their privileges. After the elimination of Lavrenti Beria and Georgi Malenkov, the protectors of Imre Nagy, Rákosi managed to get rid of him. Yet he was unable to reestablish the old order. The myth was dead and could not be resurrected.

A major obstacle was that there was no way of stopping the revolt of the Communist writers. They could not be relieved of their functions and be kicked out of their jobs. In the new situation, it was no longer possible to put them in jail. The party did not want to risk the scandal of preventing the publication of the works of writers so much revered and honored until that time.

The rituals of party life demanded a monthly party meeting. Communist writers belonging to the Writers Union had opportunity to stand up, ask disagreeable questions, and express their views. One meeting followed another, and their content became known in public.

The editor of *Irodalmi Ujság* (Literary magazine) belonged to the circle that supported Imre Nagy. Yet censorship based on the reliability of the editor did not function anymore, and the weekly became increasingly popular. The editor, Miklós Molnár, was relieved of his duties, but his successor, György Hámos, former editor of a magazine for police members, continued to attack the Rákosi leadership in an even bolder way. Hámos had to go too, but even the third editor, Endre Enczl, did not change the direction of the weekly.

Encouraged by the example of the writers, other sectors were emboldened also. The party meetings of the different artistic unions, the universities and the scientific institutions became more and more open. As if rolling down a hill, the snowball of dissent became an avalanche. It started as an inner party struggle, but later spread into magazines, weeklies, and dailies. The first serious Hungarian films were born, and they gave a highly critical appraisal of Communist reality. Meetings were organized at last in the big halls of the universities, where nonparty members, students, and their professors could join the discussions. The first proclamations were written, which demanded sweeping reforms.

On October 23, 1956, the people of Budapest joined a protest march organized to dislodge the still-remaining Muscovites (Hungarian leaders loyal to Moscow) from the party leadership. The demonstration turned into a revolution, and it became clear that those leading the revolution would not be satisfied with some sort of reformed communism. The people wanted a total change: a multiparty system, free elections, and the departure of the Soviet troops stationed in Hungary.

The Compromise of Kádár

On November 4, 1956, Soviet tanks crushed the revolution. Janos Kádár, who was put in power, could pacify the country only with terroristic methods, arrests, and more than 200 executions. The strategy broke all resistance, allowing Kádár to finish the collectivization of the farms.

But in the early 1960s, Kádár changed course. He rid himself of the old Communist guard and decided to implement all the reforms instigated by Imre Nagy that were still compatible with communism. Kádár's declaration that "Who is not against us, is with us" opened the door to a compromise with the Hungarian intellectuals. This statement meant that the party was ready to accept those who did not support it actively. Nobody codified this compromise but it worked for more than twenty years.

Under Kádár, the control mechanisms remained the same, but the walls limiting freedom were pushed further back. The direction of Hungary's intellectual life was now in the hands of György Aczél, an intimate friend of Kádár. Aczél, a pragmatic politician, preferred praxis to theory. He decided to reconcile the party with at least the leading intellectuals. Imprisoned writers were released and pardoned. Aczél, himself an interesting personality, managed to gain the friendship of leading writers and artists such as Gyula Illyés, the poet laureate of the country; László Németh, novelist, playwright, and the theoretician of the "third way"; and Tibor Déry.[12]

The main argument for gaining the goodwill of the leading intellectuals and the country at large was the notion of comparative freedom. Compared with the situation in the other socialist countries, political conditions in Hungary were tolerable. It became a slogan of those years that Hungary was "the happiest barracks in the socialist camp." Intellectual freedom was greater than anywhere in the Eastern bloc.

The theory of social realism was abandoned in these years, and even officials spoke with contempt about the Zhdanovian ideas. The official standpoint was to support literature and art that professed humanistic ideals and expressed them in a comprehensible and somewhat realistic form. Abstract and experimental art was tolerated.[13] The doors were opened to Western literature, art, and films, although not totally. Percentages were still prescribed: More works by authors from the Soviet Union and the other socialist countries than from Western authors had to be published. Aczél (for some unknown reason) hated Eugene Ionesco, and during Aczél's reign no play of the Romanian-born author was permitted to be produced in Hungarian theaters. As years passed, there were increasingly fewer forbidden works. By the end of the Communist regime, only anti-Communist literature and pornography remained prohibited.

Through use of metaphors, writers in literature, theater, and films[14] were able to express thoughts that censorship prevented scientific studies, essays, and journalism from formulating (since these required direct language). It was part of the compromise of the Kádár period that those in power agreed not to decipher the metaphors of the writers and the poets. There were always exceptions, and some works remained banned for years. One of the best plays of

Sándor Weöres, *The Beast with Two Heads,* although published, had to wait some fourteen years until it received permission to be produced in the theaters.[15] Critics were scolded sometimes for siding with the writers against the party, but in general they were not treated very harshly. In the last years of the decaying regime, no works were banned.

After the collapse of the Prague Spring of 1968, it became increasingly difficult to maintain the compromise. The fiasco of the Hungarian economic reform proved that the system was irreparable.

The End of the Compromise

Censorship became less and less efficient in the 1970s and 1980s. The chief editors and the directors of the publishing houses and of the theaters found themselves in a schizophrenic situation. Editors knew that their fame and the success of their publications depended on their boldness in publishing critical texts, but these, of course, would be disliked by the hierarchy. As the contradictions and absurdities of the regime became increasingly apparent, however, even the editors began to like the witty, well-written attacks on the regime. Nevertheless, they did not want to risk the loss of their positions and could not forget that their careers were linked to those in power. Even a small change at the top could bring about an editor's downfall.[16]

Endre Illés, the head of the Szépirodalmi Kiadó (Publishing House of Belles Lettres) and György Kardos, a veteran leader of the Hungarian KGB and later the head of the rival publishing house Magvetö, are cases demonstrating the schizophrenia. These individuals were ready to take some risks and publish manuscripts refused by others. The two had the necessary connections to Aczél and were able to convince him to give his approval to a given book. In the process, they widened the space of liberty.

At the end of the 1980s, however, the old compromise no longer functioned. The most respected old writers, artists, and scientists died one after the other, and Aczél discovered he was unable to develop friendly relations with the members of the younger generation. Aczél's aides, who had to defend the contradictions and inconsistencies of their patron, were wary in the increasingly hopeless fight. Death took its toll among them too, and Aczél had to give up and retire.

Although most of the intellectuals considered themselves in opposition to the regime, they did not dare to cross the boundaries of legality. Only a very few writers (György Konrád, István Eörsi, and György Petri) who felt somewhat protected by their international fame and some young people challenged all forms of censorship. Following the Russian, Polish, and Czech example, they began to publish the so-called samizdat newspapers and books, most of the time openly advertising the name and the address of the publishers.[17] The police intervened and confiscated the printed material and the mimeographs. On occasion, the publishers were imprisoned for one or two days and some of them were even beaten, but the state had no desire to bring them before a court.[18] These were already the times when the

Hungarian government took pride in proclaiming there were no political prisoners in the country. In reality, this was the price the government had to pay to get new loans from the West so as to maintain the economic balance of the country.

In these circumstances, a police raid on a publishing house or an ideological attack in the party newspaper (printed in 600,000 copies) amounted to an advertisement free of charge. The controversial writings that appeared in the samizdat press (which could reach only a very few people) were read the same evening on Radio Free Europe (RFE). When Hungarian radio and television began to compete with the RFE and the other foreign television channels, it became once more worthwhile to tune to the Hungarian broadcasts.[19] Under the last Communist government, headed by Miklós Németh, freedom of the press was nearly restored.

Conclusion: The Censorship of Money and the Parties

After the end of the Communist era, the new freely elected government introduced total press freedom, limited only by some articles of the Constitution that outlawed the propagation of race hatred and incitement to use antidemocratic methods to overthrow the legally elected government.

Anybody was entitled to establish a newspaper. Consequently, there are now more quarterlies, monthlies, weeklies, and dailies than readers can cope with. Most of the newspapers have been short-lived. The competition has been vigorous and papers have eliminated each other. The editors have quickly discovered that printing these papers costs more than they have been able to bring in. When owners run out of money, they have to give up, and with the establishment of new papers the competition does not ease.

It is a somewhat disappointing experience for journalists when they discover that total press freedom means total freedom for the owners of the media. For journalists, it means that, in principle, they have the right to choose between the owners—between the different offers. Unfortunately, there are few offers for high-level journalism.

The major figures of the international press arrived in Hungary very quickly, and each of them bought one of the big and influential morning papers or started a new one, most of them tabloids.[20] Media magnates such as Robert Maxwell (now deceased), Rupert Murdoch, and others have been welcomed as saviors of the Hungarian press. They bring in the necessary capital to modernize the management and the printing of these newspapers. And for the moment they defend the independence of these newspapers from the ruling party and the government, some members of which are starting to behave like the old state-party, trying to impose their own devotees—journalists who are ready to propagate the ideology of the governing coalition (which supports fervent nationalism, militant clericalism, and demagogic populism).

Those in power now are trying to establish their own newspapers and to gain control of the direction of the national radio and television. Since the Hungarian banks remained under state control, it was not very difficult to force the bank directors, who all got their posts in the old era, to sponsor with millions of forints a newly established daily called *Új Magyarország* [New Hungary]. Another new daily—established with very little Hungarian money—gave up very quickly its professed independence and rallied to the government camp in the hope of receiving the money needed to maintain itself.

The newly appointed directors of radio and television try to preserve the independence and the impartiality of their institutions, but because they must rely on government money, their resistance is weak. The television news and the political broadcasts, which have begun to attain a European level, are once more as bad and as biased as in the old times; only the political direction is different.

The cultural magazines, widely read by the intellectuals, are also in an economically difficult situation. Before the political changes, these magazines were totally financed by the state. Now, in the days of press freedom, the government is unable to continue to sponsor all of them. Committees appointed by the Ministry of Culture are given money to distribute among these magazines, but there is never enough to maintain them all. If these monthlies and quarterlies want to survive, they will have to find other sponsors which becomes more difficult. Most of these papers contain much worthy material, and it is always a loss if some of them have to give up.

The change to a market-oriented economy forced the book publishing industry to carry out radical changes. The state-owned publishers have had to reduce their staff in order to remain competitive in a market where newly founded small book publishers are trying to find their place.

In the beginning, a lot of political literature was published, especially books that were banned before (Koestler, Orwell, Solzenitzyn). But for the moment, the market is totally saturated, and it is difficult even to sell thrillers. To publish valuable books with a relatively small readership (under 20,000–30,000 copies) becomes very difficult; such a publisher must find sponsors to pay for the financial loss.

The Hungarian filmmakers, too, have many complaints. Censorship has disappeared, but now there are no funds to produce Hungarian films. Most of the film directors are out of work, even some of the best ones. Hungarian film is in a crisis, and the cause is not only the lack of money.

Theater (especially the National Theater) cannot avoid becoming the scene of the ideological clashes that split the country in two. The former head of the National Theater, although a talented young director, received his appointment during the old times; it was foreseeable he would be removed. The new director is a young critic, well known for his sympathies for the ideals of the new establishment in power. After his nomination, some twenty actors severed their links with the theater.

These kinds of conflicts are well known in the West. But they are new to Hungary, whose people hoped that after all these difficult years, they would enter a wonderful new age of justice and happiness. After such difficult historical experience, however, they should have known that this utopia could not be realized.

Notes

1. György Aczél, János Kádár's right hand and since November 1956 in charge of all cultural affairs, said to Paul Lendvai, a Hungarian-born Austrian journalist, that "there is no censorship in Hungary. The leaders of the press, the different mass medias and other public forums decide themselves independently but with responsibility what sort of opinions can be expressed in public." See _Valóság_, 1980, p. 12. Nevertheless, in his book _Socialism, Nation, Culture,_ Aczél acknowledges some limitations on press freedom. He states that there should be no liberty for reactionary ideas, warmongering, incitement against peace and humanity, views praising fascism, and race hatred (p. 169). Such views are condemned by the Hungarian Constitution and by the Charter of the United Nations, and even most of the capitalist countries have laws prohibiting the spreading of such views.

2. Mentioned here are only the most important publications about censorship published in the samizdat papers:

- _Profil_ [Profile] by János Kenedi. A collection of short writings, published in Budapest in 1977 and in the _Magyar Füzetek_ [Hungarian booklets], No. 2.
- Ferenc Köszeg, "Könyvkiadói cenzura Magyarországon" [Censorship in the Hungarian book publishing industry], _Beszélö_, No. 5-6 and No. 9, December 1982 and February 1984.
- György Bence, "Cenzurázott és alternative közlési lehetöségek a magyar kulturában" [Censored and alternative possibilities of publication in Hungarian culture], published in _Hirmondó_, No. 18, August-September 1985.
- György Konrád, "A cenzura reformja" [The reform of censorship], _Hirmondó, ibid._
- Zsolt Krokovai, "Le a cenzurával?" [down with censorship?], _Beszélö_, No. 16, 1986.

3. In the first month of 1945, the provisional government of Hungary decreed that the publication of all sorts of printed material required authorization by the government (Decree #390, 1945, Prime Minister Office).

4. One of the first fake trials was that of the so-called Magyar Közösség (Hungarian community). It seems that some civil servants working in the Ministry of Agriculture met regularly and dreamed of the "wonderful old times." Probably their meetings were taped by the Hungarian secret police. This insignificant case was purposely blown out of proportion, and politicians who belonged to the right wing of the Smallholders Party and the Peasant Party were implicated in the affair. Even the prime minister (Ferenc Nagy) was accused of high treason. He had to resign and leave the country. The international press voiced some doubts, but the leaders of the other parties allied with the Communist Party, rejected these accusations, and declared there were no irregularities during the trial.

5. Pál Demény was freed only in 1957, but had to wait for his rehabilitation until 1989, when his case was at last reported in the mass media. Demény published two books giving an account of his imprisonment: _Rabságom_ [My captivity, 1989] and _Zárkatársam Spinoza_ [My cell-mate, Spinoza]. Demény, elected to parliament, died in 1989 during a session of it.

6. Ministerial decree number 29,909 (1945) stated that to establish a private theater, one had to apply for permission from the Ministry of Religion and Education.

7. The best-known case was that of Béla Bodó, a well-known writer of children's books. In those times he was still an unknown assistant editor of a daily, _Népszava,_

and was on duty the night the obituary of Stalin was printed. The next morning an unforgettable misprint appeared in the newspaper. The original sentence wanted to express the "deep mourning" of the Hungarian people; what appeared was "ordered mourning." In Hungarian there is only one letter difference between "megrendült" (deep mourning) and "megrendelt" (ordered). Bodó was immediately imprisoned, but he was lucky: Soon afterward, Imre Nagy became prime minister, a general amnesty followed, and Bodó was released.

8. The editor of the theater column of *Szabad Nép* wrote a devastating review of a new Hungarian play. Although he was totally right, the criticized play was one of the first products of social realism, a play about workers in contemporary Hungary. The party chose to defend the play and its author, and the critic was forced to admit his mistake. I do not want to mention names, as both the author and the critic are still living. The critic became a well-known anti-Communist and played a leading role in the events leading to the 1956 revolution.

9. During the Kádár times, a special office was created called the Kiadói Föigazgatóság (the chief management office of book publishers). No manuscript could go to print without its stamp of approval. The periodicals were controlled by the Tájékoztatási Hivatal (Office of Information), whose main role was to prevent the free circulation of information. Foreign travels of journalists had to be approved by this office. It controlled the distribution of foreign newspapers.

10. István Örkény wrote in 1951 a very bad novel called the *Házastársak* [Married couples]. In those years he was a convinced Communist and wanted sincerely to adapt himself to the prescriptions of social realism. Although critics praised his book, Örkény knew it was weak. Wanting to revert to his old style, he wrote a short story called "Lila tinta" [Violet ink]. This innocent tale about young lovers who behaved quite naturally and spoke the everyday language of young students came under heavy fire from the party, which accused the author of idealizing prostitution. József Révai, the chief ideologue of the party, personally led the attack against Örkény.

11. Mikhail Bulgakov wrote an amusing satirical play about this process, based on his experiences at the Art Theater, titled *The Purple Island*.

12. Aczél declared at the Thirteenth Party Congress: "It is the first time in the history of our country that a set of values was established which was accepted not only by the artists themselves but also by the responsible critics and the readers. None of the important artists were obliged to do work against the will of those in power." See *Népszabadság*, March 27, 1985. A well-known story from those years is that one of the great old men of Hungarian poetry declared: "Naturally I have poems which cannot be published under the present conditions. But I myself would not want it." Reported by Gy. Bence, *Hirmondó*, August-September 1985.

The "third way" writers represented a line that did not endorse the bureaucratic communism but leaned toward nationalistic, socialist political ideas.

13. Nevertheless, already in the early 1970s some artists again had trouble with the regime. One of them was György Galántai, who tried to organize some avant-garde expositions in a small chapel in Balatonboglár each summer between 1970 and 1973. In the end, police intervened at the instigation of the party newspaper. See *Népszabadság*, December 16, 1973; reported by *Hirmondó*, August-September 1985.

The Inconnu ("unknown") Group (Tamás Molnár and his friends) decided in 1983 to defy all form of censorship. Their openly stated aim was to create antigovernmental political art. Their first declarations came out in a book published by a samizdat house. They stated: "Confront! Collect documents! Publish them! That means: do what is not permitted!" They, too, were harassed by the police, who tried to ruin them economically but refrained from putting them in jail. The legal base for this police action was a decree that considered these infringements of the law as petty offenses punishable only by fines. Reported by *Hirmondó*, August-September 1985.

14. Yvette Biró, "Il y avait un film en l'Europe de l'Est," *Lettre Internationale*, Paris, Spring 1991.

15. To withhold works for years was one of the leadership's favorite methods of Hungarian censorship. Permission was given to publish them only when those in power decided that the banned work had lost its political threat and that no harm would result if it appeared. Some films waited for ten years, such as *The Witness* by Peter Bacsó. Gyula Hernádi's novel *Azég katonái* [The soldiers of heaven], written in 1961, was first published in a periodical in 1981 and in book form only two years later. This novel is still the author's best work—once again proof that a really good work is able to resist the erosion of time.

16. Even Aczél could not evade this schizophrenic attitude. As he said in an interview to a French journalist, "The Party has to be its own opposition." György Aczél in *Valóság*, 1980, p. 290.

17. The most important samizdat newspapers were *Beszélö* (from December 1981; it has appeared legally since 1990) and *ABC Tájékoztató* (which in 1983 became *Hirmondó*). The most important samizdat publishers were AB Independent Publisher, published by Gábor Demszky, now mayor of Budapest; ABC Independent Publisher, published by Jenö Nagy; and Magyar Október Szabadsajtó [Free press of Hungarian October].

18. Blacklists were used not without some results. Those who published in samizdator without permission in the West got on the blacklist and were not allowed to publish in the legal publications. But as the samizdat writers became increasingly famous in the West (Konrád, Szelényi, Haraszti), it became clear that some exceptions had to be made—for István Eörsi, Sándor Csoóry, and others. In the end even this method became useless.

19. The samizdat newspaper *Hirmondó* in its August-September 1985 issue published the minutes of a meeting held at the Agit-Prop department at party headquarters. At this meeting, permission was given to the international hotels in Budapest to put in the rooms television sets able to capture the programs transferred by satellites. At the time, the party still hoped it could maintain the ban on such viewing by Hungarian citizens, although in most of western Hungary, one could easily receive the Austrian programs. All restrictions were abolished in 1989.

20. The national and local dailies have a circulation of about 2.5 million, and 82 percent of this figure is already attributable to foreign investors. Axel Springer publishes 15 percent, Bertelsmann AG 14 percent, News International (Murdoch) 7 percent, Mirror (Maxwell) also 7 percent, and Hersant 5 percent. Springer bought some provincial newspapers. The former central organ of the Communist Party belongs now to Bertelsmann AG, and the *Magyar Hirlap* (which used to be the paper of the Hungarian government) was taken by Robert Maxwell, who bought more than 50 percent of the shares. He also bought *Esti Hirlap* (The evening news), which was the organ of the Budapest Committee of the party. The *Magyar Nemzet* was sold, with the active help of the Antall government, to Hersant, which has a reputation of sponsoring right-wing newspapers such as the *Figaro* in Paris. Other foreign companies got their share too—for example, Funk (11 percent) and Westdeutscher (5 percent).

5

Censorship in Castro's Cuba: "Against the Revolution, Nothing"

Roger Reed

Censorship in Fidel Castro's Cuba has always been comparable in its goals and methods to censorship in other Communist countries. However, at a time when the government of the former Soviet Union was relaxing its restrictions on freedom of expression, the government of Cuba was cracking down harder than ever.

Castro did not introduce the practice of censorship in Cuba. For years, the dictator Fulgencio Batista had tried to control the press by bribing journalists.[1] From time to time, Batista appointed censors for certain periodicals or permitted newspapers to publish only official reports on the activities of antigovernment guerrillas.[2] However, censorship under Batista was limited and very inconsistent. Batista even allowed the publication in the Cuban press of twenty-five attacks against him by Castro, including two major revolutionary manifestos issued while Castro was fighting in the mountains.[3]

When the rebels chased Batista from power in 1959, one of their first moves was to close down several newspapers. By 1961, the Castro regime had taken over or forced out of business all independent newspapers and magazines.[4] Batista never went this far.

Castro's willingness to use extreme measures distinguishes his government from traditional dictatorships that impose censorship but allow some opposition press to exist. For example, the military dictatorship of Augusto Pinochet in Chile allowed for eight years the publication of as many as eight magazines critical of the government. Even after 1984, when most of them were forbidden to publish, the opposition magazine *Hoy* was allowed to continue.[5]

The experience in Nicaragua was somewhat similar. Although the Sandinistas imposed tight censorship on the opposition newspaper *La Prensa* and shut it down briefly several times, *La Prensa* never ceased to exist.[6] It was always a leading—and perhaps the loudest—voice of the opposition. In February 1990, an anti-Sandinista coalition led by *La Prensa* co-owner Violeta Chamorro was swept into office in nationwide elections. In stark contrast, the owners and editors of independent newspapers in Cuba were all chased out of the country three decades earlier.

Censorship may be defined broadly as "control of communication by restricting what can be written, exhibited, or said."[7] Obviously, this covers much more than banning books. In Cuba, censorship includes suppressing all independent publishing houses.[8] In fact, the entire communications industry is owned and controlled by the government. This enables the authorities to deny publication to anybody for any reason. Also, since the government is the only employer in the country, it may punish writers simply by firing them from whatever jobs they have and by denying them employment elsewhere.

The ultimate penalty in Cuba is imprisonment. Over the years, dozens of Cubans have gone to prison—and some of them are still there—for having violated criminal laws that restrict freedom of expression. Writers are not the only ones who have been arrested. Anyone who speaks to foreign journalists, who writes anti-Castro graffiti on a wall, or who simply keeps a "forbidden" book at home risks falling prey to the state security police.[9] The recent crackdown on human rights activists has contributed to a veritable reign of terror that encourages self-censorship.

Even among communist countries, Cuba is conspicuous for its failure to afford legal protection to dissidents. Unlike in the (former) Soviet Union, North Korea, and Vietnam, the government of Cuba is not legally obligated to respect the guarantee of freedom of expression provided in Article 19 of the International Covenant of Civil and Political Rights; the Cubans never signed or ratified this treaty.[10] Furthermore, freedom of expression is not guaranteed by Cuba's Constitution. According to Article 39, "artistic freedom is free as long as its content is not contrary to the Revolution." Article 52 provides that Cuban citizens have freedom of speech and expression only when it is "consistent with the purposes of socialist society."[11]

Castro indicated the sweeping scope of censorship in Cuba when he gave a famous speech in 1961 entitled "Words to the Intellectuals." Speaking to an audience of writers and artists, he told them what they would be allowed to express: "With the Revolution, everything; against the Revolution, nothing."[12]

The Object of Censorship

When Castro delivered his famous speech, he described the rationale for prohibiting everything "against the Revolution" as being that the revolution has "the right to exist" and that this right must take precedence over rights claimed by individuals.[13] In other words, the survival of the revolution has priority over freedom of expression. This is an argument based on the need to protect "national security." Civil liberties in many other countries, including the United States, have been restricted under the same pretext.

Obviously, censorship aimed at "defending the revolution" is also censorship aimed at keeping Castro in power. However, the object of censorship in Cuba is not only to suppress opposition to Castro. Another important object is to insulate the Cuban people from ideas and information that would discourage them from accepting the official ideology.

Castro is not a traditional Latin American dictator. He never intended simply to overthrow the Batista dictatorship and take power. Castro had a much more ambitious plan: to destroy the old culture and build a new society by changing the very mentality of the Cuban people. As early as September 1959, Castro was saying that it is necessary "to begin to transform the mind, through an effort of consciousness and opinion, in order to go marching down the road we have to take."[14] He insisted that "the workers must be taught to think as a class."[15]

Che Guevara shared Castro's attitude about the importance of political education. In August 1960, he was already demanding "very profound changes in the mental contexture of the people. Individualism as such . . . must disappear in Cuba." Everyone should act, he said, "in absolute benefit of the collectivity."[16] Changing the basic attitudes of the Cuban people required, as Che put it, "erasing our old ideas."[17]

Eventually, Che began calling for the creation of a "New Man"—a "true revolutionary" prepared to make enormous personal sacrifices for "the most sacred causes."[18] Che believed that the transition from capitalism to socialism is not a "mechanical" process. It is not enough, he said, to nationalize the means of production—it is also necessary to create revolutionary "consciousness." Che claimed that his concept of the New Man as an indispensable element in the transition to socialism constituted an original theoretical contribution to Marxism-Leninism.[19]

Castro quickly adopted this project. In 1968, Castro said that "the great task of the Revolution is basically the task of the forming [of] the New Socialist Man . . . the man of truly revolutionary consciousness."[20] This language has been repeated again and again by Cuban leaders. The platform adopted by the Communist Party in 1986 said that the ultimate aim of the revolution is the creation of "a qualitatively superior personality—socialist man, whose characteristics already manifest themselves in the social consciousness of the Cuban people."[21]

According to Cuban literary theoretician Desiderio Navarro, the Communist Party seeks to create the New Man through the elaboration and implementation of a "cultural policy."[22] The two main components of this cultural policy are (1) the dissemination of propaganda supporting revolutionary values and (2) the censorship of all ideas and information deemed counterrevolutionary.

Castro believes that all means of communication, including art and literature, should be used to convey a revolutionary message to the masses. In 1965, he said, "I don't think there has ever existed a society in which all the manifestations of culture have not been at the service of some cause or concept. Our duty is to see that the whole is at the service of the kind of man we wish to create."[23] Later pronouncements were even more explicit. For example, the 1971 National Congress on Education and Culture declared that radio and television are "fundamentally instruments of great efficiency in the formation of the consciousness of the new man. . . . Art is a weapon of the Revolution."[24]

Cuban authorities recognize, however, that propaganda alone is not enough.

As long as people have access to alternative ideas and information, it is easy for them to analyze the government's version and reject it. For this reason, propaganda is commonly accompanied by censorship intended to shield the populace from antigovernment influences.

An excellent statement of how propaganda and censorship go hand in hand was made by the Communist Party of Cuba at its First Congress in 1975. It proclaimed that all cultural activity in Cuba is aimed at "the formation of the new man in the new society." The party then added that the revolution "has the duty to reject any attempt to use art as an instrument or pretext to diffuse or legitimate ideological positions adverse to socialism."[25]

The use of propaganda and censorship to create a New Man is not unique to Cuba. It is a practice common to all communist countries. Stalin even said that writers were supposed to be "engineers of human souls."[26] As for the creation of a New Man, this has been an ambition of Russian revolutionary thinkers ever since the mid-nineteenth century.[27] Konstantin Chernenko declared in 1983—shortly before he became secretary-general of the Soviet Union's Communist Party—that "the formation of the new man" is "a condition that is indispensable to the construction of communism."[28] This tenet has been embraced by all Soviet-style regimes. For example, the statutes of the Institute for Cultural Exchanges with France in Ho Chi Minh City state: "The only products of culture or propaganda that may be imported, kept, or put in circulation are those which . . . contribute to the construction of the new man in Vietnam."[29]

The Methods of Censorship

The Cuban government uses several methods to suppress freedom of expression. These methods fall into three main groups: (1) the nationalization of the communications industry, (2) the punishment of Cubans who violate restrictions on freedom of expression, and (3) the denial of access to foreign sources of information.

Nationalization of Communications

As previously mentioned, Castro's government completely eliminated the opposition press within three years of taking power. There was no decree outlawing independent newspapers. Instead, Castro and his allies invented the *coletilla* (little tail), a written rebuttal newspaper employees attached to and printed at the bottom of all articles they considered counterrevolutionary. Outraged at the imposition of *coletillas,* the heads of several newspapers resigned. Other periodicals fell victim to "economic strangulation," which included the denial of official advertising and pressure on commercial advertisers to withdraw. Two of the last holdouts, the newspapers *Diario de la Marina* and *Prensa Libre,* were taken over by armed militia.[30]

Castro replaced the "bourgeois" press with newspapers that were owned and operated by the regime. The government's media empire also included all television and radio stations. As Castro put it, "We did not hesitate to nationalize the mass media, snatching it away from reaction and imperialism in order to put it at the service of the people and their heroic cause."[31]

The government controlled the film industry as well. No film could be made outside the official cinema institute, ICAIC. One of the most famous cases of censorship in Cuba involved a short documentary about Havana nightlife entitled P.M. It was made in 1961 by two independent filmmakers with East German film bought on the black market. The authorities confiscated P.M. claiming that it presented a "distorted" version of Cuban reality.[32]

In addition, all publishing houses with editorial independence were closed down. One of these, El Puente, was dissolved in 1965 after Castro charged that a book of short stories El Puente planned to publish—*Con temor* by Manuel Ballagas—was "immoral."[33] The director of El Puente, poet José Mario, was sent to a work camp.[34]

The nationalization of the communications industry made it easy for the government to stop the publication of any book it found ideologically unacceptable. For example, Reinaldo Arenas, one of Cuba's most famous writers, submitted his novel *El mundo alucinante* to the Unión publishing house in 1966, but it was rejected for political reasons. Arenas finally sent the manuscript to Paris, where it was published in French.[35]

Many other books have been censored in Cuba, but we rarely know about them because censorship there is almost never publicized. When a book is banned in a democratic country, the mass media commonly howl in protest— witness the scandal that erupted in Great Britain when the government banned the book *Spycatcher*. There are no comparable scandals in Cuba, where news of censorship is itself censored. This is not difficult in a country where the government has the exclusive power to decide what is reported in the press.

The Cuban media monopoly does not always work perfectly. Film director Nicolás Guillén Landrián managed to make a documentary at ICAIC entitled *Coffea Arábiga,* which dealt with Castro's plan to grow a "green belt" of coffee plants around Havana. Nobody knew the background music to the film until it was shown at a 1969 ceremony in honor of the tenth anniversary of ICAIC. To their horror, the distinguished guests discovered that the film included a sequence in which Castro is seen climbing the podium at the Plaza de la Revolución in Havana to the music of "The Fool on the Hill" by the Beatles.[36] Needless to say, *Coffea Arábiga* was never shown to the public in Cuba—even though film critic José Antonio Evora calls it the best documentary ever produced by ICAIC.[37]

Punishment for Violations of Restrictions

One of the most powerful weapons in Castro's arsenal is the law against "enemy propaganda." This law prescribes up to fifteen years in prison for anyone who "incites against the social order, international solidarity or the socialist State, through oral or written propaganda or any other means."[38]

Dozens of Cubans have been convicted of breaking this law. For example, prize-winning playwright René Ariza was arrested in January 1974 after the police at the Havana airport discovered short stories, poems, and plays of his in the baggage of a Spanish medical student returning to Madrid. At Ariza's trial, a member of the writers union testified as an "expert" witness and said he had analyzed Ariza's short stories and found they constituted counterrevolutionary material "without artistic value." The court found Ariza guilty of producing enemy propaganda and sentenced him to eight years in prison. He spent almost five years in various jails, military hospitals, and work camps, where he was forced to cut sugarcane and do construction work. He was released in December 1978 and moved to San Francisco.[39]

Another writer, Rafael Saumell, was arrested in October 1981, when police came to his house and seized manuscripts and a typewriter. He was tried, convicted of the crime of enemy propaganda, and sentenced to five years in prison. In its written decision, the court listed the short stories it found "counterrevolutionary";[40] they were part of a book Saumell had submitted to the writers union for publication. Saumell was incarcerated from 1981 to 1986. After his release, he was not allowed to return to his job as a television scriptwriter and could find work only as an insect exterminator and by collecting bottles in the street and returning them for deposit.[41]

The Cuban government even accused a cartoonist of producing enemy propaganda. Luis Ruiz was arrested in March 1980 after trying to send his drawings out of the country. The court said his "caricatures" had "diversionist and counterrevolutionary content" and sentenced him to six years in prison.[42]

The height of absurdity came when a court convicted Mario Gastón Hernández Martínez in 1983 for translating a book about the prophecies of Nostradamus. He was sentenced to three years in prison for the crime of enemy propaganda. According to the court, specialists from the writers union called the book "diversionist, anti-communist, and anti-Soviet."[43] Delegates at the United Nations Commission on Human Rights found this outrageous. A representative from West Germany pointed out that Nostradamus lived in the sixteenth century.[44]

Even if the government chooses not to imprison somebody, it can simply fire the person. For example, poet Yndamiro Restano was dismissed from his job at Radio Rebelde in 1985 when he tried to put out a small independent newspaper. When I talked to him in Havana in 1988, he was working as a shoe salesman.[45]

Another way to punish objectionable writers is to expel them from the official writers union. This ensures that they will not be able to publish anything in Cuba. For example, the novelist Guillermo Cabrera Infante was expelled from the writers union in August 1968 after having written articles in foreign magazines criticizing the Cuban Revolution.[46] It then became impossible to buy anything by Cabrera Infante in Cuban bookstores—not even his brilliant apolitical novel *Tres tristes tigres*.

One of the most devastating ways of punishing a writer is to force the person to make a humiliating self-criticism. For example, the poet Heberto Padilla was arrested in 1971 and kept for more than five weeks in prison, where he was drugged and beaten. Hours after his release, Padilla appeared before an audience of writers and artists and told them that he was "sick and negative" and called himself "foolish . . . completely poisonous . . . corrosively counterrevolutionary." He admitted that the poems in his book *Fuera del Juego* were full of "bitterness" and "skepticism," and he denounced his book *Provocaciones* as well as his novel *En mi jardin pastan los heroes.*[47] The Padilla case became an international scandal. Several dozen world-famous intellectuals like Jean-Paul Sartre protested in the newspaper *Le Monde* that Padilla's forced "confession" was reminiscent of "the most sordid moments of the Stalinist epoch, its prefabricated trials and its witchhunts."[48]

The tactics used against Padilla were resurrected almost twenty years later when another poet, Tania Díaz Castro, helped organize a human rights group in Cuba. She was arrested in March 1990. Charged with the crime of "illicit association," she was forced to appear on Cuban television and to "confess" that she had been "manipulated" by U.S. diplomats.[49] Hours after her release from prison in September 1990, she appeared at another televised press conference and charged that the head of the Cuban Commission on Human Rights, Gustavo Arcos, was "egoistic" and "arrogant."[50] These declarations, which were obviously made under extreme duress, had no more credibility than the self-criticism made earlier by Padilla.

The campaign against dissent in Cuba shows no sign of abating. Cuban courts continue to mete out punishment, including stiff prison sentences. For example, former philosophy professor Elizardo Sánchez and two other human rights leaders told foreign correspondents in Havana that the July 1989 trial and execution of General Arnaldo Ochoa, by firing squad, was "a public assassination dressed up in judicial clothes."[51] A few days after this was published in U.S. newspapers, Sánchez and his two colleagues were arrested. They were convicted of "spreading false news" and given prison sentences ranging up to two years.[52]

On some occasions, the Cuban authorities have resorted to terrorism aimed at intimidating critics of the government. For example, persons in civilian clothes attacked the headquarters of Cuba's only vegetarian society in August 1989 and burned its library.[53] The heads of this society, Orlando Polo and Mercedes Páez, are pacifists who had organized peace marches to protest Cuba's involvement in the war in Angola. The state security police forces are suspected of having organized book-burnings.

Terrorism in Cuba does not, however, include killing journalists. In 1989, thirty-five journalists were murdered in Latin America, most of them in Colombia, El Salvador, and Peru.[54] At least the government of Cuba has not gone this far.

Denial of Access to Outside Information

Foreign newspapers, magazines, and books that challenge the official orthodoxy in any way are banned from public circulation in Cuba. Publications as innocent as *Paris Match* and *National Geographic* are not sold on newsstands anywhere in Cuba. The José Martí National Library in Havana is reported to have an entire floor of forbidden publications, but access requires special authorization.[55]

Castro also took additional measures to isolate the Cuban population from the winds of freedom blowing in the Soviet Union before it disintegrated in 1991. In August 1989, the Cuban government banned the circulation of the Soviet periodicals *Sputnik* and *Noticias de Moscú*.[56] A few months later, *Noticias de Moscú* ran an article criticizing the persecution of Cubans who listen to foreign radios and engage in "immature political conversations."[57]

Conclusion: The Evasion of Censorship

The effort of the Cuban government to stop the free flow of ideas and information has not been a total success. In the first place, the authorities have never been able to impose a total blackout on news from the outside. For years, some Cubans have managed to tune in to the Voice of America and even commercial radio stations in Miami. Besides, some information has filtered in via letters from abroad, telephone communication with relatives in the United States, and tourists from Canada and Europe. Of course, the mail is tightly controlled, phone calls are monitored and sometimes interrupted, and Cubans are discouraged from talking to tourists.

The veil of censorship has also been pierced by Radio Martí, an anti-Castro radio station owned and operated by the U.S. government. In 1985, it began broadcasting to Cuba twenty-four hours a day from Washington, D.C. The Cuban government has been jamming Radio Martí on AM since May 1990.[58] Nevertheless, Radio Martí apparently continues to be heard widely in Cuba on short wave.

Other stations that broadcast to Cuba on short wave include *La Voz del CID*, which is the "voice" of an organization known as Cuba Democrática y Independiente (CID). Based in Miami, CID is headed by Huber Matos, a rebel army *comandante* who was imprisoned by Castro for twenty years. (In October 1959, Matos wrote Castro a letter in which he complained about "the communist problem" and asked to resign. Two days later, Matos was arrested and accused of "treason.")[59]

In spite of the constant threat of reprisals, some people in Cuba have resisted censorship by creating clandestine literature that does not conform to the rules promulgated by the government. Much of this literature was written in prison. Political prisoners like Armando Valladares, Angel Cuadra, Jorge Valls, and Ernesto Díaz Rodríguez managed to smuggle their poetry out of prison and to have it published abroad.[60]

More recently, some dissidents have circulated openly within Cuba essays that sharply criticize Castro and his government. Since November 1989, a small group called Criterio Alternativo (Alternative Viewpoint) has been producing articles that are copied mechanically in limited numbers on old, worn-out typewriters. This group was founded by José Luis Pujol, a translator of English and Russian who began sending letters of protest to Castro in 1985. He was later joined by essayist Roberto Luque Escalona and other intellectuals.[61]

By Cuban standards, Criterio Alternativo is extremely daring. In one of his essays, Pujol called the one-party system in Cuba "profoundly anti-democratic" and demanded "radical change," including free elections.[62] Luque even wrote a book in which he charged Castro as being a "monstrous personality" and challenged him to hold a plebiscite. When the authorities discovered the book was going to be published in Mexico, Luque was fired from his job at the University of Havana.[63]

Why has the government tolerated the existence of Criterio Alternativo? For one thing, its members deny that they are conspiring against the government and insist that Criterio Alternativo is simply "a group of analysis and debate." As evidence of their good faith, they send copies of all their work to Castro and the Council of State.[64] It is possible that the authorities—or at least some of them—find the analysis useful.

Castro is apparently beginning to realize what students of totalitarianism learned long ago: that censorship can end up denying ideas and information to the authorities themselves. Polish essayist Leszek Kolakowski writes:

> A closed system in which information is measured out according to one's place in the hierarchy of power is bound to prevent the rulers themselves from being properly informed, thus frustrating their efforts to acquire an undistorted image of events and resulting in wrong decisions.[65]

For example, when accurate production statistics are withheld or falsified, it becomes impossible to set prices that reflect the relationship between supply and demand. The resulting shortages breed corruption, high prices on the black market, and popular discontent.

In a desperate attempt to salvage the economy, the Cuban government launched a "rectification" campaign in 1986. Within the framework of this campaign, officials encouraged "debate" so long as the system itself remained off limits to criticism.[66] Castro still seeks to escape an avalanche of demands for reforms that could sweep him and his colleagues out of power. He does not intend to share the fate of Augusto Pinochet, Daniel Ortega, and his comrades in Eastern Europe.

Notes

1. The newspaper *Revolución* published a list of journalists who had been receiving monthly "subsidies" from the Batista government. "¿Subvenciones?" *Revolución,* January 30, 1959, p. 1.

2. Carlos Ripoll, "The Press in Cuba, 1952–1960: Autocratic and Totalitarian Censorship," in *The Selling of Fidel Castro: The Media and the Cuban Revolution,* ed. William E. Ratliff (New Brunswick, NJ: Transaction, 1987), pp. 86–94.

3. Jorge Dominguez, *Cuba: Order and Revolution* (Cambridge, MA: Belknap Press of Harvard University Press, 1978), p. 124.

4. Humberto Medrano, "Como se suprimió la libertad de la prensa," *Cuadernos* (Paris), March-April 1961, supp., pp. 8–17.

5. The eight magazines were *Mensaje, APSI, Análisis, Fortin Mapocho, La Bicicleta, Pluma y Pincel, Hoy,* and *Cauce.* See *Periodismo independiente: ¿Mito o realidad?* ed. Fernando Reyes Matta and Jorge Andrés Richards (Santiago, Chile: Instituto Latinoamericano de Estudios Transnacionales, 1986), pp. 13–31.

6. See Jaime Chamorro Cardenal, *La Prensa: The Republic of Paper* (New York: Freedom House, 1988).

7. Melvin Berger, *Censorship* (New York: Franklin Watts, 1982), p. 77.

8. Interview with poet José Mario in Madrid October 30, 1987. Mario was the director of El Puente publishing house in Havana until 1965, when it was dissolved.

9. Interview with Elizardo Sánchez in Havana March 19, 1988. Sánchez was arrested in 1980 when the security police searched his house and found books from the People's Republic of China. He was convicted of the crime of "enemy propaganda" and sentenced to five years and nine months in prison.

10. *Human Rights: Status of International Instruments* (Geneva: United Nations Center for Human Rights, 1987), pp. 25–27.

11. *Constitución de la República de Cuba* (La Habana: Editora Política, 1981), pp. 20–22, 26. Article 61 provides that no freedom may be exercised "contrary to what is established in the Constitution and the law, or contrary to the existence and objectives of the socialist state, or contrary to the decision of the Cuban people to build socialism and communism."

12. Fidel Castro, "Palabras a los intelectuales," *La Revolución Cubana* (Mexico: Ediciones Era, 1983), p. 363.

13. *Ibid.*

14. Fidel Castro, *Ideología, conciencia, y trabajo politico/1959–1986* (La Habana: Editora Política, 1987), p. 4. Castro said this on September 13, 1959.

15. *Ibid.*, p. 6. Castro said this on May 29, 1960.

16. Ernesto Che Guevara, "Debemos aprender a eliminar viejos conceptos," in Guevera, *El socialismo y el hombre nuevo* (México: Siglo Veintiuno Editores, 1985), p. 21. Che said this in a speech that is often cited as "El médico revolucionario."

17. *Ibid.*, p. 23.

18. Guevara, "El socialismo y el hombre en Cuba," in *El socialismo y el hombre nuevo*, pp. 13, 15. This essay was originally published in 1965.

19. *Ibid.*, pp. 7, 13. See Michael Lowry, *El pensamiento del Che Guevara* (México: Siglo Veintiuno Editores, 1987), pp. 17–23. Also see discussion in *Che: Selected Works of Ernesto Guevara*, ed. Rolando E. Bonachea and Nelson P. Valdés (Cambridge, MA: M.I.T. Press, 1969), pp. 27–28.

20. Fidel Castro, "Conciencia Comunista significa que el día de mañana las riquezas que hacemos entre todos las disfrutaremos por igual entre todos!" *Granma,* July 27, 1968, p. 3. See Richard Fagen, *The Transformation of Political Culture in Cuba* (Stanford: CA: Stanford University Press, 1969), pp. 13, 17.

21. *Programa del Partido Comunista de Cuba* (La Habana: Editora Política, 1987), pp. 45–51.

22. Desiderio Navarro, "El papel conductor del Partido marxista-leninista en el terreno de la cultura," *La Gaceta de Cuba,* January 1976, p. 7.

23. Interview by Lee Lockwood, *Castro's Cuba, Cuba's Fidel* (New York: Vintage, 1969), p. 111. See César Escalante, "Lo fundamental en la propaganda revolucionaria," *Cuba Socialista,* September 1963, pp. 18–31.

24. "Declaración del Primer Congreso Nacional de Educación y Cultura," *Casa de las Américas,* March-June 1971, pp. 15, 18.

25. *Tesis y Resoluciones: Primer Congreso del Partido Comunista de Cuba* (La Habana: Editorial de Ciencias Sociales, 1978), p. 468.

26. This was announced by Andrei Zhdanov at the First Congress of Soviet Writers in 1934. See John and Carol Garrard, *Inside the Soviet Writers Union* (New York: Free Press, 1990), pp. 29–43.

27. See Michel Heller, *La machine et les rouages: La formation de l'homme soviétique* (Paris: Calmann-Lévy, 1985), pp. 20–27.

28. *Ibid.*, p. 13. Chernenko wrote this in *Pravda,* June 15, 1983.

29. Jacques de Barrin, "Les contraintes économiques et politiques maintiennent la coopération avec la France à un niveau modeste," *Le Monde,* February 4, 1983, p. 4.

30. Medrano, "Como se suprimió la libertad de la prensa."

31. Fidel Castro, *Bilan de la révolution cubaine: Rapport central au 1er Congrés du Parti communiste cubaine* (Paris: François Maspero, 1976), p. 41.

32. Fausto Canel, "Orlando Jiménez Leal y el 'affaire' P.M.," *Linden Lane Magazine,* April/September 1987, pp. 14–17; Fausto Canel, "El caso PM: censura y revolución," *Linden Lane Magazine,* October/December 1987, pp. 14–17.

33. Interview with Manuel Ballagas in Miami July 22, 1988; José Mario, "Allen Ginsberg en La Habana," *Mundo Nuevo,* April 1969, p. 52.

34. Interview with José Mario in Madrid October 30, 1987. Mario was sent to UMAP (Military Units to Aid Production) camp in 1966.

35. Interview with Reinaldo Arenas in New York November 21, 1987. See Georgina Dopico Black, "The Limits of Expression: Intellectual Freedom in Postrevolutionary Cua," in *Cuban Studies,* ed. Carmelo Mesa-Lago (Pittsburgh: University of Pittsburgh Press, 1989), Vol. 19, pp. 107–142.

36. Interview with Nicolás Guillén Landrián in Miami December 14, 1989.

37. José Antonio Evora, "Santiago Alvarez et le documentaire," in *Le cinéma cubain,* ed. Paulo Antonio Paranagua (Paris: Editions du Centre Pompidou, 1990), p. 130.

38. This law was created in January 1974, when Article 140.1 was added to the Social Defense Code. It became Article 108 in the 1979 Penal Code and is Article 103 in the current Penal Code.

39. Interview with René Ariza in Miami April 20, 1988. The court document containing the conclusions of the prosecuting attorney, who called Ariza's stories "counterrevolutionary propaganda," is reproduced by Néstor Almendros and Orlando Jiménez Leal, *Conducta impropia* (Madrid: Playor, 1984), pp. 188–189.

40. Written decision of the Court of Crimes against State Security of the People's Provincial Tribunal of the City of Havana in the case of Rafael Saumell, Case no. 63 of 1981. This document is dated May 13, 1982.

41. Interview with Rafael Saumell in Havana March 31, 1988.

42. Written decision of the Court of Crimes against State Security of the People's Supreme Tribunal denying appeal by Edmigio López Castillo and Luis Ruiz. This document is dated March 12, 1981.

43. Written decisions of the People's Municipal Tribunal of Diez de Octubre and the Court of Crimes against State Security of the People's Provincial Tribunal of the City of Havana. These documents are dated September 23, 1983, and August 22, 1983, respectively. They are transcribed in *Estudio del informe de la misión realizada en Cuba de acuerdo con la decisión 1988/106 de la Comisión de Derechos Humanos,* United Nations document E/CN.4/1989/46.,

44. Goetz-Alexander Martius, deputy representative of the Federal Republic of Germany, on the floor of the commission on February 28, 1989.

45. Interview with Yndamiro Restano in Havana March 29, 1988.

46. "Expulsion," *La Gaceta de Cuba,* July-August 1968, p. 16.

47. Heberto Padilla, "Intervención en la Unión de Escritores y Artistas de Cuba," *Casa de las Américas,* March-June 1971, pp. 191–203. See Heberto Padilla, *La mala memoria* (Barcelona: Plaza and Janés, 1989), pp. 148–199.

48. "De nombreuses personnalités s'émeuvent de l'arrestation du poète Heberto

Padilla," *Le Monde,* April 9, 1971, p. 3; "La lettre des intellectuels à M. Fidel Castro," *Le Monde,* May 22, 1971, p. 6.

49. David Pitt, "Cuba Seizes 11 Human-Rights Militants," *New York Times,* March 13, 1990, p. A3; "Testimonios sobre la provocación en la Embajada de la República Checa y Eslovaca," *Granma Resumen Semanal,* August 5, 1990, p. 6.

50. "De soldados idiotas de Estados Unidos califican a grupúsculos contrarevolucionarios," *Granma Resumen Semanal,* September 16, 1990, p. 9. Two months after her release, Tania Díaz Castro was sentenced to one year of restricted liberty for "illicit association." See "Juzgados ocho cubanos por asociación ilícita," *Granma Resumen Semanal,* December 9, 1990, p. 5.

51. Interviews were reported by Julia Preston, "Castro's Iron Response on Drugs Masks Issues," *Washington Post,* August 1, 1989, p. A14; and Don A. Schanche, "Kin Vainly Seek Remains of Executed Cubans," *Los Angeles Times,* August 4, 1989, p. 7.

52. See Amnesty International, *Political Imprisonment in Cuba* (London: Amensty International, December 1989), pp. 3–5.

53. Mercedes Páez reported this incident by telephone on August 31, 1989, to human rights activist Ariel Hidalgo in Miami. See Pablo Alfonso, "Queman biblioteca de grupo naturista," *El Nuevo Herald,* September 2, 1989, p. 3.

54. Sonia Goldenberg, executive director of the Committee to Protect Journalists, reported this at a meeting of the Inter-American Press Association. See Mirta Ojito, "Inicia reunión de la SIP en Kansas City," *El Nuevo Herald,* October 16, 1990, p. 4A.

55. Eusebio Mujal-León, *The Cuban University Under the Revolution* (Washington, D.C.: Cuban American National Foundation, 1988), p. 34.

56. "Una decisión inaplazable, consecuente con nuestros principios," *Granma Resumen Semanal,* August 13, 1989, p. 9.

57. Mimi Whitefield, "Arrecia crítica de prensa soviética a Cuba," *El Nuevo Herald,* March 8, 1990, p. 1A.

58. "Neutralizadas las transmisiones radiales en ondas medias de Estados Unidos en más de 70 municipios de todo el país," *Granma Resumen Semanal,* June 24, 1990, p. 9. Officials at Radio Martí contend that the jamming on AM is effective only in Havana.

59. Interview with Huber Matos in Miami August 24, 1989.

60. For example, Armando Valladares, *Desde mi silla de ruedas* (Coral Gables, FL: Ediciones Interbooks, 1976); Angel Cuadra, *Poemas en correspondencia (desde prisión)* (Miami: Solar, 1979); Jorge Valls, *Donde estoy no hay luz y está enrejado* (Madrid: Playor, 1981), Ernesto Díaz Rodríguez, *La campana del alba* (Madrid: Playor, 1984).

61. The organization of Criterio Alternativo was announced by José Luis Pujol in a letter to Fidel Castro on November 6, 1989.

62. José Luis Pujol, "discusión en la cuerda floja," *Criterio Alternativo,* June 27, 1990, pp. 7, 12.

63. Roberto Luque Escalona, *Fidel: El juicio de la historia* (México: Editorial Dante, 1990), pp. 178, 183. The information about the reprisal against Luque is taken from the jacket of the book.

64. Telephone interview with Criterio Alternativo member María Elena Cruz Varela on April 1, 1991. She was in Havana; I was in Miami.

65. Leszek Kolakowski, "On Total Control and Its Contradictions: The Power of Information," *Encounter,* July-August 1989, p. 68.

66. "Partido Comunista promueve amplio debate nacional," *Granma Resumen Semanal,* July 1, 1990, p. 1.

PART THREE

Authoritarian Systems

6

Censorship in Latin America

Richard E. Sharpless and Ilan Peleg

Censorship in Latin America has a long history. Indeed, it is part of the cultural tradition. It was practiced from the first decades of the European conquest and continued through colonial times and most of the postindependence era. In the recent period—about which this chapter is primarily concerned—censorship was an important tool of the authoritarian military states. Today, as the Latin American countries renew their efforts of political pluralism and democratic processes, overt censorship has diminished. Yet freedom of expression remains, at best, a tentative value, desired by some, derided by other. The past's legacy weighs heavily on the present.

The intellectual climate of the Spanish colonial world, for example, was not favorable for the dissemination of new ideas. Both church and state, usually acting in concert, closely controlled education, publications, the theater, public spectacles, associations, and other means of expression. There were restrictions on the publication and distribution of books; authors were banned; works were condemned on grounds of heresy, immorality, obscenity, and subversion. After Spain became champion of the Counter-Reformation, conditions became more repressive. The church, fearing contamination of faith and morals, established its *Index Librorum Prohibitorum* of forbidden books. That even the colonial economies suffered from their lack of exposure to the discoveries of the scientific age and its related technologies made no difference. The numerically small, literate colonial elite, for its part, was content with its privileges and exclusiveness and did not challenge the prevailing orthodoxy. Yet within this framework, the quality of scholarly, literary, and artistic works was often remarkably high, tributes to both the human imagination and the pervasive hold of the prevailing culture.

The Spanish colonial world—and its Portuguese counterpart in the Americas—was authoritarian and hierarchical, a reflection of the Iberian mother countries. In this respect, it mirrored the other European states of the late Renaissance. At the apex of a pyramid of caste and class was the dynastic monarchy, from which all power emanated. Its authority was God-given; its institutional structures were modeled on the "natural" order. Truth, the province of a few wise (also, well-placed) individuals, resided near the center of power.

The printing press, that recent invention, was viewed as an instrument of power, a conveyer of truth. It was a means of informing and directing from the center of power downward. Its product was meant to support and enhance the authority and policies of the dynastic state. The notion of a private press unaccountable to the center of power was inconceivable; in exchange for a monopoly on publishing granted by the dynastic state was the expectation of upholding the established power, which always retained the right to censor.[1] Thus, from its earliest days in the Hispanic world, the press—the first modern form of mass communication—was the servant of the state. This was universally accepted throughout most of the colonial era.

The right of the state to control the flow of ideas and information was not challenged until the final decades of the eighteenth century, when the European Enlightenment made an impact on Spanish and Portuguese America. In Spain itself a new dynasty, the French-related Bourbon, was interested in renovation and renewal; for the colonies this translated into policies favoring governmental efficiency and economic reform. The Bourbons were open to the scientific and technological aspects of the Enlightenment, and these found expression in the Americas. The Bourbons were alarmed, however, by the radical philosophical and political ideas of the Enlightenment. Efforts to encourage new economic thinking and technical progress combined with increased censorship of free expression in other spheres created an intolerable tension. When the creole intellectual Antonio Nariño, for example, printed a translation of the French "Declaration of the Rights of Man and of the Citizen" in 1794 on his private press, he was imprisoned for subversion. Yet his formation of a group to discuss new ideas five years earlier was tolerated, even encouraged.

Inevitably, a new rationalist, utilitarian spirit took hold among important sectors of the Spanish American elite. This was expressed in the many new periodicals and newspapers that appeared. Although most were short-lived or suppressed by the authorities, several, like the *Gazeta de Guatemala* (published between 1797 and 1816), provided forums for the discussion of innovative ideas, however disguised or indirect the form. As the concept of the individual as a rational being possessed of the inalienable right to the search for truth spread, so also did the notion of a free press.

There remained a large gap, nevertheless, between the concept and reality. The severity of the independence struggles, with their class, racial, and regional dimensions, contributed to an atmosphere of intolerance and resulted in an intensely partisan press. In the aftermath of these wars, constitutions were written in many of the new republics that codified Enlightenment ideals, but political turmoil and struggles for power hampered freedom of expression. The newly independent Argentina of the dictator Juan Manuel de Rosas illustrates the point. He controlled the Buenos Aires press and made it a subservient mouthpiece of his regime while waging all-out war against ideological opponents like the liberal intellectual Domingo Sarmiento.[2] Only in certain places and times did a relatively unfettered and uncensored press exist. A notable example was Brazil, but even there "freedom of the press" was tempered by the fact that newspapers and publications generally reflected the views of the dominant, politically active minority. If newspapers at times appealed to a broader public, it was often in the form of demagogic incitement to popular demonstrations in favor of some cause.

The integration of Latin America into the North Atlantic economy during the second half of the nineteenth century established the basis for national consolidation and economic modernization. At the same time, powerful national elites (in particular, notable large landowners) adopted the philosophical rationale of positivism—with its emphasis on order, authority, and material progress—to impose authoritarian regimes that ensured stability, economic growth, and concentration of wealth in the hands of a small minority.[3] Economic prosperity and political order provided opportunities for cultural expression, at least for the privileged few. Literature and the arts, influenced both by European movements and a rising artistic nationalism, flourished in cities like Buenos Aires (the Paris of South America) and Bogotá (the Athens of the continent). The press, however, remained largely a tool of the elites and reflected their values and interests. The emerging urban middle sectors, industrial working class, and rural poor, who paid the costs of modernization, had limited outlets for expression. Opposition was met by repression.

The authoritarian ethos characteristic of previous eras carried over in large measure to the period of nationalist and broadly "populist" development when the export economies collapsed after 1930. Elements of the old elite, the newly professionalized military, the politically mobilizing middle sectors, and their allies in the working class formed broad coalitions that sought national development, economic independence, and, occasionally, social justice. When in power, these regimes spanned the political spectrum. Depending on their levels of national development, they were rightist and leftist, military and civilian, dictatorial and electoral. They had in common, however, an understanding of the crucial role of mass communications for their agendas. Many of these governments established state control over radio and, later, television. Nominally independent radio stations and other media frequently were subjected to both direct and indirect official pressure. National film industries sometimes government-supported, channeled financing in politically expedient directions. Newspapers, which by and large remained partisan organs of individuals or political parties, suffered harassment, censorship, or outright government takeovers. Although freedom of the press was a critical issue among competing political groups, it did not flourish.[4] Regimes as different as those of Juan Perón in Argentina and Fidel Castro in Cuba censored and controlled the media. Even relatively stable and moderate governments like those of post-1940 Mexico exerted strong influence over mass communications through licenses, subsidies, advertising, bribes, and control of newsprint.

The failures of both liberalism and populism to secure balanced socioeconomic development, political stability, and social justice, combined with factors such as the cold war and the growing influence of Marxism, precipitated a major crisis in the 1960s and 1970s. In one country after another, beginning with Brazil in 1964, military governments took power.[5] The new rulers justified their actions by proclaiming the need to restore national unity, order, and stability in the wake of the social conflicts caused by modernization. Politics, especially the "demagogic" politics of popular mobilization and class struggle, required purging. Only the military, with its traditions of patriotism, self-sacrifice, discipline, and overriding concern for the welfare and security of the nation, could guarantee this process.[6]

The military had played a pivotal role in the Latin American republics since independence. In keeping with the Iberian tradition, the military as an institution enjoyed considerable autonomy. Especially after professionalization of the services began in the late nineteenth century, soldiers saw their primary role as safeguarding the integrity of the nation. This meant not only defending the frontiers against foreign enemies but also guaranteeing the national welfare. Above any ephemeral constitution or transitory government was the sanctity of the nation, and the military was its guardian. This interpretation of its mission permitted repeated military interventions against "self-serving" politicians and special interests who put their own concerns before the nation's.

The military governments of the 1960s and 1970s added other dimensions to their role. Above all was a concern for national security, viewed as threatened by the populist mobilization of the working class and the urban and rural poor and by the widespread influence of "foreign" collectivist ideologies among students, intellectuals, and many middle-class politicians. This reaction included alarm at the appearance of armed movements advocating radical socioeconomic change similar to that of revolutionary Cuba—movements that pledged to eliminate the armed forces as principal pillars of the existing system. In essence, the new military governments regarded anyone who opposed them as an enemy. And they considerably broadened the definition of national security to include, in the words of a Brazilian theoretician of the 1964 coup, "everything that in one way or another affects the life of the nation."[7]

Another element of the soldiers' mission was economic development, which was viewed as an integral component of national security and national defense. Since at least the beginning of the twentieth century, the military had advocated industrialization and technological advance. In several of the larger Latin American countries, military industries were an important part of this process. Now, after what was regarded as the failure of civilian politics, the military authorities took on the developmental responsibility. Through their control of the state, they centralized authority and marshaled resources necessary to further the national well-being.

In the past, most military interventions had ended after order was restored in the political realm and civilian rule subsequently reestablished. The military governments of the 1960s and 1970s expected their tenure in power to last longer while they fundamentally restructured political, economic, and social institutions. They moved against all existing or potential opposition, especially groups and individuals of liberal or Marxist orientation they believed had infected and undermined the social order with subversive ideas. Constitutional limits were ignored and rule by decree instituted; political parties were banned and politicians silenced, jailed, exiled, and even killed; trade unions, student federations, and other associations were smashed or subverted by intervention; military-directed agencies staffed by nonpolitical technocrats were established to oversee economic policies. The broad area of culture was given special attention: Universities were closed or taken over, faculties purged, and curricula cleansed of subversive content. Governmental agencies were assigned to control and censor the media. Publishing houses, newspapers, and radio stations that did not agree with the objectives of the military were closed. Political commentators, journalists, writers, artists, folksingers—indeed, the entire array of those involved in intellectual or cultural endeavors—came under close scrutiny, or worse. In June 1980, the *Index on Censorship* published a provisional list of seventy-one Argentine writers and journalists who had "disappeared" and presumably were killed by agents of the military government.[8]

The harsh measures, which included widespread use of torture and the creation of an atmosphere of terror among the civilian population, were justified as necessary for the restoration of order and progress, respect for hierarchy and authority, and the revival of values centered on God, nation, and family.[9] In reality, the philosophical jumble of spirituality, traditionalism, nationalism, anti-Marxism, morality, and duty that the military regimes used to rationalize their takeovers disguised their deep-rooted fear of the popular and democratic challenges of the modern world. Theirs was a desperate attempt to expunge the previous fifty years of Latin America's history.

Brazil

The model for the "national security state" was Brazil. There, in late March 1964, a military coup supported by the most conservative political groups ousted the civilian government of João Goulart during a time of economic crisis, political polarization, and attempted government mobilization for socioeconomic reforms. Subsequently, the generals imposed an authoritarian political structure that served their development goal of rapid economic growth based on export-driven industrialization funded in large measure by foreign capital, a strategy that gave little attention to the issue of equitable distribution. The result was widening disparities of income, a falling standard of living for the middle and working classes, and impoverishment for many. The policy required control of the popular political forces of Brazil's relatively industrialized, modern society. This included, naturally enough, control of the media.

The military government amended the Constitution by a series of Institutional Acts that conferred virtually unlimited power on the executive. One of these, Institutional Act Number 5 of December 1968 and an accompanying Complementary Act, dissolved the congress and state and local representative bodies. It also imposed strict censorship on all media. Overall supervision of cultural activities was vested in a Conselho Superior de Cultura (High Council for Culture), formed shortly before Act 5, which was described in practice as a board of censors.[10] Precedent for the High Council was established earlier in Brazil's history during the populist dictatorship of Getulio Vargas when, in the 1940s, his Department of Press and Propaganda monitored writers and intellectuals.

The Ministry of Justice and the federal police also were granted broad censorship powers. An agency of the latter, the Censorship Division of Public Entertainments, required the registration of all magazines, national and foreign, before distribution. Legal orders issued by the Ministry of Justice proscribed everything from art exhibits to theater performances. Additionally, a series of official edicts further restricted freedom of expression. Decree Law Number 1077 of January 1970, for example, justified prior censorship of books and periodicals on the grounds that they might "stimulate licentiousness, propagate free love, and . . . destroy the moral values" or that "use of these . . . is part of a subversive plan which puts national security at risk."[11] The National Security Law of January 1979, which took effect after the suspension of Act 5, made it a criminal offense, punishable by imprisonment, to disseminate material in any media that was "incompatible with the Constitution . . . incited people against the constitutional authorities . . . offended the head of a foreign government . . . [permitted the] use of communications media for the execution of a crime against national security," and used the media for creating "subversive propaganda."[12] The impact of these measures was described by the Brazilian writer Clovis Mouro in 1979:

> Fourteen years of censorship in Brazil: a culture demeaned, crushed, humiliated. Books, radio, television, theater, cinema, and universities clothed in the straitjacket of a new Inquisition. Hundreds of books seized, burnt, destroyed, or withdrawn from circulation. Writers, playwrights, and radicals imprisoned, without being able to protest; all lines of defense sealed off. A climate of cultural terror gradually accumulated; at any time anyone might be accused, tortured, or assassinated.[13]

Censorship was accompanied by repression, which included the arrest of writers, journalists, artists, and intellectuals deemed subversive and charged, for example, with violating the National Security Law. The detained were almost always subjected to police interrogation, sometimes tortured, and brought before military courts for trial. The more fortunate, perhaps, simply had their works banned; others, like the numerous contributors to the *New History of Brazil,* which was seen as having Marxist tendencies, were deported; still others were imprisoned; not a few, like the journalist Vladimir Herzog, were killed.[14]

Academics suffered similar fates. Special official decrees permitted administrators to expel students without allowing appeal, to dismiss faculty members without giving them the right of defense because of their ideological leanings, and to rid libraries of offensive books. Hundreds of students and faculty were imprisoned. Major universities were depopulated as a result, and the level of instruction declined substantially.[15]

Such draconian measures of censorship and repression were seldom reported in the media. Indeed, as a result of censorship or self-censorship, which became a means of survival, the quality of journalism declined significantly. Controversial subjects were avoided; news reporting and programming emphasized the bland and innocuous. The large national media, often controlled by those closest to the regime, conformed to the official line. Many of the smaller newspapers—the so-called fringe press—failed to survive.

The sweeping, often generalized texts of the censorship laws allowed for broad interpretation by enforcing authorities. The results sometimes touched on the absurd: In 1978 Lenin shared with two of Brazil's leading pornographers the honor of being most censored; in an effort to simplify matters for the censors, Edict Number 427 of 1977 automatically banned all foreign publications that had in their titles the words "revolution," "struggle," or "sex." Commenting on the abilities of the censors, Helio Fernandez, editor of the much-targeted newspaper *A Tribuna da Imprensa,* noted: "The most enlightened of the censors must have a mental age of about five years and the accumulated subservience of 500."[16]

Humor, of course, was a last defense in tragedy. For most of Brazil's artists and intellectuals who opposed the regime, there was no other recourse. Their associations, like the Brazilian Union of Writers, at first protested the banning of books and the imprisonment of members, but were finally reduced to silence. Silence, in fact, became the prevalent mode of survival, except for the most courageous. Censorship and repression had the desired effect—or as art critic Geraldo Mayrink observed in comparing Brazil's cultural climate in 1979 to the end of an all-night party: "The guests are drunk and glutted with authoritarianism. All they want to do is go home."[17]

The key word in Mayrink's remark is "authoritarianism." Despite the measures taken to enforce censorship, the military government did not achieve the pervasive type of mind control characteristic of the totalitarian regimes of Eastern Europe. The theories of the national security state did not become an established dogma like Marxism-Leninism, which offered a systematic, elaborated explanation of human existence. If the generals' efforts had a philosophical rationale, it was rather toward the establishment of a modern-day version of the corporate state, that idealized vision of an organic, integrated social order so much apart of the Iberian tradition. As already noted, strong state authority that tolerated little opposition was central to that tradition. Censorship was one of its components.

Further, the regime had come to power with substantial civilian support among those groups most threatened by the populist challenge. Businesspeople, professionals, technocrats, elements of the middle class, sectors of the church, and even intellectuals, members of the media, and nationalists backed the measures to restore order. Eventually, some of these groups turned against the government's policies, especially those that allowed an inordinate influence for foreign capital, and voiced their criticisms. The military leaders, themselves at times divided, vacillated over how to deal with opposition. But criticism, even that from the cooperating media was never entirely stifled. One result, from the mid-1970s, was a growing public demand for the return of civilian rule, including a freer media. It was a demand the generals finally did not resist. The restoration of civilian government in the 1980s brought with it greater freedom of expression. Though Brazil's media still have not fully recovered from the restrictions of the recent past, the "climate of cultural terror" described by Clovis Moura has largely dissipated.

Chile

Until September 11, 1973, the Latin American country with one of the strongest traditions of free discourse and an open press was Chile. Great pride was taken in the high rate of literacy, a flourishing literature that produced two Nobel Prize winners, and a sophisticated, vibrant press that expressed a broad range of cultural and political viewpoints. These features were the result of more than a half century of accommodation and compromise by the country's political elite, which had adapted to a measure of democratic participation by the citizenry uncommon on the continent.

The political system encouraged a high level of political consciousness, which in turn both stimulated and was fostered by the media. Yet the country's economic institutions and social structure did not match the advanced level of its politics. By the 1960s, as the problems of economic dependency and underdevelopment in general worsened, the clamor for change among the middle and working classes intensified. A reformist Christian Democratic administration between 1964 and 1970 achieved only partial successes; this contributed to further political polarization. In November 1970, after a highly charged political campaign, the Socialist Salvador Allende won the presidency at the head of a Popular Unity coalition of Communists, Socialists, radicals, and other leftist groups. Allende pledged to carry out sweeping socioeconomic reforms.

The Allende administration ended in 1973, but still provokes controversy among supporters and detractors, Chileans and foreign observers. There is no question that nationalizations, land reform, factory seizures, and programs to redistribute wealth and improve conditions for the working classes and poor caused an enormous reaction. Political parties, from the Christian Democrats in the center to the National Party on the right, opposed the administration in the legislature. Middle-class housewives, businesspeople, and elements of the working class protested in the streets. Multinational corporations and the U.S. government took measures to undermine Allende. By late August 1973, the country was in chaos, and the military, despite a long history of noninterference in civilian politics, took power.

Unlike the relatively bloodless Brazilian coup of 1964, the Chilean takeover was brutal. Allende was killed along with hundreds, perhaps thousands, of his supporters. In the months and years immediately after the overthrow, tens of thousands were rounded up, interrogated, often tortured, imprisoned, or exiled; many "disappeared." The ruling military junta closed Congress, dissolved the Popular Unity parties, suspended civilian politics, and assumed executive and legislative functions. Military courts were established to judge former administration figures and opponents of the new regime.

The coup, repression, and authoritarian dictatorship were justified on the grounds that the country's internal order was being undermined by subversive ideas—that is, Marxist doctrines. The military's task was to restore "liberty" and the "basic moral foundations from which the Western and Christian civilizations derive."[18] Expurgating the effects of the "corrosive" foreign ideology, which had penetrated all areas of the nation's social and cultural life, required drastic measures. That meant, of course, control of freedom of expression. For the generals, it was precisely the various cultural and intellectual forms—from the written and spoken word to film and the plastic arts—that had given expression to the national threat. The leader of the military government, General Augusto Pinochet, said:

> To begin with, communism was allowed direct or indirect control of fundamentally influential media and was given ample facilities for political action and propaganda. Later its vocabulary and ideas were gradually adopted by democratic sectors, who from the habit of dialogue inadvertently became imbued with its myths and slogans.[19]

In the immediate aftermath of the coup, the military shut down and confiscated all communications media that had supported the Allende administration. As a Chilean journalist observed, the 44 percent of the population that had voted for Popular Unity in the March 1973 elections suddenly found itself without any means of public expression.[20] The crackdown soon spread beyond newspapers and radio stations to other areas of cultural and intellectual life: Bookstores were raided and books considered subversive were burned; publishers were forced to destroy suspect stocks; popular theaters were closed; the universities were occupied by the military with officers appointed as rectors; the two university-affiliated television channels (the third was state-owned) were placed under military control. Journalists, academics, writers, and artists fell victim to the repression. The lucky merely lost their positions; many were imprisoned, interned, deported, and even killed.[21]

Media that had been critical of Allende usually continued to function. These included, for example, two of the largest newspapers, *El Mercurio* and *La Tercera,* owned respectively by the wealthy Edwards and Pico Cañas families. But all media were censored. Most magazines, for example, had to submit proofs of their articles to a government agency, the National Directorate of Social Communications, for approval.[22]

The period of direct censorship lasted several months; after that, what was called "implicit" censorship took effect. The surviving media found it expedient to practice self-censorship and back the junta, printing and broadcasting government-managed news. In any case, there were additional methods of enforcing conformity: editions could be and were seized, a particular blow to small magazines; paper supplies were cut off; advertisers were encouraged to run ads only in media that supported the military; radio station licenses were revoked; and editorial personnel were threatened by anticommunist paramilitary groups known to have links to the military.[23]

In the mid-1970s, the regime, isolated internationally and widely criticized for its human rights violations, allowed a number of opposition publications to appear. One of these was the news weekly *Hoy,* affiliated with the Christian Democratic Party.[24] Several periodicals of the Roman Catholic Church, including the critical Jesuit monthly *Mensaje,* also circulated. The readership of such magazines, however, was small compared with that of the progovernment dailies, and their impact relatively limited. Further, despite the fact that they did not print far-left articles, they were subjected to various forms of official harassment, including temporary suspensions and judicial prosecution for printing material the government considered objectionable.[25]

The limited liberalization allowed newspapers and magazines did not extend to the electronic media. Radio, for Chileans the most popular means of receiving information, continued to be closely monitored. The largest independent network, Radio Cooperativa, lost most of its affiliates through license cancellations in the 1970s, though eventually it managed to regain them.[26] Like other privately owned radio stations, its programs were frequently censored.

The government considered television the most important outlet for its views, and the three existing channels remained under firm control. As a result, programming was upbeat and bland as the government attempted to project the image of a society operating peacefully and normally. A journalist noted, "Television either offers a diet of escapism (through sports and soap operas), promotes consumerism (the latter being an important part of the economic model initiated in the late 1970s), or markets the government itself."[27] What news coverage occurred was highly slanted; occasionally, it was manufactured. The Catholic Church charged, for example, that news about terrorist activity in the Santiago slums featured captured arms and revolutionary literature planted by the police.[28]

Books also continued under censorship. In the late 1970s, several decrees required that all Chilean and foreign books receive prior approval from a censorship board before distribution. An additional burden was placed on the book publishing industry when a 20 percent value-added tax paid prior to distribution was placed on previously exempt books.[29] The combination of the tax and the purposely delayed approval by the censorship board had a devastating impact on the market. And the book-reading public's recourse to libraries offered no solution: "Subversive" books were culled from library shelves. At the Santa Maria Technical University in Valparaiso, librarians worked for four days to remove "Marxist" books.[30]

Government policies changed somewhat with the promulgation of a new Constitution in 1981. Article 19 allowed for freedom of expression and private ownership of media and prohibited the state from establishing a monopoly over mass communications. Prior censorship was permitted, however, but only to uphold "general norms" in the area of artistic activities, apparently a safeguard against pornography. Further potential restrictions were embedded in Article 8, which permitted prosecution of anyone propagating ideas of a "totalitarian character or based on class warfare."[31]

Although the new Constitution at least technically allowed for a considerable range of media freedom, it was in fact additionally circumscribed by "transitional articles" in effect until the transfer to civilian rule in 1989. These gave the executive the authority to restrict freedom of information if it contributed to the disturbance of public order and to suspend freedom of information during a time of emergency.[32] The latter provision was invoked when a state of siege was declared in November 1984 during massive demonstrations against the regime. In the ensuing crackdown on the press, six of seven opposition publications were closed indefinitely; the seventh, *Hoy*, was allowed to continue publication under prior censorship. The mainstream media also were affected: Only political news approved by the government could be reported.[33]

This new assault on the media after more than a decade of authoritarian rule underscored the importance the means of communication had achieved in Chile. In the absence of a legislature, political parties, and other forums of public debate, the media, especially the press, had become the principal means of dissent—of criticism of the government. The state of siege had been interpreted widely as an effort by Pinochet to regain control by striking at the center of opposition, the press, that despite enormous difficulties, had exposed the corruption, deficiencies, and high level of public discontent with the regime.[34]

Chile's journalists, its cultural and intellectual workers, can rightfully claim an important place among those whose opposition contributed to the pressure for transition to civilian rule. Through the long years of dictatorship and under conditions that literally threatened—and sometimes cost—life and limb, the bravest of them fought to uphold the value of freedom of expression. Organizations like the Chilean Journalists' Association and the Society of Authors' Permanent Committee for the Defense of Freedom of Expression indefatigably battled against government censorship and repression. Today, as the country's popular forces and elected civilian government struggle to restore democratic institutions, writers and artists face formidable new obstacles: a diminished number of publishing houses and the high cost of books; the concentration of newspaper and radio station ownership in the hands of powerful small groups that profited from military rule; economic difficulties that have resulted in unemployment, low wages, and the use of free-lancers rather than full-time staff.[35] Clearly, the battle for freedom of expression in Chile is not over.

Conclusion: Beyond the National Security State

The reappearance of elected civilian governments in Latin America during the 1980s has not meant the total defeat of authoritarianism. The soldiers simply have withdrawn to their barracks, discredited in various degrees by universal condemnation of their human rights violations, by the region's worst economic decade since the 1930s, or, in the case of Argentina, by military defeat. That they have demonstrated they are not much more capable than previous civilian governments of solving grave national problems of unity, balanced development, and social justice does not mean their permanent demise. In virtually every Latin American country, the military remains a potent force that exerts considerable influence on politics. Further, the constitutional changes, legal statutes, and policies the military implemented to control freedom of expression in many cases remain intact. The fear instilled by years of repression still works its effects. And the powerful civilian groups who supported the military are present as well, with no intention of surrendering place to democratic forces they frequently despise.

Argentina provides a case in point. The military government that ruled the country from 1976 to 1983 exercised the usual types of censorship—harassment of publishers, banning of books, closing of magazines and newspapers[36]—but rather than institutionalize control of the media, the leaders took more direct actions. Over 100 journalists and writers "disappeared." The journalists were among the thousands of victims of the military's "dirty war" against subversion. When civilian rule was restored, a massive public outcry demanded that those responsible for such crimes be punished. Under pressure, the government of President Raùl Alfonsín launched investigations and brought officers of the former regime to trial. The response of the military's supporters in the media was hostile. The largest circulation newspapers opposed the government's initiatives; they continued to treat the military with circumspection, either from fear of reprisals or agreement with its policies. Their selective self-censorship was not practiced by all media, but when magazines, radio, and television stations did run articles or air programs on human rights abuses, they often were threatened.[37] Government-run television stations and agencies that provided public forums for discussion of the issue were forced to cancel programs for fear of bombings.

Supporters of the military, far-right, and anti-Semitic groups continue their assault on Argentina's struggling democracy through the media. The Catholic church has campaigned against pornography in publications and television. Although Argentines enjoy more freedom of expression than at any time in recent history and have access to a wide range of opinions and viewpoints, their freedom is at best tentative. As one commentator noted, those who would destroy it have "created a tense climate which menaces attempts to break with the past."[38]

Civilian governments like Argentina's struggle to achieve the stability necessary for continued freedom of expression, but the press in particular in one of the few Latin American countries to avoid recent military rule faces other daunting problems. In Colombia, the combination of control of national politics by a close-knit civilian oligarchy, a military allied with it, and widespread violence involving revolutionary groups and drug traffickers has resulted in severe limits on the free flow of information.

Colombians have long taken pride in the diversity of their press; newspapers representing the spectrum of political views from right to left have circulated freely. But virtually every newspaper is allied with a political group and slants the news accordingly. The most influential national newspaper, *El Tiempo,* with close ties to the Liberal Party, is in reality very conservative and frequently serves as a mouthpiece for the government. With large parts of the country under virtual military control because of guerrilla and drug activities, *El Tiempo* has been accused of reporting only the military's version of events and ignoring human rights violations.[39] Similar charges have been made against other major newspapers. During the presidential administration of Belisario Betancur (1982–1986), efforts to achieve peace by incorporating the main revolutionary groups into the political mainstream reportedly were undermined by opposing military and conservative civilian elements who provided "disinformation" to the government and press.[40]

The drug trade also has adversely affected the press. Virtually every institution and sector of Colombian society has been tainted by the billions of illicit dollars flowing into the country from the sale of cocaine. The ruthless drug lords (*narcotraficantes*) have spread corruption and terror in their efforts to survive. The media have exercised varying degrees of self-censorship in covering the issue, usually because of fear. Periodical offices and radio stations have been bombed; at least thirty journalists investigating the drug trade have been murdered, including Guillermo Cano, editor of the leading Bogotá daily, *El Espectador*.[41] In defense, journalists in recent years have cooperated in coordinating news stories about the drug trade, which then run unsigned in the press. Tactics like this, along with the government's campaign against the *narcotraficantes,* have diminished attacks on journalists, but the threat remains.

Colombian journalists work under extreme conditions: a nearly thirty-year "state of siege" that permits the government to suppress information and prosecute reporters of unfavorable news; distortion of material by media allied with particular political groups; harassment and misinformation by the military; and personal insecurity when covering the activities of guerrilla, drug, and paramilitary groups.[42] Under the circumstances, it is remarkable that journalists still find the courage to work and fight for a free and open media. Perhaps the crucial test for them—and for Colombia—will come as new political forces supported by a disillusioned public challenge the old order.

As the twentieth century ends, the struggle for freedom of expression in Latin America that began 200 years ago continues. The writers, artists, and intellectuals presently engaged find themselves contending against those who see the open exchange of ideas and information as a threat to their power, wealth, and privileges. Yet there is another, perhaps more difficult, level of opposition: a tradition, born in bloody conquest and nurtured through generations of domination, that is profoundly antidemocratic. Within that tradition, monopoly of power assumes monopoly of truth; toleration and compromise are regarded as weakness. Changing such age-old cultural norms requires more than the writing of laws; it requires nothing less than the transformation of attitudes and behavior, both collectively and individually. Freedom of expression, the concomitant of democracy, must be believed in as well as practiced.

Progress has occurred. Legal frameworks have been constructed, and constitutions, even those written by governments of the national security states, have at least formal guarantees, for example, against censorship. The elected civilian governments that now rule have honored freedom of the press in varying degrees. The retreat of authoritarianism in Latin America and elsewhere and the global trend toward democratic processes provide positive influences. In addition, the universal concern for human rights, of which freedom of expression is a part, and the work of international organizations like Americas Watch, International PEN, and Article 19 give support to media workers that extends beyond national boundaries. Finally, the advances in communications technology have resulted in enormous progress in the diffusion of ideas and information and thus rendered obstruction more difficult.

There is now the expectation that a new era is opening in Latin America. It is evidenced by the discrediting of old ideologies of both the Left and the Right, by the cultural revival in countries like Argentina and Brazil, and by the restoration of constitutional rule. But although the international and continental climate for freedom of expression has turned favorable, the men and women who fought for it recently in Latin America continue to face daunting problems. Not the least of them is the way of thinking expressed in "Press Conference" by the Chilean poet Mauricio Roblés:

> Freedom of the press yes
> Yes there is freedom of the press for any
> Person who does not contravene our norms.[43]

Notes

1. Fred S. Siebert, Theodore Peterson, and Wilbur Schramm, *Four Theories of the Press* (Urbana: University of Illinois Press, 1956), pp. 2–3.

2. A good account of Sarmiento's travails is found in Alison W. Bunkley, *The Life of Sarmiento* (Princeton, NJ: Princeton University Press, 1952). See also, D. F. Sarmiento, *Life in the Argentine Republic in the Days of the Tyrants: Or Civilization and Barbarism,* tr. by Mrs. Horace Mann (New York, 1868).

3. Brian Loveman and Thomas M. Davies, Jr., eds., *The Politics of Antipolitics: The Military in Latin America* (Lincoln: University of Nebraska Press, 1978), p. 6.

4. Robert Jones Shafer, *A History of Latin America* (Toronto: D. C. Heath, 1978), p. 621.

5. The military took power in the following South American countries in the years indicated: Brazil (1964), Argentina (1966, 1976), Chile (1973), Peru (1968), Uruguay (1973), Bolivia (1964), Ecuador (1972). Paraguay was under military rule throughout the 1960s and 1970s. In Central America and the Spanish Caribbean, the military was the dominant political force in all but Costa Rica and, nominally, the Dominican Republic, during those decades. Mexico was a one-party state.

6. Loveman and Davies, *The Politics of Antipolitics,* p. 12.

7. Quotation in Victor Vilanueva, *El Caem y la revolución de la fuerza armada* (Lima: Institute of Peruvian Studies, 1972), p. 233.

8. "Disappeared Writers and Journalists," *Index on Censorship,* Vol. 9, no. 3, June 1980, p. 50.

9. Thomas G. Sanders, "Military Government in Chile," in Loveman and Davies, *The Politics of Antipolitics,* pp. 272–273.

10. Maria da Glória, "Mutilating the Written Word," *Index on Censorship,* Vol. 8, no. 4, July–August 1979, p. 28.

11. Ibid., p. 27.

12. Extracted from "The National Security Law," *Index on Censorship,* Vol. 8, no. 4, July–August 1979, p. 25.

13. Quotation from Clovis Moura, "Climate of Terror," *Index on Censorship,* Vol. 8, no. 4, July–August 1979, p. 8.

14. Ibid.

15. Ibid., p. 10.

16. Da Glória. "Mutilating the Written Word," p. 27.

17. Ibid., p. 28.

18. Quoted from a speech by General Augusto Pinochet Ugarte, in Loveman and Davies, *The Politics of Antipolitics,* p. 204.

19. Ibid., p. 205.

20. Pablo Portales, "Journalists in Chile," *Index on Censorship,* Vol. 13, no. 2, April 1984, p. 23.

21. Jorge Edwards, "Books in Chile," *Index on Censorship,* Vol. 13, no. 2, April 1984, p. 20.

22. Portales, "Journalists in Chile," p. 23.

23. "Chile: No News Allowed," report of the Committee to Protect Journalists, May 1985, p. 19. This is a report on conditions of journalists in Chile resulting from the visit to that country in December 1984 of a group of North and South American journalists sponsored by the committee and the Inter-American Press Association.

24. Ibid., pp. 6–7.

25. Ibid., pp. 16–17.

26. Ibid., p. 11.

27. Quotation from ibid., p. 9.

28. Ibid., p. 10.

29. Edwards, "Books in Chile," p. 21.

30. Michael Sanders, "Book Burning and Brutality," *Index on Censorship,* Vol. 3, no. 1, Spring 1974, p. 135.

31. "Chile," in Kevin Boyle, ed., *Article 19: Information, Freedom, and Censorship (World Report 1988)* (New York: Times Books, 1988), p. 73.

32. Ibid., pp. 73–74.

33. "Chile: No News Allowed," p. 26.

34. Ibid., pp. 25–26.

35. Portales, "Journalists in Chile," p. 35.

36. Daniel Divinsky, "Publishing, etc., in Argentina," *Index on Censorship,* Vol. 14, no. 4, August 1985, p. 46.

37. "Argentina," in Boyle, *Article 19,* pp. 64–65.

38. Quotation from ibid., p. 66.

39. "Colombia," in Boyle, *Article 19,* p. 79.

40. Ibid., p. 78.

41. Ibid., p. 80.

42. For a report on working conditions of journalists in Colombia, see Article 19 Publications, *Freedom of Information and Expression in Colombia* (London, Article 19, 1988).

43. Quotation from Mauricio Redolés, "Press Conference," *Index on Censorship,* Vol. 14, no. 4, August 1985, p. 47.

7

Censorship in the Middle East:
The Case of Arabic Literature

Anonymous

Quis custodiet ipsos custodes?
—Juvenal

Dimensions of Censorship

Before discussing the situation in the Arabic-speaking countries, I would like to explore censorship as a general phenomenon in greater detail. In the most literal sense, "censorship" is an activity carried out by someone with the title of "censor," a Latin word for an official who conducted the census and, as an additional function, oversaw the maintenance of public morality. The *Oxford English Dictionary* (*OED*) (1971) provides the following definitions for the word "censor": "An official in some countries whose duty it is to inspect all books, journals, dramatic pieces, etc., before publication, to secure that they shall contain nothing immoral, heretical, or offensive to the government." The *Standard College Dictionary* (*SCD*) lists a definition that is similar but not entirely so: "An official examiner of manuscripts, plays, etc., empowered to suppress them, wholly or in part, if politically or morally objectionable."

Among the similarities, one notes that both definitions talk in terms of an "official" position, and both single out the dramatic genre for special mention. Among differences, the *OED* definition focuses on prevention, whereas the emphasis in *SCD* is on the power to suppress. The latter uses general terms such as "politically . . . objectionable"; the former mentions "offensive to the government." Finally, and this is significant in the context of the Arab world, the *OED* definition alone includes heresy among its categories. What these definitions seem to agree on, however, is that the primary objects of the censor's attention are normally materials that challenge or offend the sensitivities of authorities in a particular country or region relating to politics,

---

It is, no doubt, an apt reflection of the contents of this chapter that the author prefers to remain anonymous.

morality (and as the definitions cited show, that usually implies sexual morality), and religion.

Although in this chapter I investigate the activities of officials and government agencies in the Arab world that are fulfilling this kind of function, it should be emphasized that the phenomenon of censorship and, in particular, its impact on literature and those who create it are not confined to a process of review whereby an official or a committee of such people decide on the dissemination of a work. In an old adage, there are many ways of skinning a cat. To most Western readers, the profession of creative writer may not seem a particularly dangerous, life-threatening one, but evidence collected by numerous international agencies makes it abundantly clear that in many areas of the world—including several countries of the Arabic-speaking region—it most certainly is such. A quotation from a work that brings together writings by censored, imprisoned, or assassinated writers from all over the globe and comments of those who endeavor to help them will suffice:

> The Writers in Prison Committee of International PEN has on its books today a total of 480 novelists, poets and other authors who are languishing in prison or labor camp somewhere in the world, who have "disappeared" or are interned in psychiatric hospitals.
>
> But a writer does not have to be incarcerated in a prison cell or a psychiatric ward, he does not have to be abducted or murdered, to be silenced by a regime which does not approve of him. To be banned, censored, unable to publish his work, can, to a dedicated writer, be a "fate worse than death"—and it is a fate that is shared by thousands in every part of the globe.[1]

In this chapter, I focus on the text and the reader, leaving discussion of the author until last because it seems clear that one of the more distressing aspects of censorship in Third World countries such as those of the Arab world is that the status and treatment of authors provide the context for many of the most significant differences from what I would term "censorship tactics" as commonly encountered in Western societies.[2]

Attacks on the availability of books and other modes of communication can come from many quarters within society. The most obvious avenue for what I term the "evaluation" of scripts is the censor's office in its various manifestations; this includes any agency whose function is covered by the dictionary definitions previously cited. All nations have officials of such a kind within one or another sector of society. The board that assigns "ratings" to films, the local public library committee, and the school board all are examples of such an evaluative mechanism with the authority to exercise control over access to printed and other materials. However, the results of the activities of such agencies are, needless to say, most prominently seen in those countries that attempt to control the lives of their citizens to the maximum degree possible, a category into which a number of countries in the Arab world clearly fall.

Even if a work manages to survive these screening mechanisms, there remain several ways of preventing public access to it. These include the imposition of difficult or impossible publication requirements and refusal on the part of bookstores to stock the work[3] or of libraries to place it on their shelves. In the Third World, a common tactic is to seize controversial works after their publication, which brings considerable financial loss to the publisher and, more often than not, the author and offers a strong disincentive to publish such works in the future.

It goes without saying that the measures just outlined will have an impact on the creator of the works given such treatment. In dealing with the artist as an individual member of society, the regimes that choose to exert such controls have a further battery of options open to them. Torture, imprisonment, and expulsion of authors are all regrettably common in many countries. The imposition of such punishments on members of the creative community is clearly intended to have an exemplary effect, and it clearly succeeds in this aim. Only the most courageous writers will be prepared to take the considerable risk that may be involved. Although these measures may be direct, intimidating, and inhumane, there are also other less physical modes whereby authorities can make the life of a creative writer miserable. One of the most commonly encountered will be a requirement that writers belong to some type of writers union. Whereas trade unions in the West are often seen, particularly in their historical context, as a means of protecting the rights of workers, this is not the pattern for writers unions—at least in those countries that form the focus of this chapter; instead, they serve as a means of exercising controls over writers rather than of protecting their interests. Issues of the *Index on Censorship* have been filled with accounts of the establishment and policies of such organizations, and noted later, the Arab world provides some clear examples of such procedures.

The consequences of this situation regarding creative writers and their works are many. One of them is simply a resort to silence, a cessation of all creative activity in favor of "a regular job." A more subtle decision involves a shift to a different genre of writing that is less subject to control. For example, the cited definitions of "censorship" single out the dramatic genre for particular mention, and, if the Arab world can serve as any kind of example for other cultures, this "popular parliament" has offered censorship authorities a broad arena for interference and suppression.[4]

Whether authors are expelled from their home countries and from contact with their readers or make a personal decision to pursue a writing career in a more conducive environment, the result is still the same: exile. This is the fate or choice of a large number of Arab authors, something that emerges as an anticipatable consequence of the situation discussed here.

Contemporary Arab Societies:
Historical and Political Background

A principle enshrined in the common law if not in the constitutions of most Western democracies is the "public's right to know." When the right is curtailed in some way, for whatever reason, the action will normally be challenged. In contrast, many litterateurs in the Arab world today function in societies where that right is either controlled to varying degrees or else nonexistent, a situation that may be seen as resulting not only from the current political system under which their nation and its society operates but also from the historical background against which that political system has evolved. Also significant is the worldview entertained by the region as a whole and by its individual political leaders in their relationships with not only each other but also those of other world regions.

Although the events of the more distant past can provide some justifications for the shape of the Middle Eastern map today, it remains true that most of the borders currently in place were not drawn by the indigenous inhabitants of the region, and many of these are of relatively recent creation.[5] Citizens of the Middle East constantly draw attention to this factor and further point out that it is only since the conclusion of World War II and the subsequent withdrawal of colonial forces from the region that the individual nations have managed to obtain full control over their life and destiny. Nor should the use of the word "withdrawal" be seen as implying a well-planned or mutually agreed process. Change came, more often than not, as the result of revolution—a movement aimed both at ridding the country of foreign domination and at transforming the prevailing political patterns. These goals were shared by the revolutions in a number of Arab nations, but local circumstances necessarily made the sequence and emphases different from one country to another. In the case of Egypt, for example, the revolution (in 1952) was a relatively bloodless one, initially aimed at overthrowing a corrupt monarchical regime. In other countries, the same process took the form of bloody internal political feuding, as in Iraq (1958), or a prolonged and bitter battle against colonial forces, as in the "War of a Million Martyrs" in Algeria (1954–1962). Thus, although the very course of these processes of change varied widely, the major aim of the Arab world since the beginning of the century—namely, the achievement of control over the national destiny—became a reality.

While these varied processes of change were under way, the attention of the entire region was also focused on another issue, one that has continued to occupy the attention of every nation and thus to be reflected in a large number of literary works: the establishment of the state of Israel. Ever since the announcement of the Balfour Declaration in 1917 (a document whose terms were totally incompatible with those previously agreed upon with the Arabs under the Sykes-Picot agreement of 1916), the Arabs in Palestine had been resisting the idea of a Jewish national home in the region. With the declaration of the state of Israel in 1948, the conflict assumed an entirely different and more global level. As war has followed war (1948, 1956, 1967, 1973, and 1982), the fate of the Palestinian people has become for a large number of creative writers in the region a continuing symbol of their personal and communal malaise and sense of powerlessness, a yardstick against which other struggles, national and international, have to be judged.

As the forces of the foreign powers (France, Britain, and Italy) left the region and as monarchs and other leaders of anciens régimes were replaced or assassinated, new structures had to be established, new national and international links had to be forged, and new understandings of societal rights and obligations had to be reached. Each Arab nation undertook this complex tasks in different ways, a logical consequence of the variety of emerging circumstances—such as the availability of natural resources and expertise and ethnic, religious, and linguistic diversity. All this activity took place against the background of a pattern of world politics that came to be known as the cold war. Within such a scenario, the Middle East was a natural—indeed, time-worn—venue for the exercise of such rivalries.

During this period in the modern history of the Middle East, President Gamal Abdel Nasser was among the leaders in the region not only to take advantage of Soviet financial support but also to make full use of these connections to study and imitate the model of societies within the Soviet bloc regarding such matters as the creation of an internal security apparatus, the supervision (and suppression) of the publication media and the creation of an atmosphere of suspicion and fear through which to exert control over as many aspects of the life of each individual in the society as possible. A regular feature of this policy of control involved the nationalization of the publication media—newspapers, magazines, radio, television, and films—and the consequent control of the public's access to information.[6] As a U.S. writer noted, "To their astonishment, and with mixed feelings, the Egyptians found that their revolution had produced despotism."[7] During the latter part of the 1950s and into the 1960s, the governments of the Arab world kept a tight rein on the dissemination of information and began to acquire the necessary skills in the use and abuse of the broadcasting media for propaganda purposes.

The new political and societal alignments that resulted from the various revolutionary processes were clearly a ready and legitimate topic for the creativity of litterateurs. The 1950s and 1960s witnessed an enormous growth in literary production and in critical discussion of it. In the latter context, there was much debate on the role of the writer in the new society, much of it under the banner of "commitment" (*ilitzām*). The famous Beirut journal, Al-Ādāb, was founded for the specific purpose of promoting commitment in literature and criticism of it. M. M. Badawi describes the general environment as follows:

> The Arab poet or writer . . . [a]s a result of a growing sense of individuality, both politically and psychologically, and an increasing awareness of his place in his society, . . . is now expected to have a message, to maintain his artistic integrity and not to sell his poetic or prose wares to the highest bidder, or to serve a cause in which he does not believe, sincerity now being regarded as the prime consideration.[8]

Within such frames of reference, writers were clearly to be regarded as participants in the nation's political process and advocates of the social transformations that were perceived to be necessary. This perception was (and still is) often expressed through a requirement that writers join an official writers union so that the government's "expectations" could be conveyed quickly and efficiently.[9] Writers might not be required to foster and reflect official policies in a direct manner, but the very least that seemed to be expected was that they not venture beyond certain clearly defined boundaries. As long as the topics were confined to those aspects of the emerging societal fabric that were seen to be positive—freedom from foreign domination, new opportunities in education, the reform of agricultural policy, and the like—the publication opportunities were fully open and the resulting works were afforded considerable publicity.

However, there were a number of authors who remained uncertain; one such, according to his own words, was the 1988 Nobel laureate Najib Maḥfūẓ who wrote no works of fiction between 1952 and 1957, when he began work on *Awlād Ḥāratinā* (Children of our quarter, translated into English as *Children of Gebelawi*) that was to appear in the columns of *Al-Ahrām* in 1959 and thereafter to be banned. Such uncertainties have by no means been diminished with the passage of time.[10] However, for those writers who, nursing the illusion that they were free to describe what they saw and felt frankly and accurately or having courage to do so in any case, decided to discuss the more negative aspects of the new and emerging societal fabric, the situation soon emerged to be very different indeed. It is perhaps appropriate that some of the most graphic accounts of the treatment to which some writers were subjected come from works of fiction, but even for this genre, the message that emerges is clear enough.

> I saw my homeland for which I had been prepared to go through the very tortures of Hell itself applying those very same tortures to anyone who fell into the hands of the authorities. From the Arab Gulf to the Atlantic Ocean I heard a cry. I heard weeping and the sound of sticks and plastic hoses. Capitals and casbas, the secret police were everywhere, on mountaintops and in the valleys below, men in neat civilian suits walking to and fro like a thousand shuttles on a thousand looms, hauling off to the centres of darkness people by the tens and hundreds.[11]

The picture of the various societies of the Arab world that emerged as a result of this situation was normally the one the governments wished to see in the public domain. There was a general awareness among intellectuals of the falseness of that picture, but it took a major catastrophe to bring about full knowledge of the scale of the problem and thereafter a certain degree of change. That event was the June 1967 war when, for a considerable period of time, people in the Arab world (those without access to the British Broadcasting Corporation's World Service, at least) were under the impression that a tremendous victory for the Arabs was imminent.[12] In the atmosphere of self-examination and recrimination that followed that cataclysmic event in modern Arab history, debate on every aspect of Arab society, its bases and values, was lengthy and heated. Egypt bore the brunt of the defeat, militarily and politically. Even though his own people demanded that he continue as leader, Nasser never recovered his former position of prominence in the region. What did change, to a certain extent at least, was the general atmosphere in the country, something to which Anwar al-Sādāt made frequent reference early in his presidency. In May 1971, he instituted what was termed the "Correctional Revolution" *(thawrat al-taṣḥīḥ)* aimed at the promotion of freedom of speech; people were supposed to be able to speak *bi-kulli al-ṣarāḥa* (absolutely frankly.) Even though other means were found to exert such control over writers as was deemed necessary, it cannot be denied that the situation was more open than had been the case previously.[13]

Although the situation may have changed in certain countries of the region and particular circumstances may vary, Arab litterateurs certainly do not share the freedoms enjoyed by their Western colleagues. The Syrian poet and literary critic Kamal Abu Deeb describes the situation in the following way: "restrictive, authoritarian regimes that have annulled the right of man to think, reflect, act, cogitate, and conduct research outside the bounds of a zone that is both predetermined and preimposed."[14] Another writer puts it as follows: "In the Arab World the word is not merely forbidden: it's so beset that it feels as though it's being throttled. And it's not just the written word, but the spoken too."[15]

However, there is one country, Lebanon, that has been and still is an exception to this description. One of the most disarming yet potentially encouraging facts to emerge from the devastating civil strife that has torn that country apart since 1975—the war being, no doubt, one regrettable result of the very societal diversity that has stimulated freedom of publication—is that in spite of the lethal bombardments the different communities continue to hurl in each other's direction, books and journals continue to be published as presses are moved on a regular basis from one underground garage to another.[16]

The general situation in the Arab world, as these works are being written, is aptly summarized in the following verdict to be found in the first paragraph of the English introduction to the 1987 Report of the Arab Organization for Human Rights (Cairo, 1988): "The continued inability of the Arab world to formulate a covenant or charter expressing the Arab concept of the important cultural and ethical value of human rights is clearly indicative of apathy and discord."

Censorship of Literature in the Arab World

The very existence of censorship—let alone discussion of its nature and modus operandi or critical comment on its implementation and effects—is a taboo topic in the Arab world. In a word, the existence of censorship is censored. As can be seen from the notes to this chapter, information used here comes predominantly from three primary sources outside the Arab world: the *Index on Censorship*, published in English by Writers and Scholars International in London; the publications of the Arab Organization for Human Rights (AOHR), based in Geneva and with an office in Cairo;[17] and Al-Nāqid, a monthly journal in Arabic published also in London by Riyāḍ Najīb al-Rayyis. In fact, al-Rayyis is quite specific about the aims of his journal: "The dream in founding Al-Nāqid was to be able to write for a free Arab publication in exile, far removed from the pressures of politics, party feuds, and police terror found in the Arab World."[18]

These sources make it clear that the methods I have noted whereby access to literary works can be controlled or prevented are to be found throughout the Arab world. However, although general patterns are reasonably clear, the detail that is provided is far from consistent. The most information by far is about writers from Egypt, Israel, and the occupied West Bank, the measures that are taken against them, the literary works that are the object of the censors' scrutiny, and so on.[19] There are also several reports concerning the general situation in Morocco, although most of them concentrate on the censorship of the press. However, when there are reports on litterateurs, the news almost always concerns the imposition of sentences of imprisonment that seem particularly severe.[20] This information becomes available because the society involved either allows (or is unable to prevent) the reporting of such facts to the publishers of censorship information. In some cases, that situation extends to giving permission to one or another human rights organization to maintain an office. However, if conclusions are based solely on the amount of information available, these nations would appear, in terms of the published information on censorship, as the pariahs of the region. Needless to say, that statement is in no way intended to condone or excuse the variety of censorship activities involved in those countries, but it does point to the fact that the relative silence of sources on a number of other countries by no means implies that the situation is less severe; indeed, a diametrically opposite conclusion is almost certainly the correct one. In a word, what cannot be discovered or verified is probably far greater and more serious than what can be.

The inferences that can be drawn from the few reports that appear concerning the situation in Iraq and Syria, for example, are far from encouraging. Even when they live in Western countries, authors of reports about these countries write under pseudonyms for fear of reprisals. The reports themselves talk of authors being executed or simply disappearing.[21] With regard to the Gulf states, the traditional moral values maintained within those societies obviously have a direct impact on the kinds of literary works that are permitted to appear. Yet variations can also be found, and it is impossible to detect any general patterns. The interest in women's rights that has been a feature of much societal discourse in the West recently has been reflected in recent reports regarding the treatment of two female writers in this region.[22]

However, information on these and other nations of the Arab world is extremely scarce. The occasional reports that do appear make it clear that creative writers are by no means able to compose without constraints, but the wide variety of local political and social situations involved would require a separate treatment of each region that is clearly beyond the scope of this chapter. Thus, rather than attempting to survey the censorship of Arabic literature on a regional or generic basis, I illustrate the categories already outlined with some exemplary cases, using the same sequence as already adopted: actions relating in turn to text, reader, and author.

Within the general area of the handling of literary texts by official censorship authorities, there is one genre that has been adversely affected throughout the Arab world: drama. I wish to make it clear that in making such a blanket statement, I am referring to drama as *performance,* the latter being an aspect of this literary genre without which, in the opinion of the majority of theorists, it ceases to have any distinct generic validity. Texts of dramas have been written and published in large numbers, and numerous dramatists have become famous in their own countries and, in a few cases throughout the region—for example, Tawfīq al-Ḥakīm, Yūsuf Idrīs, and Alfred Faraj from Egypt; al-Ṭayyib al-Ṣiddīqī from Morocco; Saʿdallāh Wannūs from Syria; and ʿIzz al-dīn al-Madamī from Tunisia. However, because the process of transferring the text of a play to the stage involves reading committees, acting troupes with their directors and actors, the theater management, and the theatrical press—the vast majority of them under state control—it should come as no surprise to learn that there is hardly a dramatist in the Arab world who at one time or another has not encountered difficulties in seeing his or her creations performed in front of an audience. Countless plays have been banned, either at the outset, during production, or after one night or even several weeks of performance. Under such circumstances, many playwrights have stopped writing altogether, moved to other genres, gone into exile, or entered into some combination of these actions.[23] Furthermore, it should be remembered that this theatrical tradition, which does not share with its Western models a lengthy period of development, has been forced relatively early in its modern history to confront the effects of cinema and television, both of which continue to vie with the theater for the services of a rather small cadre of actors and with the public for its attention.

These factors, coupled with the prevalence of domestic farces and the blatantly political message of much officially sponsored "serious" drama, have produced a situation that in almost every region of the Arab world has been termed a "theater crisis" *(azmat al-masrah)*. The status of theater texts and performances of them are also reflected to a degree in the reception of another, perhaps less obvious literary genre: poetry. Many Arab poets continue to fulfill a traditional role as public performer and catalyst of popular opinion. Thus, collections of poetry, as texts, are subjected to much the same kind of censorship as is the case with other genres, but poetry—as an expression of opposition to official policies and views—has been able to take advantage of that same modern technology that may be working to the disadvantage of theater—the development of an underground cassette distribution network. Among the more famous examples of this phenomenon are the Egyptian poet Ahmad Fuʾād Nigm (Najm) and his colleague, the singer Shaykh Imām, and the notorious Iraqi poet Muzaffar al-Nawwāb, whose poems contain savage attacks on virtually every leader in the Arab world, thus placing him at the top of the wanted list of almost every secret police organization in the region.[24]

As for writings that lack the advantage of performance for their expression but that find their only availability in book form, the almost complete control of publication produces a situation that clearly favors the famous and those who are prepared to operate within certain established terms of reference. The Egyptian critic Sabry Hafez has the following to say on the subject:

> In other words, the tongue of a whole generation has been prohibited from any genuine political activity, and surrounded by deformed values and fallacies. This generation [of the 1960s] has grown up in a paternal society, in the fullest and worst sense of the word, where the governor and his corrupted

bureaucratic establishment considered themselves the only possible substitute for all political and social systems and organizations. When this unfortunate generation started to express its rebellious visions, it conflicted not only with the heavy fist of censorship, but also with the reluctance of the previous generation who dominated the literary establishment and benefited from it, in a literary and economic manner.[25]

Beyond publication lies distribution; here the Arab author faces a situation that is both capricious and chaotic. Works tend to be published in relatively small runs that, because of a lack of storage facilities and the quality of production, tend to have a very short shelf life. If that is the situation within each country, the distribution of works among the different countries of the Arab world (and indeed in the West) is entirely ad hoc. The creation and maintenance of interest in literary works are thus very much the hostage of attention in the press and efficient distribution networks. Reports of "difficulties" are widespread.[26]

Civil authorities are not the only ones to request the censorship of literary works. In instances of protests from religious sources, the case of Najib Mahfūz is already well known. It was during the course of his Nobel year (1988–1989) that the *Satanic Verses* affair reached its acme, incidentally distracting a good deal of the Western audience's attention from his oeuvre. Mahfūz's courageous defense of Rushdie's right to express himself (even though Mahfūz did voice his own strong distaste for *Satanic Verses*) led to a death threat against Mahfūz and focused attention once again on his work, *Awlād Ḥāratinā*, translated into English as *Children of Gebelawi*.[27] This novel, an allegorical account of the history of mankind's encounter with religion, was serialized in *Al-Ahrām* in 1959 and immediately banned under pressure from Al-Azhar, the mosque university in Cairo. It was nevertheless published in Beirut in 1967 and has been unofficially available in Egypt ever since.

After this work was mentioned in the Nobel Prize committee's citation, journalists attending the celebration of Mahfūz's award asked President Hosni Mubārak of Egypt a trap question: Mr. President, do you think all our prizewinner's works should be republished in Egypt? In the excitement of the celebration, the president replied that of course he did, and the next morning, Cairo's newspapers carried headlines to the effect that the president of Egypt had made that declaration. Only a short time afterward, the Shaykh of Al-Azhar published a decree reconfirming the ban on the publication of *Children of Gebelawi* in Egypt.[28] Mahfūz's response to this was typically laconic: "Not all the works of any author are necessarily suitable for publication in his homeland." He had in fact already acknowledged that the Nobel Prize was a Western prize and reflected a particular set of expectations and standards, but here he was expanding on the ramifications of that statement into the realm of censorship. More recently, the religious authorities in Egypt, apparently desiring to quash any attempts at emulating Rushdie's experiment, have instigated a charge of blasphemy against a young novelist.[29]

Issues such as the banning of books and performances of various kinds and the regulation, deliberate or not, of book and magazine distribution clearly have a direct impact on readers in the Arab world. These are perhaps the most obvious and direct but not the only avenues of control. In the case of Mahfūz's *Awlād Hāratinā*, for example, copies manufactured in Beirut must have been imported in some manner. Certain countries monitor the importation of books very carefully. Several reports in the *Index on Censorship* discuss the confiscation of materials in Morocco, and the situation seems particularly tight in Saudi Arabia.

Cases of censorship involving individual Arab writers are regrettably varied and numerous; the instances cited here can serve only as examples of a phenomenon that is widespread. As already noted, not even Mahfūz has been immune from this treatment, most famously with *Children of Gebelawi* but also on other occasions during the presidencies of both Nasser and Sadat.[30] However, one fate Mahfūz has, to my knowledge, avoided is that of actual imprisonment—the fate of many Arab litterateurs and the topic of several works of fiction. Among the more graphic examples are " Al-'Askarī al-Aswad" (The black policeman), written in 1962 by Yūsuf Idrīs,[31] and *Sharq al-Mutawassit* (East of the Mediterranean), written in 1977 by 'Abd al-Rahmān Munīf.[32]

But in the link between personal experiences and their reflection in fiction, few cases can match that of the Egyptian fiction writer Sun'allāh Ibrāhim. Imprisoned for five years (1959–1964) for "political activities," he emerged to begin writing *Tilka al-rā'iha* (That smell) (1966), a disarmingly accurate portrayal of the life of a released prisoner and the disorientation brought about both by his attempts to reintegrate himself into society and by the constant surveillance of the security forces. The work was immediately banned, issued in incomplete form in 1969, and only published in complete form in Casablanca in 1986.[33] In this and two later works of fiction, Ibrāhim presented an utterly disillusioning picture of the treatment to which creative writers were exposed, what is described in the *Index on Censorship* as "the experience of a generation."[34] Nor has such treatment been reserved for male writers. The world-famous Egyptian feminist writer Nawāl al-Sa'dāwi was incarcerated for her political views and outspoken statements toward the end of the Sadat era; in fact, she emerged from prison only after his assassination in 1981.[35]

The other area on which detailed information is available is Israel and the occupied territories. The famous Palestinian poet Mahmūd Darwish eventually decided to pursue his career outside his homeland because "his life there [in Israel] had become intolerable from daily harassment, frequent imprisonments and continuous house arrest."[36] Darwish's colleague, Samih al-Qāsim, was imprisoned by the Israeli authorities when he did not submit one of his collections of poetry to the military censor; as he puts it, his book was arrested, and he was sequestered. After an outcry involving telegrams from such figures as Jean-Paul Sartre, Allen Ginsberg, and Arnold Wesker, he was released.[37] When another poet, Tawfīq al-Zayyād, was asked by Israeli authorities where he had learned his Hebrew, he responded: "In your jails." Even Emīl Habībī, the famous author of such works as *Al-Waqā'i' al-gharība* . . . and for several years a member of the Israeli Knesset, reports that he is not free to publish.[38] Finally—and as previously discussed, drama is analyzed particularly carefully—it is no surprise that Israeli censors have paid close attention to the performance of Arabic plays in both Israel and the occupied territories; the successes and tribulations of the famous Ḥakawātī troupe are strong evidence in this regard.

The authors mentioned here are all alive today (as of mid-1992) and have recounted their experiences with great courage. However, the attention of the censor has not been confined to living writers and their texts. The works of the medieval mystic and littérateur Ibn 'Arabī (1165–1240) were found to be heretical and were impounded in Egypt,[39] and that most famous of authorless texts, *A Thousand and One Nights* was declared obscene and withdrawn in 1985.[40]

In concluding this list of examples, I must again stress that the most specific information is available only about those countries that permit its release. These circumstances are bad enough, but they must be regarded unfortunately as the tip of a very large iceberg, the full dimensions of which may never be known.

Conclusion

Writing this chapter has not been the kind of pleasant and fulfilling experience one normally associates with the preparation of a contribution to one's field of specialty. To the obvious reason of the general distastefulness of the subject matter must be added the fact that it is highly unsatisfactory to begin and proceed through a project and yet be well aware that much of the information needed is not available. Such seems to be the lot of anyone who would write about censorship.

As part of the conference convened by Writers and Scholars International In London and later published in 1984 as *They Shoot Writers, Don't They?* a British novelist has these words to say, and they may serve as a most fitting conclusion to this necessarily incomplete survey:

> But the worst, most insidious effect of censorship is that, in the end, it can deaden the imagination of the people. Where there is not debate, it is hard to go on remembering, every day, that there is a suppressed side to every argument. It becomes almost impossible to conceive of what the suppressed things might be. It becomes easy to think that what has been suppressed was valueless anyway, or so dangerous that it needed to be suppressed. And then the victory of the censor is total.

The novelist in question was Salman Rushdie.[41]

Notes

1. George Theiner, "Introduction," in *They Shoot Writers, Don't They?* ed. George Theiner (London and Boston: Faber and Faber, 1984), p. 12. A short listing of assassinated writers can be found on p. 13.

2. I concentrate in this section on examples from outside the Arab world

because the remainder of the chapter is devoted to the Arab world and writers in Arabic.

3. As happened in both the United States and Britain with Salman Rushdie's *Satanic Verses* when bookstores were threatened with violent repercussions. Indeed, one London bookstore was bombed for carrying the book.

4. The expression "popular parliament" is used by Khayrī Shalabī in the Egyptian theater journal *Al-Masraḥ* 29 (May 1966), p. 65.

5. The problem of the independence of Kuwait and its borders with Iraq is precisely such an issue.

6. Fāḍil al-'Azzāwī makes the following comment on this matter: "When a regime nationalizes mankind in the name of adherence to a national, religious, or class credo, it simply condemns itself to death. The selfsame credo will die when its only goal turns out to be a closed room haunted by specters. The real crisis for Arab man is that of freedom of conscience above all else." See "Kayf tafsid al-thawrāt?" [How do revolutions go bad?], *Al-Nāqid*, Vol. 13 (July 1989), pp. 16–24.

7. Milton Viorst, *New Yorker*, July 2, p. 45, col. 1. He is contrasting the reactions of Najīb Maḥfūz to the Nasser period with those of Tawfīq al-Ḥakīm, the famous Egyptian playwright.

8. M. M. Badawi, *An Anthology of Modern Arabic Verse* (London: Oxford University Press, 1970), Introduction, p. ix; idem, "Commitment in Modern Arabic Poetry," *Cahiers d'histoire mondiale* [Journal of world history], Vol. 14 (1972): 858 ff.

9. Anon., "Repression in Iraq and Syria," *Index on Censorship* (hereafter *IC*), Vol. 13, no. 2 (April 1984), p. 34. The dissolution of the Jordanian Writers Association is noted in *IC*, Vol. 16, no. 9 (October 1987), p. 37, and Vol. 16, no. 10 (November-December 1987), p. 37, together with an announcement about required membership in a new writers union. The Egyptian journal *Al-Kātib* (November 1975) contains discussion of the articles of the writers union, including one to the effect that "The Union Council, by vote of two-thirds of its members, may draw a member's attention to deviations from proper conduct or to offences against the by-laws and order of the Union."

10. Muhammad Muhammad Al-Baqqāsh, "Hal naktub li-al-qurrā' am li-al-raqāba?" [Who are we writing for, readers or the censor?], *Al-Nāqid*, September 15, 1989, pp. 79–80.

11. Jabrā Ibrāhim Jabrā, *Al-Baḥth 'an Walīd Mas'ūd* (Beirut: Dār Al-Ādāb, 1978), p. 249. It should be noted that "from the Arab Gulf . . . to the Atlantic Ocean" is a sardonic reference to one of Nasser's most quoted phrases. Compare also the comments of the Egyptian critic Farīda al-Naqqāsh: "prisons and torture, police chases and a constricting surveillance, exile . . . thousands of masks—false names and hideaways." *Al-Ādāb* (February-March 1980), p. 33. Farīda al-Naqqāsh is herself the subject of a report in the *IC* for having written a work published in Beirut in 1980 entitled *Al-Sijn . . . Al-Watan* [The prison . . . the homeland]; see Marilyn Booth, "Farīda al-Naqqāsh Banned from Writing in Egypt," *IC*, Vol. 12, no. 3 (June 1983), pp. 20–22.

12. The impact of this situation is graphically portrayed in Ḥalīm Bakarāt's novel *'Awdat al-ṭā'i r ilā al-baḥr* (Beirut: Dār al-Nahār, 1969), translated into English by Trevor Le Gassick as *Days of Dust*, (Wilmette, IL: Medina Press International, 1974).

13. It needs to be observed that the sorry record of President Sadat with regard to freedom of expression and censorship, seen at its most notorious in such measures as the Law on Shame (*IC*, Vol. 9, no. 4 (August 1980), pp. 65–66) and in the purge

of university teachers (*IC*, Vol. 11, no. 1 (February 1982), p. 37), and the continuing battles in Egypt between creative writers and censorship authorities, as reflected on a regular basis in the *IC* reports were reported without hindrance presumably because of the relative freedom of access to information and transmission of it outside the country as compared with other countries in the region. This aspect of the reporting of censorship is discussed further later in the chapter.

14. Kamal Abu Deeb, "Al-Kitāba wa-al-Sulṭa" [Writing and authority], *Al-Nāqid* 26 (August 1990), p. 40.

15. "'Alī Hāshim, "Man sa-yataghayyar: Al-raqīb am al-kātib?" [Who is going to change: The censor or the writer?], *Al-Nāqid* 16 (October 1989), p. 55.

16. The traditionally favorable situation in Lebanon is described in the Arab Organization for Human Rights (AOHR) report (in Arabic) for 1989, p. 131. Adel Darwish and Haifaa Khalafallah held a pessimistic view of the 1983 situation; see "Lebanon: Last Refuge of the Written Word Destroyed," *IC*, Vol. 11, no. 6 (December 1982), p. 26: "Beirut was not only a safety valve whereby Arab intellectuals could publish works they could not publish at home, it was also an important source for Arabists and non-Arab scholars of material written in or about the Arab world, even if the materials were banned everywhere else in the Middle East." Although the situation is clearly not ideal, the volume of publication emerging from Beirut is nevertheless remarkable.

17. AOHR maintains records on violations of personal liberties in the Arab world and since 1986 has published a detailed annual account of its findings in Arabic, *Huqūq al-insān fī al-waṭan 'Arabī*, with a general introduction and country-by-country details. AOHR also publishes annually an English version of the introduction to each year's report. The aim of the organization is "to ensure respect for the right of Arab Citizens everywhere so that their natural aptitudes, freed from all restrictions, can contribute to the development and advancement of the Arab World." Introduction (in Arabic) to *AOHR Report for 1988* (Cairo, 1988), p. 5; English version (Cairo, 1989), p. 1.

18. *Al-Nāqid* 8 (February 1989), p. 5. It should be noted that this is in response to an article by Mamdūh 'Adwān in Syria in *Al-Nāqid* 7 (January 1989), pp. 18–19, about the courage of writers in exile as opposed to those who remain in their homeland.

19. Sherif Hetāta, in *IC*, Vol. 12, no. 3 (June 1983), p. 16, describes the situation in Egypt as follows: "Actual freedom of expression in Egypt is still very limited . . . in the sphere of publishing, in the availability of books, and in our universities." The Palestinian poet Samīḥ al-Qāsim has the following to say about the situation in Israel: "Talking about freedom and democracy . . . Israel is pure hypocrisy." *IC*, Vol. 12, no. 6 (December 1983), pp. 30–32. The reports of AOHR contain regular accounts of "massive violations of human rights by the occupation authorities in Palestine." See, e.g., English introduction for 1987 (Cairo, 1988), p. 6; Arabic report for 1988 (Cairo, 1988), pp. 132–144; English introduction for 1988 (Cairo, 1989), p. 8; Arabic report for 1989 (Cairo, 1989), pp. 104–120; English introduction for 1989 (Cairo, 1990), pp. 19–27; Arabic report for 1990 (Cairo, 1990), pp. 122–136.

20. "How Morocco Treats Its Dissidents," *IC*, Vol. 13, no. 6 (December 1984), p. 30; "Eliminating the Outspoken Press in Morocco," *IC*, Vol. 14, no. 2 (April 1985), p. 25; "Blindfold Justice," *IC*, Vol. 18, no. 1 (January 1989), pp. 19–21.

21. On Iraq, see, for example, Raad Mushatat [pseud.], "At Home and in Exile," *IC*, Vol. 15, no. 2 (February 1986), p. 28. One report provides a list of 114 Iraqi

intellectuals who have either left the country or been expelled; see *IC*,Vol. 10, no. 4 (August 1981), p. 42. For Syria, see *IC*, Vol. 11, no. 3 (June 1982), p. 47; Anon., "Repression in Iraq and Syria," *IC*, Vol. 13, no. 2 (April 1984), p. 34; and *IC*, Vol. 16, no. 6 (June 1987), pp. 25–26. The AOHR report (in Arabic) for 1988 notes that "hardly anything in Syria escapes the censor's attention. Even Friday sermons in the mosque have to be submitted in advance to the Ministry of Religious Affairs before being delivered. All information media are subjected to the very strictest censorship" (p. 95, and, for the similar situation in Iraq, p. 123). See also the English introduction to the AOHR report for 1989 (Cairo, 1990), p. 10.

22. For example, Dr. Su'ād al-Sabbāh, the Kuwaiti poet, was banned from publishing or writing; see *Al-Nāqid* 13 (July 1989), p. 15; and *IC*, Vol. 18, no. 6-7 (July-August 1989), p. 78. In the United Arab Emirates, poet Dhabia Khamees was arrested; see *IC*, Vol. 16, no. 10 (November-December 1987), p. 39. On the general situation in the Gulf states, see Anon., "Keeping the Lid On," *IC*, Vol. 14, no. 2 (April 1985), p. 24.

23. See *IC*, Vol. 12, no. 3 (June 1983), p. 24. In *Al-Talīa'* (February 1976), p. 166, is this observation: "Had the right circumstances for a flourishing drama existed, such producers could have been replaced by others or a new younger generation of dramatists could have taken its place beside the older one. However, this generation has moved to the novel, not the drama. They realize their works will never be performed on stage; they will remain unfulfilled unless performed."

24. For Ahmad Fu'ād Nigm, see *IC*, Vol. 2, no. 3 (Winter 1973); Vol. 10, no. 5 (October 1981), p. 11; and Haifaa Khalafallah, "Unofficial Cassette Culture in the Middle East," *IC*, Vol. 11, no. 5 (October 1982), pp. 10–12. For Shaykh Imām, see Marilyn Booth, "Sheikh Imām the Singer: An Interview," *IC*, Vol. 14, no. 3 (June 1985), pp. 18–21. For Muzaffar al-Nawwāb, see *IC*, Vol. 11, no. 5 (October 1982), pp. 10–12; for a translated poem, "Jerusalem," see *Nimrod*, Vol. 24, no. 2 (Spring-Summer 1981), pp. 135–138.

25. Sabry Hafez, "Innovation in the Egyptian Short Story," in *Studies in Modern Arabic Literature* ed. R. C. Ostle (Warminster, England: Aris and Phillips, 1975), p. 110. I freely acknowledge that this description is not a little dated with regard to the situation in Egypt to which it originally referred (although complexities still remain). However, I believe the quotation certainly remains an apt depiction of circumstances in many other parts of the Arab world.

26. In Algeria, for example, "the position of artists and writers is also extremely difficult . . . many writers had difficulties with the censor and the State-owned distrbution company." See *IC*, Vol. 18, no. 1 (January 1989), p. 18. One of the editors of *Al-Nāqid* discusses difficulties that have been encountered: "As far as censorship organizations in the Arab World allow us, we do our very best to distribute *Al-Nāqid* and get it out into the Arab markets. It is quite beyond our powers to cope with the situation as long as censorship 'chains' transcend the normal bounds of reasonable logic. Has it occurred to any of our readers that *Al-Nāqid* is not to be distributed in one Gulf State because it 'offends public decency'?" 'Abd al-Ghani Muruwwah, "Lusūs al-kutub marratan ukhrā" [Once again book thieves], *Al-Nāqid* 9 (March 1989), p. 57.

27. Najib Mahfūz [Naguib Mahfouz], *Children of Gebelawi*, trans. Philip Stewart (Washington, DC: Three Continents, 1981).

28. See *IC*, Vol. 18, no. 3 (March 1989), p. 36.

29. See *Christian Science Monitor*, July 24, 1990.

30. Nasser himself is said to have been extremely annoyed by the negative image of Egypt depicted in *Tharthara fawq al-Nīl* [Chatter on the Nile] (1966); apparently

only the personal intervention of Tharwat 'Ukāsha, the minister of culture, prevented further action. Mahfūz was one of the writers who was suspended from membership in the writers union (and thus from all publication activity) for a short time during the early years of the Sadat regime.

31. Translated by Catherine Cobham as "The Black Policeman" in *Rings of Burnished Brass* (London: Heinemann; and Washington: Three Continents, 1984). Idrīs was imprisoned from August 1954 until September 1955; see P. M. Kurpershoek, *The Short Stories of Yūsuf Idrīs*(Leiden: E. J. Brill, 1981), p. 28.

32. Translated into French by Kadhem Jihad as *A l'Est de la Mediterranée* (Paris: Sindbad, 1985).

33. Until 1986, the English translation of the work by Denys Johnson-Davies, *The Smell of It* (London: Heinemann, 1971), seems to have been the only complete version.

34. "The Experience of a Generation," trans. Marilyn Booth, *IC*, Vol. 16, no. 9 (October 1987), pp. 19–22.

35. See Nawāl al-Sa'dāwī, *Mudhakkirāt min sijn al-nisā'* (1983), translated as *Memoirs from the Women's Prison* by Marilyn Booth (London: Women's Press, 1986); also "In the Women's Prison," *IC*, Vol. 14, no. 4 (August 1985), pp. 36–43. Dr. al-Sa'dāwī's husband, Sherif Hetāta, like his wife a writer of fiction, suffered a much longer term in prison. He was released in 1964.

36. See *IC*, Vol. 12, no. 6 (December 1983), p. 45 (on the refusal of the United States to grant him a visitor's visa), and *IC*, Vol. 13, no. 4 (August 1984), pp. 30–32 (for details of his life in Israel.)

37. See Theiner, *They Shoot Writers*, p. 124; and interviews in *IC*, Vol. 11, no. 4 (August 1982), pp. 19–21, and *IC*, Vol. 12, no. 6 (December 1983), pp. 30–32.

38. For accounts of both authors, see *IC*, Vol. 11, no. 4 (August 1982), pp. 19–21. Habībī's famous novel is translated into English by Salma Khadra Jayyusi and Trevor Le Gassick as *The Secret Life of Saeed, the Ill-Fated Pessoptimist: A Palestinian Who Became a Citizen of Israel* (New York: Vantage, 1982).

39. See *IC*, Vol. 8, no. 3 (May-June 1979), p. 66.

40. See *IC*, Vol. 14, no. 4 (August 1985), p. 51, and Vol. 14, no. 5 (October 1985), p. 65.

41. Salman Rushdie, "Casualties of Censorship," in Theiner, *They Shoot Writers*, p. 87.

8

Freedom of Expression in the Third World: The Human Rights of Writers in Developing Countries

Ilan Peleg

This chapter is a methodical inquiry into writers' human rights within a comparative analytical framework; it identifies patterns of artistic oppression in the Third World, patterns relating to various dimensions of such oppression.

First, I review briefly the legal status of censorship in developing countries. Second, I examine the objectives of governments involved in artistic oppression. For example, some governments oppress artists as a means of eliminating political opposition to the regime in power; others oppress any criticism of the existing social order; some governments persecute intellectuals as a class; and others react only to what they see as obscenity, a threat to national security, or other specific considerations. In terms of objectives, there seems to be an interesting spectrum ranging from total opposition to any expression of political or social idea on the part of individuals—or even opposition to individuality itself—to a more benign, specific political censorship. I examine this spectrum by asking the following question: To what extent, and in what cases, is artistic oppression used to perpetuate the state's ideology by eliminating any challenge (or challenger) to the dominant belief system in a society? This segment of the chapter is based on the distinction between macro- and micro-objectives of censorship.

Third, I discuss the methods of artistic oppression prevalent in today's Third World. Some governments use brute force to prevent the free expression of ideas (e.g., death squads in different parts of Latin America), but most adopt at least some kind of legal fiction in persecuting their writers. Whereas some governments have a broad-based definition of censorship, others define more specifically topics that are out of bounds for artists. Islamic fundamentalist regimes (Iran, Libya), for example, are narrow in their interpretation of artistic freedom, with emphasis on obscenity, protection of religious values, and so forth. The punishment for artistic deviation from the politically determined norms ought also to be examined. It ranges from temporary or even permanent banning of works or creators to expulsion of writers from artists unions (as a means of depriving them of a livelihood), and from imprisonment to the imposition of the death penalty (as in the case of South Korea's most acclaimed poet, Kim Chi-ha). Although my primary focus is not the penalty repertoire used by governments, I do investigate the pattern of harshness/leniency used to deal with writers; the intensity of oppression of artists is of special significance. This part of the chapter is based on the distinction between censorship against authors and censorship against books.

The Legal Status of Censorship

Most developing countries take a legal approach to censorship. They carefully define in their constitutions and legal codes the causes for which persons might be punished, even though their definition of the illegal might not always be compatible with international standards. For example, Idi Amin's Uganda was, from a legal point of view, unique:

> Among the hundreds of thousands of Ugandans who have been murdered since Idi Amin took power . . . there have been remarkably few journalists, writers and broadcasters. Many more, however, have fled the country, and others have either abandoned their dangerous profession or have stayed on in their jobs to toe the government line. In Amin's Uganda *there are no censorship laws,* nor is there any code of conduct for writers—write it and you die.[1]

In other countries, violence committed outside the legal framework of the state is often carried out, tolerated, and even encouraged by the regime, despite the fact that, formally, freedom of expression is constitutionally guaranteed. Thus, in Augusto Pinochet's Chile, Article 19 (clause 2) of the 1980 Constitution provides for freedom of expression as well as private operation of the press and the media. Nevertheless, the Chilean media has been, on occasions, "vulnerable to guerrilla attacks": Radio stations and broadcasters have been assaulted, and "known dissenters have been killed in supposed armed confrontations (enfrentamientos), which are widely believed to be staged executions."[2]

In the People's Republic of Congo, a Marxist state, freedom of expression is guaranteed by Article 16 of the Constitution, but in practice, "the Party [Parti Congolaise du Travail] exercises direct control over the content and means of all communication within the country."[3] Article 19 noted that the voicing of "any opinion which is unacceptable to the ruling party" or the advocating of "any reform of the law or constitution" is, in practice, a criminal offense in the People's Republic.[4]

It seems that in Pinochet's Chile the constitutionally guaranteed freedom of expression was often violated through extrajudicial means, but in the Congo it is violated through legal or semilegal means. Both methods are quite common in developing countries.

The legal basis for limitations on the freedom of expression is rather diverse. In many countries, there is censorship against what is abstractly defined as the national interest, the state's interests, and other such generalized formulas. Angola has a 1983 law according to which the unauthorized divulgence of a secret that is "of fundamental interest to the State" or that "could affect the country's interest or be used to combat the development of the country's revolutionary process" might result in a severe penalty.[5]

In China, where the 1982 Constitution formally guarantees the right of expression, Article 51 of the document states that "the exercise of citizens of the People's Republic of China of their freedoms and rights . . . may not infringe upon the interests of the state, of society, and of the collective."[6] Writers and artists in China have been accused from time to time of such vague crimes as "spreading doubts about socialism in the mind of the young."[7]

Under the 1980 Egyptian Press Law, it is an offense to "advocate opposition to or hatred of state institutions."[8] The Egyptian poet Abdel Rahman Abonoudy, who has been critical of various aspects of Egyptian life and the government policy toward Israel, was summoned for investigation by the security service under the 1980 Law of Shame.[9] In Malaysia, the authorities not only can ban any publication thought "prejudicial to the national interest"[10] but also prohibit publication or distribution of materials judged by the minister of home affairs as endangering bilateral relations, public morality, security, and public order or even if it might "alarm public opinion."[11]

In Nigeria (Decree no. 4, 1985), the government has the power to close newspapers and radio and television stations for twelve months if they are deemed "detrimental to the interests of the federation."[12] In South Korea, the poet Yang Sung Woo was accused of and convicted for "defamation of state" through literature in accordance with Article 104, Section 2, of the criminal code; the poet was imprisoned for three years for publishing a poem called "Notes of a Slave" in the May 1977 issue of the Japanese monthly *Sekai*.[13] The Zambian Constitution (Article 22) guarantees the right to hold opinions and to communicate ideas freely, but Article 53 of the penal code empowers the president to prohibit publications that in his or her opinion are "contrary to the public interest."[14]

Often the limitation on free expression is imposed not in the name of the state or the nation in general but in the name of the specific regime in power or the social order it represents. Thus, among African states, Angola reserves the right to punish those who threaten "the country's revolutionary process";[15] the People's Republic of Congo cracks down on those who "challenge the authority of the single-party state"[16] or advocate a change in the constitutional order;[17] and Zambia, despite Article 22(1) of its Constitution that guarantees "freedom of expression without interference," forbids "the espousal of alternative political arrangements" in the country.[18]

Communist regimes in the Third World typically protect what they define as "the social order." Thus, under Cuba's Penal Code, anyone who writes, distributes, or possesses any material that "incites against the social order or the internal solidarity of the socialist State" is punishable. Many of the regime's political prisoners have been sentenced under this provision. Thus, Ariel

Hidalgo, a Cuban academic and writer, was convicted in the early 1980s in accordance with Article 108(1) of the Penal Code (enemy propaganda) for "incitement against the social order"; he was sentenced to an eight-year prison term.[19]

In some Third World countries, censorship is applied, by law, against those who criticize the ruler(s); here the level of specificity is remarkable in comparison to those countries where the state, the nation, the people, and the social order are protected. In the Central African Republic, "insults against the representatives of the public authority" are outlawed;[20] in Nigeria, holding the government or officials up to ridicule is prohibited.[21] In Pinochet's Chile, Article 417 of the Code of Military Justice makes it an offense to "slander the armed services"; thus, journalists accusing military officers of oppression might be prosecuted.[22] In Tunisia, as in other countries, criticism of the head of state is strictly prohibited.[23]

The legal basis for censorship is quite often very specific. In numerous Third World countries there are provisions against blasphemy: In Egypt, it is an offense to "challenge the truth of divine teachings."[24] In Trinidad and Tobago, an individual "must not attack another's belief or religious practices in a way which would amount to blasphemy."[25] As the Salman Rushdie affair indicates, the antiblasphemy sentiment in the Third World is quite powerful.

In many countries, there are provisions against written and pictorial material of a sexual nature. The Undesirable Publications Act (1967) in Singapore is applicable to publications the government considers sexually permissive.[26] The Indian Penal Code has strong provisions against obscenity, as does the Indecent Representation of Women (Prohibition) Act;[27] the Pakistani law and practice are even more severe.[28]

Some countries have specific regulations as to what line ought to be taken politically. In Morocco, no political organization can challenge the government's position on the Western Sahara or promote a political system other than the current monarchy.[29] Some systems prohibit the support of Marxism: Chile bans activity "intended to propagate ideas of totalitarian character or based on class warfare,"[30] and South Korea has a law prohibiting the praising or encouraging of communism. In 1978, the translator and publisher of a collection of essays about life in China, *Dialogue with 800 Million People* (written by John Kenneth Galbraith, Harrison Salisbury, Edgar Snow, and others), were sentenced to three and a half years in prison for violation of the Anti-Communist Law.[31]

Communist countries have similar laws punishing persons for anti-socialist activities and opinions. In China, for example, writers have been prosecuted for "spreading doubts about socialism" and accused of "spiritual pollution" whenever they deviated from the ideological line of the regime.[32] Vietnam's 1986 Penal code defines "propaganda against socialism" as a punishable crime.[33]

In sum, almost every Third World country today has legally sanctioned censorship of one type or another, and many have extralegal censorship as well. It even might be argued that in many countries, censorship is expanding, not contracting.[34] Most governments in the Third World tend to be authoritarian, and because censorship is one of the main characteristics of such a regime, censorship is rather common today in the Third World. The slogan "bread rather than freedom" often applies to censorship. Writers throughout the Third World continue to be judged not merely by the quality of their work but by their political opinions. Most governments in the Third World consider censorship, next to sheer military and police force, as their most powerful instrument of power.

The Objectives of Censorship

In this section, I consider the question of the objectives of censorship and limitations imposed on free expression. There are numerous objectives, goals, and ends to censorship, and a useful way of classifying them is to distinguish between what might be called macro-objectives and micro-objectives. The first category, *macro-objectives,* includes the general goals of censorship: maintaining the existing political and social order and eliminating internal or external opposition to it; keeping what might be called the "ideological purity" of the existing order; protecting the national interest or national security; or even preventing publications that offer an alternative historical interpretation to the one preferred by the existing regime.

The *micro-objectives of* censorship include various types of activity: curbing blasphemy, religious intolerance, or religious radicalism; maintaining morality (often through antipornographic policies); protecting the body politic from ethnic strife and separatist literature; guaranteeing that a specific policy or even an individual is not attacked; protecting the country's international relations or preventing outside interference; keeping the army or other societal institutions intact, and so forth.

Macro-Objectives

In numerous countries in the Third World, there is a fundamental, overarching goal for the censorship policy of the government: to maintain the political and social order—to prevent a regime change and to eliminate any opposition to it. In Nepal, member of parliament Rupchand Bista and editor-publisher Keschav Raj Pindali were arrested in late 1986 for publishing a satirical poem that was critical of the country's partyless system.[35] Vietnam introduced in early 1986 a new penal code that included punishments for "propaganda against socialism," "cultural sabotage," and the distribution of "decadent and counter-revolutionary books and magazines";[36] the new code was designed to maintain the results of the Tranh Loc program ("purification of culture") introduced by the victorious North Vietnamese in September 1975.[37] In South Africa, a government board banned Jack Cope's novel *The Dawn Comes Twice* on the grounds that it was "prejudicial to the safety of the state, the general welfare, and peace and good order."[38] In all three of these cases, a regime used censorship as a tool for maintaining the existing social and political order.

In many censorship cases throughout the Third World, the focus on not only eliminating any opposition but also maintaining the existing order is rather pronounced. In Morocco, the rule is simple, straightforward: The monarchy cannot be criticized.[39] In Iraq, not only the president is beyond criticism but so also are people and institutions acting on his behalf, such as the army, the Ba'ath Party, the National Assembly, and the government in general: Insulting any of these could result in a public execution.[40] The dean of the faculty of arts of Kuwait University, Dr. Khaldoun al-Naqib, was arrested and dismissed from his post for writing a book critical of the government, *Society and the State in the Gulf and the Arabian Peninsula.*[41]

Revolutionary regimes take a particularly strong position against nonconformity. The International PEN's Writers in Prison Committee reported in 1988 that five Vietnamese authors were charged with the crime of "systematic counterrevolutionary propaganda," of deliberately slandering the regime, and of listening to resistance broadcasts.[42] Similarly, in the People's Republic of Congo, author Emmanuel Boundzeki Dongola had his collection of short stories, *Jazze et vin de Palme,* banned for "satirizing party members and the official scientific Marxist ideology of the state."[43] In Cuba, writers have been arrested, prosecuted, and convicted for similar crimes.[44]

Yet conservative regimes also frequently use censorship to silence opposition circles. In Colombia, the poet José Pena was found shot on May 6, 1986; it was believed he was killed by security forces because of his pro–trade union poems and songs.[45] In South Africa, numerous authors have been harassed due to their opposition roles and had their writings banned due to their contents. In Paraguay, six authors arrested for opposing the government's policies drew the attention of PEN in the late 1970s.[46] In Turkey, a journalist who wrote a book on the history of human rights and torture in the country and the publisher of the book were indicted and convicted.[47] In Egypt under both Presidents Sadat and Mubarak, writers found themselves arrested or their books banned.[48]

In almost all of these cases, the thrust of the restrictions on freedom of expression has been twofold: to insulate the population against ideas the government regards as undesirable and dangerous, and to prevent the outside world from becoming aware of what is happening inside the country.[49] The authorities have been successful on both scores.

In many countries the regime in power seems to carry out a censorship policy designed to guarantee ideological purity of the highest order. In South Korea, the police seized (February 1986) a number of books from bookstores clustered near some of the universities to "protect the students from dangerous leftist ideologies."[50] Along the same ideological line, the authorities in Indonesia banned the books *Jejak Langkah* (Steps forward) and *Sang Pemula* (The initiator) by the author Pramoedya Anta Toer; the Indonesian attorney general declared that the ban was necessary because "the books were based on the concept of social contradictions and class struggle . . . as it is generally adhered to by communist writers."[51]

Leftist regimes everywhere have traditionally relied on censorship as a means of maintaining ideological purity within their societies. In Cuba, many authors spent long periods in prison for refusing to support the ideological tone of the

Castro regime.[52] Campaigns in China against "spiritual pollution" targeting Chinese and foreign writers and condemning the "decadent culture of the West"[53] have been quite common. The People's Republic of Congo has adopted similar policies.[54]

In Iran, the Islamic republic established by the Ayatollah Ruhollah Khomeini carried out a comprehensive campaign designed to integrate Islamic tenets into all aspects of Iranian life. In the process, the regime prosecuted numerous writers and banned numerous books.[55]

Often the moves against writers and books are presented as a campaign for protecting the national or public interest. According to a Malaysian law, the authorities may ban any publication thought "prejudicial to the national interest."[56] The Israeli military government in the West Bank often bans publications it considers a threat to security and public order.[57] In Zambia, the president may censor anything he feels endangers the public interest.[58] In numerous countries, the rationale, objective, or pretext for censorship is national interest.

Similarly, although not quite identically, governments tend to perceive or present "national security" as a main objective of censorship. Even democratic societies feel they ought to strike a balance between freedom of expression and censorship when an issue involves national security matters.[59] In Israel proper (as distinguished from the occupied territories), censorship of the Hebrew press is limited to military and security issues.[60] In the two Koreas, authors are often accused of endangering the state by supporting its archenemy, the other Korea.[61] In South Africa, novels such as Nadine Gordimer's *Burger's Daughter* have been banned through the years on the grounds that they constitute a threat to national security.[62] On rare occasions, it seems, censorship might be based on potentially real security considerations. Thus, in Taiwan, the memoirs of Lin Sheng-jung, a former intelligence agent of the Nationalist Party (KMT) in the People's Republic of China, were confiscated because, according to the authorities, Lin "divulged military secrets and compromised national security."[63]

It is often very difficult to ascertain whether the accusation leveled against writers that they endanger national security is based on substantial evidence or whether it is merely or mainly a mechanism to silence political opponents of the regime in power. The accusation is simply too abstract, and the evidence is almost invariably presented in secret.

Micro-Objectives

Very often the objectives and rationale of censorship in the Third World are more specific and better defined for micro-objectives than for the macro-objectives discussed in the previous section. In the case of micro-objectives, there is a greater differentiation among societies, and some polities focus on certain types of objectives and others on other types.

One of the more commonly used rationales for censorship in the Third World is in the area of religion and religious practice: Many Third World countries have censorship laws and practices against blasphemy, and others have rules and policies against religious intolerance or religious radicalism. The publication of *The Satanic Verses* by Salman Rushdie led to its banning in numerous Third World countries, mostly Moslem states or countries with large Moslem minorities.[64] In Egypt, Najib Mahfuz's *The Children of Gebelawi* was also banned in 1988 due to pressure from orthodox religious groups; the sheikhs of Al-Azhar University described the book as "blasphemous."[65] Jordan banned John Levin's *The Danger of Islam,* claiming it contained "misleading information" about Islam and the Prophet Muhammad.[66] In Indonesia, preachers who are critical of some aspects of Islam may be banned. In July 1986, for example, Kassim Ahmad was prohibited from giving sermons or lectures on Islam because of his book *Hadis: A Reevaluation,* in which he argued that there was no proof that Islamic tradition outlined in Hadis came from the Prophet.[67]

Censorship is used in developing countries not only against books considered anti-Moslem but also those described as anti-Christian. Thus, Singapore banned Nikos Kazantzakis' *The Last Temptation of Christ* in December 1988 as a result of pressure from fundamentalist Christians.[68] Similarly, in India, a play written and directed by P. M. Anthony, *The Sixth Wound of Christ,* was not allowed to be staged in Kerala State (December 1986) because of the protests of some Christian leaders who thought the play was "derogatory to the image of Christ."[69]

Often censorship is directed toward what the authorities consider to be religious intolerance; in other cases, the censorship policy itself reflects an intolerant approach to religion on the part of the authorities, as indicated by some of the examples already cited. In Singapore, the Newspaper and Printing Act authorized the government to restrict or ban material that is "intended to generate political, ethnic, and religious unrest."[70] The Iraqi Press Code (Article 16) prohibits "defamation against recognized religion."[71]

The widespread banning of *The Satanic Verses* by numerous Third World governments indicates the depth of religious intolerance in this part of the world. Yet this well-known case is by no means unique. In Ethiopia, 40,000 Bibles sent to Lutheran congregations were withheld by the government for a few years.[72] In Indonesia, the poet F. Rahardi was prohibited from reading his work in public because his poetry was considered atheistic by the government.[73] At the same time, the Indonesian government banned the translation of the classic *On Religion* by David Hume, translations of the Old and New Testaments,[74] and twenty-one of Christian writer Herman Ambrie's books that the authorities described as a threat to religious harmony.[75] In Iran, a widespread campaign against any opposition to the teaching of the Islamic Republic has been carried out since 1979.

In recent years, Third World governments have used censorship to curb the rise of radical religion. In 1989, the Egyptian government banned *The Letters of Jahiman al-Taibi,* a collection of writings by the man who led an armed group that took control of Mecca's holy shrine.[76] In Iran, even under the shah, attacks on the clergy resulted in punishment. For example, Gholam-Hoseyn Sa'edi was repeatedly imprisoned for attacking the clergy who, for him, symbolized ignorance, hypocrisy, and parasitism.[77] In Tunisia in 1985, the police seized

130,000 publications considered to be subversive as encouraging radical Islam.[78]

Many Third World nations that face difficult ethnic problems try to solve or ease them by employing widespread censorship. In Mauritania, black writer Tene Youssouf Gueye was arrested in 1986, along with about thirty other people. They were charged with distributing publications harmful to the national interest and making propaganda of racial and ethnic character. The charges were connected to a thirty-seven-page pamphlet prepared by the group in which they alleged discrimination against blacks by the government.[79]

In Turkey, systematic action against the Kurds has occurred for decades: The campaign has been directed at several targets, including the Kurdish language and publishing in it.[80] In February 1987, *Cumhuiyet* reported that criminal proceedings had been brought against the writers, translators, and publishers of 240 publications within the previous three and a half years as a result of orders issued by two Istanbul district courts and the Istanbul State Security Court. On December 18, 1986, thirty-nine tons of books, periodicals, and newspapers were sent to a papermill and pulped. According to the February 19, 1987, *Cumhuiyet*, among the pulped publications were Penguin's *Map of the World* and *Map of Europe*, *National Geographic Atlas of the World*, the Turkish edition of the *Encyclopedia Britannica*, and *Petit Larousse Illustre*. All of them have been declared "means of separatist propaganda" by Turkish authorities for containing articles or maps related to the history of the Armenians or the Kurds.[81]

The Bolivian government has acted on occasion to curb the ethnic writings of Indian writers.[82] In Israel, any demonstration of Palestinian nationalism is considered hostile—the ban is imposed on written materials, paintings, music, theatrical works, and the like.

In some countries, the ethnic character of censorship lies not in carrying out a campaign against a minority but in trying to protect the dominant culture from outside influences. In China, a number of such cultural campaigns have been promoted by the government. Malawi banned *The Lion and the Jewel* "in defense of African tradition."[83] In Kenya, the plays of William Shakespeare were banned between 1981 and 1988 to remove "the colonial legacy."[84]

Censorship in the Third World focuses often on protection of public morals, and governments thus tend to concentrate on banning material deemed indecent and pornographic. Morality laws exist in most Third World states. In China, the authorities in 1987 seized millions of copies of D. H. Lawrence's *Lady Chatterley's Lover* and other "corrupting works."[85] A judge in Egypt ruled in 1985 that a 150-year-old version of *A Thousand and One Nights* was pornographic and ordered it seized after the public prosecutor demanded that the book be "burned in a public place."[86] All Moslem countries such as Tunisia,[87] Iraq,[88] and Kuwait[89] have strong antipornography legislation.

In South Africa, in addition to widespread censorship relating to the country's ongoing political crisis, there is strong censorship against what is considered indecency in literature. William Styron's *Sophie's Choice* was banned in the early 1980s for being too sexually explicit.[90] In Turkey, a number of nonfiction books on sexuality as well as novels considered obscene have been banned in the last few years. In October 1986, the Council to Protect Minors banned Arslan Yuzgun's *Homosexuality of Yesterday and Today in Turkey*, and a similar fate was met by Hardar Dumen's *Sexual Problems*, which was confiscated following a trial in March 1987. For an earlier book by Dumen, *Sexual Life II*, he was acquitted of charges of obscenity in December 1986.[91] In Malawi, the Censorship Board banned recently over 840 books, more than 100 periodicals, and 16 films because it considered them pornographic.[92]

On some occasions, the morally based rationale for banning books in Third World countries is quite general and even obscure. Thus, on November 1, 1978, the Argentine government banned a novel by the well-known Peruvian writer Mario Vargas Llosa, *Aunt Julia and the Scriptwriter*, because "it contained offenses against the family, the religion, the armed institutions, and the moral and ethical principles which have sustained the spiritual and institutional structures of Hispano-American societies."[93] In Brazil, the government announced on May 27, 1977, that it would censor all foreign books and magazines to ascertain that they do not "contain material contrary to public order" or "run counter to morality and good standards of behavior."[94]

In their zest to control the moral climate in their countries, some Third World governments present their actions as an attempt to protect children and young people. Turkey has enacted a special Law to Protect Minors (March 12, 1986). Although ostensibly a measure against pornography, the law is used also to restrict "items of political nature which may influence minors adversely."[95] The Council to Protect Minors banned in December 1986 Pinar Kur's novel *Unending Love*, stating that it would "corrupt minors by causing them to misunderstand the contemporary era, rendering them daydreamers."[96] Similarly, in April 1986, Erdal Oz was put on trial on obscenity charges for publishing a translation of Henry Miller's *Tropic of Capricorn*, a recognized classic.[97] The Chinese authorities have also explained antipornographic campaigns as an effort to protect young people.[98]

In addition to these commonly cited reasons for specifically targeted censorship in the Third World—censorship in the name of religion, ethnicity (nationalism), and morality—there are a few other rationales used, although much less frequently: These include protection of a particular policy or even person(s), defense of the foreign policy of a country, and the shielding of the armed forces from criticism. For example, Najīb Maḥfūẓ, the Nobel Prize—winning author from Egypt, has had many of his works banned throughout the Middle East because he supported the Camp David Accords.[99] In 1979, Jordan banned all Egyptian government publications and all books by Egyptians backing the peace treaty of Egypt with Israel.[100] Holding an opposite view on the issue is the popular Egyptian poet Abdel Rahman Abonoudy, a critic of different aspects of life in Egypt and the government policy toward Israel. In 1981, Abonoudy was summoned for investigation under the 1980 Law of Shame for what a government prosecutor termed "a friendly chat."[101]

Often the censorship policy of a government focuses on a particular person or a small group. In China, after the "Gang of Four" was arrested, their writings, which were critical of those who ordered the Gang's arrest, were banned and destroyed.[102] In Egypt, Muhammad Haikal's book about the assassination of President Anwar Sadat (*Autumn of Fury*) was not allowed to be sold in Egypt, and foreign newspapers serializing it, including the *Sunday Times*, disappeared from the newsstands: There are indications that Haikal, a close friend of Gamal Abdel Nasser, had become persona non grata in the Egypt of Sadat and Mubarak.[103] In Indonesia, a book entitled *An Imaginary Interview with Bung Karno*, compiled by Christianto Wibisono, was banned by the attorney general because, the government stated, it could "disturb peace and order"; the book dealt with the late President Sukarno.[104]

In a few cases, Third World countries have specific legal provisions designed to protect their foreign relations. For example, the Press Code (Article 16) of Iraq forbids the publication of material that might "injure the relations [of Iraq] with the friendly Arab states."[105] In Singapore, censorship is designed to prevent any outside intervention; by law, foreign publications dealing with national politics in Singapore may be banned by the government.[106]

A more common rationale for censorship among Third World nations is that of shielding the armed forces from criticism. This is not surprising because the armed forces are often the dominant political force within the Third World. Yet even in societies where the army is not in a command position, it is often protected through censorship. In Israel, a play about troop brutality on the West Bank has been banned by the censorship council, and the manager of the Haifa Municipal Theater, where the play was staged, was told that parts of the play could damage the army and incite violence.[107] In Chile under Pinochet, Article 417 of the military justice code makes it an offense to slander the armed services; the definition of slander is rather broad and has been used against journalists accusing military officers of repression.[108] In Syria, which has also been governed by military officers for many years, Khalil Brayez, author of *The Fall of Golan* and *From the Golan File*, both books critical of Syrian army actions during the 1967 war, was sentenced to a fifteen-year prison term.[109] In some countries, the censorship of expression relating to the army is truly extensive. In Iraq, there is prohibition on "dereputation of the Armed Forces and divulgence of their secrets, matters and movements"; police and other national forces are also covered by the prohibition.[110]

The censorship objectives described here, as explained by the various governments, are not necessarily and always genuine. Often the formal objective or rationale given for censorship is merely propaganda, a pretext to silence political opponents. Most of the Third World governments would like writers and journalists to reflect that government's views. Authors are tolerated and allowed to write and publish only so long as their views coincide with those who control the government.

Methods of Censorship

The methods of censorship available to the authorities in Third World countries are many and varied. Some means adopted by governments are directed against authors: They are prohibited from publishing, arrested, forced into exile, subjected to a variety of economic pressures, restricted in their movement, and, quite often, executed after a trial or even without a trial. Other means used by governments are directed against the books rather than directly against the writers: Books are banned, confiscated, and, on occasions, burned; sometimes authors are forced to remove parts of a text deemed unacceptable to the authorities.

Censorship Against Authors

Numerous authors in Third World countries have found themselves banned by the authorities, prohibited from publishing their work. In some countries, the banning of authors is truly massive. In Iran, no fewer than 4,350 authors have been on an official blacklist since 1986.[111] In Vietnam, a large-scale "cultural purification" program resulted in the publication (1975) of a list of banned authors.[112] South African authors opposed to apartheid risked banned, as discovered by writers such as Helen Joseph,[113] the Reverend Dr. Beyers Naude of the Dutch Reformed Church,[114] the poet Dennis Brutus,[115] and numerous others.

In other countries, the banning of authors is less widespread, but by no means negligible. Pramoedya Ananta Toer, Indonesia's best-known novelist, had all of his books banned in 1981; Toer's *Glass House* was banned in 1988 because—as the minister for politics and security put it—it revealed "Marx's labor theory," "continuing Leninist themes," and "the concept of social classes."[116] Also in Indonesia, all books by Herman Ambrie, a convert to Christianity from Islam, were banned.[117] Many authors have been unable to publish in Cuba due to disagreements with the Castro regime.[118] In China, similarly, an ideological test has been applied routinely.

Numerous authors in developing states have been arrested by the police or the security forces. In 1988 it was estimated by International PEN that hundreds of writers were held in prison all over the world. Although no breakdown among different types of countries was given by PEN, the figures (given in parentheses after the year) are nevertheless illuminating for purposes of this chapter because many of the writers are imprisoned in developing countries: 1981 (256); 1982 (381); 1983 (385); 1984 (351); 1985 (349); 1986 (340); and 1987 (305).[119] These figures seem to be extremely conservative; the total number of authors in detention, in developing and other countries, is probably considerably higher.

The severity of the punishment imposed on authors, in terms of the number of years they are imprisoned, is sometimes surprising. The possession of "seditious material" in Kenya—not even writing or distributing it—could bring a person up to seven years in prison.[120] Ismail Besikci, a non-Kurd Turkish sociologist, was sentenced in 1982 to ten years in prison, to be followed by five years of internal exile, in connection with his writing about the Kurdish minority in Turkey.[121] Khalil Brayez, a former captain and intelligence officer in the Syrian army (1958–1962), was sentenced to fifteen years' imprisonment for criticizing the army's performance during the 1967 war.[122] Cuban writer Ariel Hidalgo was sentenced to eight years in prison for "incitement against the social order,"[123] and persons convicted for "praising, encouraging or benefitting North Korea" through publications face similarly severe punishment in South

Korea.[124] In fact, a publisher in South Korea was sentenced in 1982 to life imprisonment for printing and distributing banned foreign books, mostly by Marxist authors.[125]

In some countries, the punishment for writing, publishing, or possessing prohibited materials is markedly less severe. Thus, in Tunisia, the owner of the large publishing house Editions Bouslama was recently fined and sentenced to fourteen months' imprisonment for printing and distributing "subversive literature";[126] author Hassan Ben Ottman was sentenced to a "mere" four-month term for writing *Abas Yafqidu as-Sawad* (Abbas loses his mind), and the sentence was eventually repealed.[127] In Egypt, the poet Ahmed Fouad Negm was sentenced in 1978 by a military tribunal to a year in prison at forced labor for composing a poem considered by the authorities as "humiliating" to the head of state.[128]

Not only may persons be imprisoned for writing, translating, publishing, printing, or distributing prohibited material, but imprisonment is used for a wide variety of offenses, including but not limited to the following:

1. Support for communist ideology[129]
2. Expression of antigovernment opinions[130]
3. Criticism of the armed forces[131]
4. Anticommunist writing[132]
5. Attacks on the clergy[133]
6. Support for a minority ethnic group[134]
7. Writing of material considered obscene or immoral[135]
8. Criticism of the social order or social practices.[136]

The imprisonment of authors is often accompanied by torture, as reported in recent cases in Syria,[137] Cuba,[138] Turkey,[139] and other countries. In some states, writers have been arrested and spent time in prison—sometimes for long periods—with no trial at all. Syrian writer Mohammad Khoja has been detained in Aleppo prison with no charge or trial for a long time.[140] Sudanese poet Mahgoub Sharif was also detained without trial.[141] The poet Jack Mapanje was detained in Malawi in 1987 but never charged with a specific crime; his poetry collection, *Of Chameleons and Gods,* has been banned.[142] As have other writers in developing countries, Mapanje has been held in prison for a long period incommunicado.[143]

In some countries, even large-scale arrest of intellectuals does not lead to public announcement, let alone discussion. In Saudi Arabia, thirty-four writers, scholars, and students were among 104 people arrested between June and August 1982, without any public announcement made by the authorities.[144] In other countries, the authorities "use imprisonment to prevent authors from writing."[145] Although most countries are selective in the imposition of prison terms on intellectuals, others use them rather broadly. In Turkey, for example, prison terms are used against left-leaning circles, separatists (pro-Kurdish or pro-Armenian), Moslem fundamentalists, and others; in 1971, Salahattin Eyuboglu was arrested on a charge of translating into Turkish Thomas More's *Utopia.*[146]

In general, the use of censorship in the form of imprisonment is widespread in many developing countries. The common use of this method has led to equivalently widespread attention in the world to those countries in which imprisonment is used most frequently. Amnesty International, Article 19, PEN, and other international organizations concerned with human rights have often focused their attention on writers in prison. These organizations were involved in defending Salman Rushdie after the threats made on his life by Iran's leaders. In 1988, Article 19 sent a letter to President Roh Tae Woo of South Korea asking him to relax censorship regulations in his country in anticipation of the forthcoming Olympic games.[147]

Obviously, imprisonment is not the only punishment available to governments in their campaign against writers. Some authors have been exiled from their countries or forced to live abroad. Postrevolutionary Iran is a case in point. According to some reports, 300–400 Iranian writers left the country after 1979 due to persecution;[148] among them were many publishers and editors.[149] Gholam-Hoseyn Sa'edi, a longtime critic of the Shiite clergy, fled Iran following the Islamic revolution,[150] but even writers not particularly hostile to the clergy found the conditions in postrevolutionary Iran threatening to their work.

A large number of African writers have been forced to live in exile, including Nigeria's foremost writer Ngugi Wa Thionga;[151] a few Malawian writers, including Frank Chipasule;[152] poet Syl Cheney-Coker, who has been in self-imposed exile from Sierra Leone since 1975;[153] the Guinean writer Camara Laye, who had to leave his country in 1964;[154] writers in the Uganda of Idi Amin;[155] and several authors, both black and white, from South Africa.[156]

Latin American authoritarianism, notably Chile's variety over the last decade, has generated its share of exiled or self-exiled writers. On March 27, 1981, the internationally known Colombian novelist Gabriel Garcia Marquez sought refuge in the Mexican embassy in Bogota and then left the country for Mexico, where he was a resident; it was reported he was being sought by the military authorities for alleged connections with the M-19 guerrilla group.[157] The well-known Uruguayan literary critic Angel Rama left his native country as well.[158] The Cuban revolution, resulting in the establishment of a totalitarian regime, led to a considerable flight of writers from the island.[159] Even some who preferred to stay in Cuba after the revolution defected on occasion; Cesar Leante, author of eight books and an adviser to Castro's Ministry of Culture, defected in Madrid (1981) when he was enroute to Bulgaria to represent the Cuba government.[160]

Many Middle Eastern writers have also found refuge outside of their native countries. Author Jamil Hatmal, along with other Syrian writers, has been forced to live in exile.[161] So has Mehmet Emin Bozarslan, a Kurdish author from Turkey, who had been punished for his campaign to preserve the Kurdish language and culture.[162] Turkish intellectuals supportive of leftist causes have also been exiled on occasion, sometimes internally.[163]

The most severe punishment reserved for authors, however, is not exile but the death penalty. Writers have been executed with or without trial; others have disappeared without a trace, murdered by "their" governments even after they have left their native countries, or tortured to death in prison.

Again, although some governments use murder on a grand scale others use it
sparingly; most governments never resort to it. In recent years, Iran has been
killing writers massively. By January 1983, only three to four years after the
revolution, the Iranian Writers Association in Exile, based in Paris, had
documented the death of thirty-nine of its members.[164] Many of those
assassinated were publishers and editors, often living in London and Paris.[165] In
1984, Scotland Yard foiled an Iranian plot designed to assassinate the poet Hadi
Khorsandi.[166] On February 14, 1989, the Ayatollah Khomeini called on all
Moslems to seek out and execute Salman Rushdie, the author of *The Satanic
Verses,* and all those involved in the publication of the book.[167] Although
under the shah's regime there were some executions of writers these were
exceptional events. "The rule was that the Shah's regime was against the work,
not against the author, against the book and not the writer."[168] Under
Khomeini, the focus of the censoring process shifted to the writers and expanded
to "the publisher, the printer, the bookbinder, and even the paper merchant."[169]
One author summed up Khomeini's approach in words that could be applicable
to other regimes as well: "Authors are tolerated and even honored only so long
as their views happen to coincide with those of the ruling ayatollahs. Those
who might have other views or wish to offer a different image of reality must,
in Khomeini's words, be 'eliminated.'"[170]

Sadam Hussein's Iraq, Iran's archenemy, has take a similar approach to
censorship. The penal code explicitly imposes severe penalties on free
expression, journalism, and publication; included is the death penalty for such
offenses as "insulting the President of the Republic or those who are acting on
his behalf."[171] As Raad Mushatat wrote in the February 1986 issue of *Index of
Censorship:* "The army is an organization to brainwash people. You are not
allowed to read anything other than government newspapers or magazines, and
if they find any other literature on you, even harmless material such as Tolstoy
or Walt Whitman, you can be accused of circulating anti-state literature and
executed."[172]

In Turkey, a left-wing publisher, Ilhan Erdost, was killed in Ankara on
November 7, 1980, by soldiers escorting him from an interrogation; the
authorities announced that an officer and eight soldiers were arrested in
connection with the murder.[173] Assassinations of authors are much less
common in Turkey and in most other Middle Eastern countries than they are in
Iran and Iraq.

In Latin America, however, the extrajudicial killing of intellectuals has not
been rare. The mutilated body of José Pena, a young Colombian poet, was
discovered on May 6, 1986, in Bucaramanga; he is believed to have been killed
by security forces because he was writing prounion poems and songs.[174]
Colombian artists associated with M-19 have been killed by the authorities.[175]
Assassinations were also reported from such authoritarian environments as
Paraguay, Chile, and Argentina while these countries were under military
dictatorships. In Guyana, Walter Rodney, one of the Caribbean's finest
historians, was killed by a bomb placed in his brother's car (June 13, 1980).
Suspicion fell on the government of Forbes Burnham.[176]

Most African regimes have not adopted assassination as a major tool of censorship. Yet writers in Amin's Uganda, along with many others, lived under continuous death threats. *Index of Censorship* summed up the situation accurately and succinctly: "In Amin's Uganda there are no censorship laws, nor is there any code of conduct for writers—write it and you die."[177] In Kenya today, many of those arrested for possession of seditious material are never brought to trial; they simply disappear[178] and could be presumed dead. In South Africa, human rights activist, researcher, and writer David Webster was assassinated on May 1, 1989, presumably by an organization associated with the apartheid regime. In a just-completed article, Webster pointed to the use of assassination as the final weapon used to silence state opponents when no options were available.[179]

Also in Asia, the censoring activity often leads to the killing of writers. China has seen in the last forty years a few waves of cultural "purification" of this sort. In Taiwan, the government admitted in January 1985 that some of its intelligence officers had been involved in the murder (October 1984) of Henry Liu, a Chinese-American journalist and author. Liu wrote critical articles of the Taiwanese government and was finishing a biography critical of Taiwan's former president, Chiang Ching-kuo.[180] In South Korea, the poet Kim Chi-ha was sentenced by a court to death.[181]

In many cases, however, dissident writers in the Third World are not even given a day in court, nor are their premature, violent deaths even announced to the public or reported to their families. The disappearance of authors is especially common in South and Central America. In Argentina, under the rule of the generals, writers frequently disappeared. This was the fate of Haroldo Conti,[182] Tilo Wenner,[183] Norberto Armando Habegger,[184] Susana Martinez,[185] and numerous others. Chile, under Pinochet, is another case in point. In Central America, cases of disappearance have also been reported. In El Salvador, for example, a few organizations reported the disappearance of the writer Edgar Mauricio Vallejo, who seems to have been abducted by the National Police.[186]

Revolutionary regimes in Africa have also been engaged in abduction and murder of writers. In Ethiopia, novelist Bealu Girma disappeared after the publication of his book *Oromiya* (Enough); his car was found, deserted, outside of Addis Ababa.[187] Authoritarian regimes such as Zaire's have been involved in similar cases, and murder became almost a way of life in Uganda under Amin. In 1979, in the middle of a performance of Byron Kawadwa's *The Chair Is Empty* in the National Theater in Kampala—a play Amin interpreted as an attack on his regime—Kawadwa and some of his actors disappeared; others fled to Kenya.[188]

Yet it is important to understand that to silence writers, governments do not necessarily have to resort to abduction, murder, or even exile: Milder threats and punishments can be quite effective. In China and other countries where one has to be a member of the writers union to publish, an expulsion from the union can go a long way toward silencing an author. In Cuba, for example, the establishment of the Union of Writers and Artists of Cuba meant increasing official control of taste and control over access to publishing houses: "The presses were in the hand of the government, and the writers received salaries from official entities, so if they did not adjust to the preferences of the authorities they could not see their works published."[189]

Milder economic pressures, such as the dismissal of authors from their posts, are also effective. Khaldoun Naqih, dean of the Faculty of Arts at Kuwait University, was fired following the publication of his book *Society and the State in the Gulf and the Arabian Peninsula*.[190] Ghazi al-Gussuibi, a renowned poet and the Saudi minister for public health, was dismissed in 1984 after the publication of one of his poems in a Riyadh daily; the authorities thought the poem was irreverent and insulting to King Fahd.[191] Osman Ahmad Osman's memoirs, *Pages from My Experience*, led to his dismissal as deputy prime minister for popular development in Egypt.[192] In Iraq, the penal code provides, inter alia, for the confiscation of "movable and immovable properties" of an author convicted for insulting the president of the republic or whoever is acting on his behalf.[193]

Dismissals from work or other such economic penalties, including fines, are not limited, obviously, to Middle Eastern countries. In Kenya, the novelist and playwright Ngugi wa Thiong'o was fired from the University of Nairobi and arrested.[194] In many constitutions and penal codes, free expression could lead to a heavy fine if it is judged, for example, blasphemous.[195] The writer Tene Youssouf Gueye, a black Mauritanian, was recently sentenced not only to four years in prison and five years of internal exile but also received a large fine; he and others were accused of arguing that the government discriminates against blacks.[196]

In Israel, the owner of a Gaza bookshop was fined 20,000 shekels (or two months in prison) for publishing and distributing political literature; earlier in the same year, 1983, Ali Safadi's bookshop was ordered sealed for six months.[197] In recent years, especially since the beginning of the Palestinian intifada (uprising), this type of policy that imposes economic penalties in order to censor has been much intensified.

In Iraq, the mere possession of banned political materials under Article 208 of the penal code can result not only in a seven-year imprisonment but also in a fine of 500 dinars.[198] In Tunisia, a much milder regime than Iraq's, prior authorization for publication is required by law. Without such authorization, those involved in the publication may incur a fine of 120–1,200 dinars.[199] The financial penalty in Kuwait is even higher and can reach $10,000 for a violation of the censorship laws,[200] and in Egypt a court fined three booksellers 500 Egyptian pounds each for distributing the classic *A Thousand and One Nights*.[201]

Beyond this rather specific means of censorship, governments in developing countries sometimes use general terror to create an atmosphere of fear to restrain the intellectuals. In Uganda during the 1970s, in Iran during the 1980s, and in Chile through almost all of this period, writers were given to understand that the expression of antigovernment sentiment could result in severe punishment. "Write it and you die!" as a censorship policy provides strong incentive for people to control their inclination to express themselves freely. In 1984, Chilean writer Enrique Lafourcade sought asylum in the Argentine embassy in Santiago after his bookshop had been raided. Lafourcade's novel, *El Gran Taimado* (The great con trick) contains criticism of the Pinochet regime.[202]

Intimidation is heavily used by both totalitarian and authoritarian regimes, although the former may use it more systematically. In Iran under the shah, the anticlerical writer Sa'edi was arrested numerous times and survived several "road accidents."[203] In those days, SAVAK (the secret police) used to summon people for "interrogations as to what [they] really meant" in a particular work—sometimes people would lose their job, were arrested, or even shot.[204] Under Khomeini, the probability of being shot increased dramatically.

Even in milder regimes, interrogation by the secret police is a common intimidation instrument and a censorship tool. In Egypt, Muhammad Abdessalim Zayyat, a former vice-premier, was briefly detained and interrogated about his book *Whither Egypt*, 3,000 copies of which were seized from the printers before it went on sale.[205] Anastasio Somoza's National Guard used similar techniques in Nicaragua, raiding publishing houses, seizing books, threatening witnesses, and the like,[206] as did the Brazilian regime of this period.[207]

Arrests for even a brief time are often accompanied by torture, whether the detainee is a writer or not. Authors have suffered their share of torture in prisons all over the Third World.[208] Detailed reports on the torture of writers have been accumulated from all corners of the globe: for example, torture has occurred in the Middle East in Syria,[209] Iran,[210] Libya,[211] and Turkey;[212] in the Far East in Vietnam;[213] in Latin America in Uruguay[214] and Cuba;[215] and in Africa in Ghana.[216]

Censorship Against Books

In 1485, the archbishop of Mainz (where Gutenberg had lived, worked, and invented the printing press) requested and obtained the first secular censorship office. In 1493, the Inquisition in Venice issued the Catholic church's first list of banned books, and shortly afterward the pope sought to make censorship universal throughout Christendom. In 1559, the *Index Librorum Prohibitorum* (Index of banned books), binding on all Roman Catholics, was established.

Since then, censorship against books—in a variety of forms, different degrees of intensity, and for different purposes—has become part and parcel of the human landscape. Censorship against books is now commonplace throughout the Third World: Books are banned, burned, confiscated, and condemned; printing facilities are closed; import licenses are revoked; authors are forced to change their work; and so forth. But the banning of books is by far the single most common censorship method in developing countries.

Banning books is sometimes pursued in a massive, comprehensive manner; in other situations, it is a much more selective policy. In South Africa, the number of banned books was estimated at 18,000 in 1988, and books are constantly added to the list in the *Government Gazette*.[217] The Chinese authorities seized 7 million books and magazines, a half million of them in Beijing alone.[218] Under Military Order 101, as amended by 718, the Israeli military government in the West Bank banned (as of 1988) about 1,600 titles.[219] Malawi has put 840 books on its list,[220] and South Korea banned 313 books between May 1 and 10, 1985, alone.[221] Against these examples of massive censorship, there are other examples of considerably more modest efforts. Article 19 reported that only one book, Mancef Marzouki's *Let My Country Wake Up,* was prohibited in Tunisia recently.[222] Between 1984 and 1986, according to Article 19, six books were on the list in Tunisia on the grounds that they harmed public morals or public order or defamed public figures.[223]

Although some governments tend to be very systematic and thorough in banning books, others display a more erratic pattern of behavior. South Korea has a prepublication review process; nevertheless, some books (having passed the review) are banned after their publication.[224] In Pinochet's Chile, similar arbitrariness has been reported. Jorgé Edwards's *Persona Non Grata,* which recounts his experiences as a diplomat in Cuba in the early 1970s, was denied entry to the country by customs officials in December 1982, then in May 1983 import was approved.[225]

In some countries, even the classics are not beyond banning. In Turkey, David Hume's *On Religion,* a translation of the Old and New Testaments, a collection of philosophical writings (Montaigne, Bacon, Russell, Sartre, and others), and one of James Joyce's novels were banned in 1986.[226] A number of books, including not only all of Maxim Gorky's works but also Plato's *Republic,* were banned from university dormitories in December 1985.[227] In the People's Republic of China, a ten-year ban on the works of Shakespeare and some German and Russian writers was lifted in May 1977; the government stated that new Chinese editions of the works of these writers would be published to mark the thirty-fifth anniversary of a speech by Mao Zedong asserting that culture serves the workers and peasants.[228]

The methodology of banning—the exact procedure through which a government controls publication—is quite varied, although the eventual goal is the same. Most governments target the writers of prohibited material, but some pursue the printers, editors, distributors, or even people who possess such material. South Africa even has lists of books that can be possessed but not distributed.[229]

Some governments have a prepublication control process: Every manuscript must be submitted to the censor before it can be printed. In Kuwait, for example, the Ministry of Information must approve all books, and it uses this authority to deny publication to a large number of manuscripts on political, religious, and moral grounds.[230] Other governments prefer postpublication censorship: Books are banned after they have appeared in print.[231] The prepublication approval system makes writers very cautious and sometimes timid; the postpublication censorship process makes publishers also very cautious, because they fear the loss of their investment if a published book is confiscated. In either case, censorship affects what is written and how and whether it is published.

The campaign against publishers today is quite extensive and covers different types of regimes. A few examples suffice: In early 1987, fifteen Chilean secret police agents invaded the premises of Terranova, publishers and printers, and removed large numbers of books, printing material, and equipment.[232] A few months later, in China, the State Publishing Administration announced there had been a large increase in the number of underground printers and publishers producing a "disturbingly large number of unhealthy and illegal works" in the PRC. By some estimates, there are around 200 such underground publishing houses.[233] From time to time, they have been raided.

Book banning is designed by governments to curb freedom of expression for any number of reasons. Some governments are particularly sensitive to material they consider obscene. South Africa is a case in point. William Styron's *Sophie's Choice* was banned there for being sexually explicit.[234] The government is quite particular in trying to control the availability of material it perceives as immoral. Andre Brink's *Kennis Van Die Aand* (Looking on darkness) was banned for eight years before the government allowed it to be published, and even then conditions were attached: The book could be sold only in hardcover and to persons 18 years and over and published only in Africaans (not English).[235] The Turkish authorities are similarly concerned about the availability of obscene material and ban both fiction and nonfiction dealing with sexual matters.[236]

Religion is often a focus of attention for censors. *The Children of Gebelawi,* the greatest work of Nobel prizewinner Najīb Mahfūz, remains banned in Egypt due to pressure from the orthodox circles; the novel has been described by the sheikhs of Al-Azar University as "blasphemous."[237] The Jordanian government banned John Lavin's *The Danger of Islam,* a nonfictional analysis the government thought contained "misleading information" about Islam and the Prophet Muhammad.[238] Salman Rushdie's *The Satanic Verses* was banned by numerous countries as blasphemous.

On occasion, governments using censorship become involved in complex religious controversies. In Malaysia, *Alkitah,* the Indonesian translation of the Bible, has been banned by the government because it contains references to Allah.[239] Yet presumably, in most cases, censorship is applied as a result of internal political pressure (Singapore banned *The Last Temptation of Christ* due to the pressure of fundamentalist Christians);[240] external interference (Egypt banned the *Letters of Jahiman Al-Taibi* at the request of the Saudi government);[241] perception that the material is an affront to the religious beliefs of the majority of the population (thus the Indonesian government's censorship against the Christian writer Hamran Ambrie); or the government's view that material is antireligious (in Ethiopia thousands of Bibles in the Amharic language destined for Lutheran congregations were withheld by the government).

Many governments use censorship as an instrument to suppress the aspirations of an ethnic minority within their jurisdiction, although South Africa uses censorship against the majority. The Israeli military government has adopted tough, comprehensive censorship policies against the expression of Palestinian aspirations in the occupied territories, and the Turkish position toward Kurdish or Armenian aspirations is similar.

In most cases, however, governmental censorship is simply a tool in the service of the ideology supported by the regime in power. Most often censorship is used against communist, socialist, or otherwise left-leaning literature. The South Korean government is second to none in the suppression of anything considered "communist." The Seoul police recently identified eighty-one publishers of communist books and seized over 100 titles.[242] Indonesia has a similar if somewhat less intensive policy,[243] as do Turkey and many other countries.[244]

In some countries, the reverse approach is adopted: Tough censorship against anticommunist or antisocialist policies (or, as it is often called, counterrevolutionary literature) is adopted by the government. In the People's Republic of the Congo, for example, Guy Menga, whose play *La Marmite de Koka-Mbala* won the Concours Theatrical Inter-African prize (which is sponsored by the French Broadcasting Corporation), left for exile after the play was banned. A short-story collection of Emmanuel Boundzeki Dongala, another well-known Congolese writer, was also banned for satirizing party members and the official scientific Marxist ideology of the state.[245]

Vietnam has taken much more vigorous action against what is considered counterrevolutionary literature. A large number of books deemed reactionary have been prohibited since the mid-1970s; in fact, the sale or possession of any literature published under the former regime is prohibited. In an effort to "purify" the country, the revolutionary government closed printing houses, bookshops, theatrical and opera companies, tea rooms, film studios, and movie theaters.[246]

Beyond these major and relatively common reasons for banning books—curbing obscenity, protecting religion, suppressing minorities, and serving the state ideology—censorship is used for less common reasons as well. In 1983, the sultan of Brunei banned a number of British books because they referred to bars, alcohol, and parties;[247] he was responding apparently to the sensitivities of Brunei's Moslem population. In other countries, books have been banned on the grounds of being a "threat to national security,"[248] disturbing "peace and order,"[249] slandering the armed forces,[250] or, simply, being "undesirable."[251]

In some developing countries, books seem to have been banned because they have been written by specific individuals or about them. In the PRC, all the works by the Gang of Four were banned following their arrest.[252] In Grenada, books by and about Maurice Bishop and Nelson Mandela have been confiscated.[253] In Malaysia, a ban imposed on *The Malay Dilemma* by Muhammad Mahathir was lifted after the author became prime minister.[254] The banning of books by opposition leaders is not uncommon in developing countries.

In some cases, censorship is directed toward books dealing with a specific policy or event in a way unacceptable to the government. In Egypt, restrictions on foreign books about Israel were lifted in 1972.[255] Nizar Qabbani's book on the Six Day War, *Footnotes to the Book of Setback,* was "universally banned throughout the Arab world."[256] Muhammad Heikal's book about the Sadat assassination, *Autumn of Fury,* published in London in April 1983, was not allowed into Egypt for sale, and foreign newspapers serializing it disappeared from the newsstands.[257] In Israel, the military banned publication of a book by two Israelis, Ami Doron and Eli Teicher, that described the country's nuclear capabilities,[258] and in Colombia, a book on a specific kidnapping by M-19, *I Am Free,* by Alvaro Gomez Hurtado, was recently banned by a judge.[259]

Just as specific is the recent ban in India of a book critical of the World Bank–aided Narmada Valley project. The volume, written by two Indian environmental experts and published in Malaysia, was withheld by the customs office in Delhi.[260] An eyewitness report on the 1984 riots in South Africa, written by Johannes Rantete, was also confiscated,[261] as was an official report on the assassination of Indira Gandhi in India (sparking protests from opposition parties and civil rights groups).[262] In brief, censorship is often general, but it is sometimes applied to specific events.

Usually, there are few ways for a banned author to react effectively against the government's prohibition. If a government is truly interested in imposing a ban and has a constitutional basis for the action, the writer is unlikely to prevail. The Afrikaans writer Andre Brink "launched literary guerrilla strategy" against the South African censors of his book *A Dry White Season;* he simply sent copies to subscribers without submitting the novel for censorship.[263] This type of tactic, however admirable, cannot prevail in the long run.

Conclusion

As this chapter amply demonstrates, censorship is very common in the Third World: There is hardly a country that does not impose substantial limitations on free expression, although some countries have many more restraints than others. Political authorities all over the Third World view many books and other published material as being dangerous on doctrinal grounds, threatening to existing social norms, or potentially undermining their power base. Both types of regimes—totalitarian ones that have a general ideology, a Weltanschauung, through which they actively seek to implement or coerce, and authoritarian types that rest on nondemocratic, power-based control over an unwilling society—use censorship as a means for perpetuating their rule.[264] The differences between these two types of regimes are marginal in the area of censorship.

Although almost every Third World country today has legally sanctioned or factually implemented censorship, it is extremely difficult to determine whether censorship in general is expanding or not. In any event, there is no indication that it is significantly on the retreat. Writers throughout the Third World continue to be judged not merely—and maybe not even mainly—by the quality of their work but by the content of their message. It could even be persuasively argued that numerous governments consider censorship as one of the most powerful instruments in their arsenal, second only to the use of military or police force against their opponents. In fact, censorship is one of the most important sources of power in the hand of any government resisting change.

Even a cursory review of the data collected by such organizations as Article 19, Amnesty International, the Helsinki Watch Committees, PEN International, and by the publication *Index on Censorship* paints a fairly bleak picture. The *World Report 1988* of Article 19 documents comprehensively the problem. So does Charles Humana in his human rights handbook.[265]

In assessing whether different countries have "independent book publishing" (his question 25), Humana in his data points out although the majority (thirty-eight) of developing countries have independent publishing houses, at least in a qualified way, there are at best twenty-two such countries where individual publishing is denied, either completely or significantly. Furthermore, Humana does not offer precise quantitative measures for many Third World countries known for their lack of any individual publishing: Angola, Burma, Burundi, Central African Republic, El Salvador, Guatemala, Guinea, Honduras, Iran, Ivory Coast, Jordan, Cambodia, Laos, Lesotho, Madagascar, Malawi, Mali, Nepal, Nicaragua, Niger, Rwanda, Somalia, Sudan, Togo, Uganda, Uruguay, and North and South Yemen (altogether twenty-eight countries). When these countries are added to those Humana identifies as lacking some form of independent book publishing, the country total increases to fifty (versus the thirty-eight countries that do have some form of it).

On the question of freedom from political censorship of the press, the picture presented by Humana (question 17) is much worse than in the case of book publishing (which governments apparently believe to be less relevant for their political power). Twenty Third World countries suffer from lack of freedom from political censorship of the press, and twenty-one have frequent violations of this freedom. In only nineteen Third World countries is there unqualified (ten) or qualified (nine) respect for this particular type of freedom. If the forty-one violators are added to the thirty-eight countries on which Humana does not include quantitative assessment (and all of these are clear violators), there are seventy-nine developing countries that violate the freedom of the press; only nineteen respect it.

Humana also evaluates the "freedom to teach ideas and receive information" (question 4). His findings indicate an almost equal distribution of nations in his four categories: Fifteen are constant violators, sixteen frequent violators, fifteen qualified supporters, and fourteen unqualified supporters of the freedom to teach ideas and receive information. But if added to his list of violators are the twenty-eight unranked nations—and most of them are constant violators—the scale tilts once again toward censorship.

A few generalizations could be reached in addition to the empirically supported finding that censorship is extremely common in the Third World. There can be no question that freedom of expression and information is essential for the functioning of democracy. Without the ability to receive information and express views freely, citizens can neither affect policy nor participate meaningfully in the process of selecting those who are to govern society. In this sense, the common, pervasive existence of censorship in Third World countries indicates the continuation of nondemocratic regimes in most of them.

This chapter indicates that *censorship and power are intimately linked:* Governments do not ordinarily use censorship to protect the population from offensive material—they typically employ censorship to protect their power base. That is probably why books are often not as strictly controlled as the mass media.[266] As material directed at an educated elite, a small minority in most developing countries, books are considered less dangerous to the power base of the ruling elite than daily newspapers, let alone radio or television.

Although it is difficult at this stage to discover clear patterns of censorship, it is evident that in most of the Third World today, censorship is the rule, not the exception: It is a norm internalized by the rulers and probably by the ruled as well. It seems that censorship is most radical when the rulers believe they have knowledge of the ultimate truth. Such ultimate truth is then used for justifying an all-encompassing control of the mind, absolute censorship. In the eyes of the censor and the regime for which the person works, censorship represents the ultimate good, whether it is to protect the nation from real or imagined subversion, to preserve social harmony, to maintain the purity of religious doctrine, or to serve any other goal.

The development thrust in the Third World often has been used, unfortunately, to support dictatorial practices of censorship, collective brainwashing, and mind control. Governments have argued that social stability must be maintained at all costs—that society must be ruled by one party and governed by one center from above. Strict censorship goes hand in hand with this kind of thinking, although there is doubt as to whether, in the long run, this type of governance and censorship indeed serves the cause of development.

Notes

The author wishes to thank Brian Walsh for data collection for this research and the Lafayette College Committee on Advanced Study and Research for its financial assistance.

1. *Index on Censorship*, Vol. 8, no. 2, March-April 1979, p. 18, emphasis added (cited hereafter as *Index*).

2. Kevin Boyle, ed., *Article 19: Information, Freedom, and Censorship (World Report 1988)* (New York: Times Books, 1988), pp. 73–76 (hereafter *Article 19*).

3. *Ibid.*, p. 23.

4. *Freedom of Information and Expression in Congo*, p. 12.

5. *Index*, Vol. 12, no. 3, June 1983, p. 42.

6. *Article 19*, p. 129.

7. Liang Heng and Judith Shapiro, *Intellectual Freedom in China*, a report of Asia Watch Committee: The Fund for Free Expression, July 1985, p. 37.

8. *Article 19*, p. 247.

9. *Index*, Vol. 10, no. 1, February 1981, p. 716.

10. *Ibid.*, Vol. 13, no. 4, August 1984, p. 41.

11. *Article 19*, p. 156; *Index*, Vol. 17, no. 4, April 1988, p. 38.

12. *Index*, Vol. 14, no. 2, April 1985, p. 40.

13. *Ibid.*, Vol. 7, no. 6, November-December 1978, p. 59.

14. *Article 19*, p. 57.

15. State Secrets Law of 1983. See *Index*, Vol. 12, no. 3, June 1983, p. 42.

16. *Article 19*, p. 23 (the Congolese position is formulated in the 1979 Constitution).

17. *Freedom of Information and Expression in the Congo, Article 19*, pp. 12 and 14.

18. Article 4 of the Constitution; see *Freedom of Information and Expression in Zambia, Article 19*, p. 15.

19. Carlos Ripell, *Harassing the Intellectuals: Censoring Writers and Artists in Today's Cuba*, The Cuban-American National Foundation, Inc., 1985, Freedom House, p. 38; *Index*, Vol. 18, no. 3, March 1989, p. 18.

20. *Freedom of Information and Expression in Central African Republic, Article 19*, p. 9.

21. *Index*, Vol. 14, no. 2, April 1985, p. 40 (Decree 4).

22. *Article 19*, p. 74.

23. *Index*, Vol. 18, no. 1, January 1989, p. 2.

24. *Article 19*, p. 247.

25. *Freedom of Information and Expression in Trinidad and Tobago, Article 19*, p. 7.

26. *Article 19*, p. 166.

27. *Ibid.*, p. 136.

28. *Ibid.*, pp. 160–161.

29. *Ibid.*, p. 278.

30. *Ibid.*, p. 73.

31. *Index*, Vol. 7, no. 4, November-December 1978, p. 65.

32. Heng and Shapiro, *Intellectual Freedom*, p. 37; see also *Index*, Vol. 8, no. 4, July-August 1979, p. 63.

33. Article 82; see *Index*, Vol. 15, no. 2, February 1986, p. 41.

34. *Newsweek*, special issue on censorship, 1988, p. 6.

35. *Index*, Vol. 16, no. 1, January 1987, p. 41.

36. *Ibid.*, Vol. 15, no. 3, March 1986, p. 41.

37. Asia Watch, Committee to Protect Journalists, *Still Confined: Journalists in Re-Education Camps and Prisons in Vietnam*, April 1987, p. 6.

38. Index, Vol. 6, no. 4, July-August 1977, pp. 71–72.

39. *Article 19*, p. 276. In Thailand, a similar policy exists. In 1984 thousands of copies of Sulak Silvaraksa's *Interviews with S. Silvaraksa: Unmasking Thai Society* were seized by police for allegedly defaming the monarchy; *Index*, Vol. 13, no. 5, December 1984, p. 43.

40. *Article 19*, p. 258. See also *Freedom of Information and Expression in Iraq, Article 19*, pp. 22–23.

41. *Index*, Vol. 17, no. 5, May 1988, p. 128.

42. International PEN, Writers in Prison Committee Report, July 29, 1988, p. 2. See also Asia Watch, *Still Confined*.

43. *Freedom of Information and Expression in the Congo*.

44. *Index*, Vol. 18, no. 3, March 1989, p. 18.

45. Amnesty International, *Artists and the Urgent Action Network* (London: Amnesty International, 1986), p. 2.

46. Writers in Prison Committee, Chairman's Report for Barcelona, September 22, 1978, p. 2.

47. *Violations of the Helsinki Accords: Turkey*, Helsinki Watch Report, 1986, New York, p. 24.

48. See *Index*, October 1981, Vol. 10, no. 5, p. 45, on the arrest of the poet Ahmed Fouad Negm who wrote a poem considered by the authorities as "humiliating" to the head of state. The same publication reported in October 1986 (p. 40) that a novel written by Muhammad Yusef al-Qa'id was banned because of its description of Egypt's problems as "cancerous bureaucracy and corruption."

49. *Article 19*, p. 40, makes this point in regard to South Africa; it can safely be generalized.

50. *Index*, Vol. 15, no. 5, May 1986, p. 41.

51. *Ibid.*, Vol. 16, no. 7, July-August 1987, p. 4.

52. *Ibid.*, Vol. 12, no. 1, February 1983, p. 43; and Vol. 18, no. 3, March 1989, p. 18, describe a few of the numerous examples.

53. *Ibid.*, Vol. 13, no. 1, 1984, p. 42.

54. *Freedom of Information and Expression in the Congo.*

55. *Index,* Vol. 14, no. 6, December 1985, p. 42.

56. *Ibid.*, Vol. 13, no. 4, August 1984, p. 41.

57. See, for example, Committee to Protect Journalists and Article 19, *Journalism Under Occupation: Israel's Regulation of the Palestinian Press,* October 1988, New York.

58. *Article 19,* p. 57.

59. For this argument, see *Index,* Vol. 18, no. 2, February 1988, p. 2.

60. *Article 19,* p. 262.

61. *Ibid.* For North Korea, see p. 145; for South Korea, see p. 151.

62. *Index,* Vol. 10, no. 1, February 1981, p. 4.

63. *Ibid.*, Vol. 15, no. 2, February 1986, p. 41.

64. India, for example, banned *The Satanic Verses* even before the Ayatollah Khomeini issued a death sentence against Salman Rushdie. *Index,* Vol. 17, no. 10, November-December 1988, p. 42.

65. *Index,* Vol. 18, no. 3, March 1989, p. 36.

66. *Ibid.*, Vol. 9, no. 2, April 1980, p. 70.

67. *Article 19,* p. 156; *Index,* Vol. 15, no. 8, September 1986, p. 4.

68. *Index,* Vol. 18, no. 2, February 1989, p. 38.

69. *Ibid.*, Vol. 16, no. 4, April 1987, p. 26.

70. *Article 19,* p. 164.

71. *Freedom of Information and Expression in Iraq,* p. 19.

72. *Index,* Vol. 16, no. 10, November-December 1987, p. 37.

73. *Ibid.*, Vol. 15, no. 3, March 1986, p. 39.

74. *Ibid.*, Vol. 15, no. 7, July-August 1986, p. 46.

75. *Ibid.*, Vol. 15, no. 5, May 1986, p. 39. Ambrie is a convert from Islam to Christianity and writes chiefly on the relations between the two religions; see also *ibid.*, Vol. 11, no. 5, October 1982, pp. 34–35.

76. *Ibid.*, Vol. 17, no. 7, August 1988, p. 34.

77. *Ibid.*, Vol. 15, no. 4, April 1986, p. 11.

78. *Freedom of Information and Expression in Tunisia,* p. 18.

79. International PEN, Writers in Prison Committee, July 1988 report, p. 22.

80. *Article 19,* p. 228.

81. *State of Flux: Human Rights in Turkey,* Helsinki Watch Report, December 1987 Update, New York, 1987, p. 26; *Violations of the Helsinki Accords: Turkey,* p. 23. The PEN Freedom-to-Write Bulletin of February 26, 1988, reported on a Kurdish publisher sentenced to thirty-six years in prison for publishing books about the Kurdish minority in Turkey (p. 4). See also John Ziman, Paul Sieghart, and John Humphrey, *The World of Science and the Rule of Law: A Study of the Observance and Violations of the Human Rights of Scientists in the Participating States of the Helsinki Accords* (New York: Oxford University Press, 1986), p. 123, reporting on the jailing of the social scientist Ismail Besikci who dared refer to the Kurds as a separate ethnic group. Besikci, who is not a Kurd, was convicted of "propaganda for communism and separatism."

82. *Index,* Vol. 1, no. 3-4, August-Winter 1972, p. 113.

83. *Ibid.*, Vol. 17, no. 2, February 1988, p. 19.

84. *Ibid.*, Vol. 17, no. 9, October 1988, p. 38.

85. *Ibid.*, Vol. 16, no. 5, May 1987, p. 20.

86. *Ibid.*, Vol. 14, no. 4, August 1985, p. 51; Vol. 14, no. 5, October 1985, p. 65.

87. Article 19 Bulletin, Issue 4, December 1988, p. 2.
88. *Freedom of Information and Expression in Iraq*, pp. 19, 21.
89. *Article 19*, p. 272.
90. *Index*, Vol. 9, no. 2, April 1980, p. 72.
91. *State of Flux*, p. 25.
92. *Index*, Vol. 17, no. 2, February 1988, p. 19.
93. *Ibid.*, Vol. 8, no. 2, March-April 1979, p. 64.
94. *Ibid.*, Vol. 6, no. 5, September-October 1977, p. 65.
95. *Article 19*, p. 229; *Index*, Vol. 15, no. 6, June 1986, p. 41.
96. *State of Flux*, pp. 25–26.
97. *Violations of the Helsinki Accords: Turkey*, p. 19.
98. *Index*, Vol. 18, no. 2, February 1989, p. 36.
99. *Ibid.*, Vol. 18 no. 1, January 1989, p. 14.
100. *Ibid.*, Vol. 8, no. 6, December 1979, p. 67.
101. *Ibid.*, Vol. 10, no. 1, February 1981, p. 71.
102. *Ibid.*, Vol. 17, no. 6, June-July 1988, p. 13.
103. *Ibid.*, Vol. 12, no. 4, August 1983, p. 41.
104. *Ibid.*, Vol. 7, no. 5, September-October 1978, p. 25.
105. *Freedom of Information and Expression in Iraq*, p. 19.
106. *Index*, Vol. 15, no. 9, October 1986, p. 50.
107. *Ibid.*, Vol. 15, no. 1, January 1986, p. 34.
108. *Article 19*, p. 74.
109. International PEN, Writers in Prison Committee Report, July 1988, p. 30.
110. *Freedom of Information and Expression in Iraq*, pp. 20–21.
111. *Index*, Vol. 18, no. 5, May-June 1989, p. 7.
112. Asia Watch, *Still Confined*, p. 6.
113. Because Helen Joseph was "listed" and cannot be quoted, no South African publisher has felt able to publish her autobiography *Side by Side*. See *Index*, Vol. 15, no. 6, June 1986, p. 40.
114. *Index*, Vol. 12, no. 2, April 1983, p. 47.
115. *Ibid.*, Vol. 12, no. 3, June 1983, p. 7.
116. International PEN, Writers in Prison Committee Report, July 1988, pp. 12–13; PEN American Center, case sheet on P. A. Toer, April 15, 1981, p. 1.
117. *Index*, Vol. 11, no. 5, October 1982, pp. 34–35.
118. *Ibid.*, Vol. 9, no. 4, August 1980, p. 69.
119. International PEN, Writers in Prison Committee Report, July 1988, p. 1.
120. *Article 19*, p. 34; *Index*, Vol. 16, no. 1, January 1987, p. 24.
121. According to *State of Flux*, pp. 26–27, Recep Marasli received a thirty-six-year prison term for a similar offense.
122. *Index*, Vol. 16, no. 6, June 1987, p. 27; International PEN Writers in Prison Committee Report, July 1988, p. 30.
123. *Index*, Vol. 18, no. 3, March 1989, p. 18. Many Cuban writers have spent more than twenty years in prison (e.g., Armanda Valladares, held in prison 1961–1983); *Index*, Vol. 12, no. 1, February 1983, p. 43.
124. *Ibid.*, Vol. 18, no. 4, April 1989, p. 40.
125. *Ibid.*, Vol. 11, no. 2, April 1982, p. 47.
126. *Freedom of Information and Expression in Tunisia*, p. 18.
127. Article 19 Bulletin, Issue 4, December 1988, p. 2.
128. *Index*, Vol 10, no. 5, October 1981, p. 45.
129. Common in South Korea (*Index*, Vol. 17, no. 2, February 1988, p. 40, and Vol. 18, no. 5, May-June 1989, p. 40), but not unknown even in Syria (*ibid.*, Vol.

16, no. 7, July-August 1987, p. 41), Brazil (*ibid.*, Vol. 1, no. 1, Spring 1972, p. 81), Pakistan (*ibid.*, Vol. 13, no. 6, December 1984, p. 43), and Cameroon (Amnesty International, *Artists and the Urgent Action Network*, p. 1).

130. The antigovernment accusation is widely used by different political systems: Nepal (*Index*, Vol. 16, no. 1, January 1987, p. 24; Vol. 16, no. 8, September 1987, p. 38); Somalia (*ibid.*, Vol. 16, no. 2, February 1987); South Africa (where the apartheid policy has been widely criticized); Turkey (where Yadcin Kucuk was tried in 1986 for the fourth time for his book *For a New Republic*—see *Violations of the Helsinki Accords: Turkey*, p. 19), and Paraguay (*Chairman's Report for Barcelona*, PEN Writers in Prison Committee, September 22, 1978, p. 2).

131. Syria (*Index*, Vol. 16, no. 6, June 1987, p. 2).

132. Widespread cause for imprisonment of writers in Vietnam, Cuba, North Korea, and China. Typically in Vietnam, Article 82 of the penal code assigns three to six years' imprisonment for "propaganda against socialism," and the distribution of decadent and counterrevolutionary books (Article 99) may result in a prison term of six months to twelve years (*Index*, Vol. 15, no. 3, March 1986, p. 4).

133. Under the shah's regime in Iran, Gholam Hoseyn Sa'edi was imprisoned nineteen times for that offense (*Index*, Vol. 15, no. 4, April 1986, p. 11).

134. This sanction is common in Turkey (for writings dealing with the Kurds) and in Israel (Palestinians). Thus, sociologist Ismail Besikci has been jailed for referring to the Kurds as a separate ethnic group; see Ziman et al., *The World of Science and the Rule of Law*, p. 123. In Mauritania, black writers have been convicted for "making propaganda of racial or ethnic character"; see International PEN Writers in Prison Committee, July 1988, p. 22.

135. Although obscenity charges can be brought against writers in most countries, some states use them more often than others, and sometimes attacks on authors are carried out on moral grounds when in reality their political and social philosophies are in question. In Turkey, Erdal Oz was put on trial on obscenity charges for publishing a translation of Henry Miller's *Tropic of Capricorn*, and so was Ahmet Altan for his novel *Sudaki Iz* [Trace on water], *Violations of the Helsinki Accords: Turkey*, p. 19.

136. For example, author Nawal el-Saadawi has been imprisoned for championing the cause of women and criticizing Arab society. *Index*, Vol. 11, no. 3, June 1982, p. 18.

137. Wail Sawwah, the author of a collection of short stories entitled *Why Did Yusuf al-Najia Die?* was tortured following his arrest. *Index*, Vol. 16, no. 6, June 1987, p. 27.

138. After Cuban writer Herberto Padilla was reportedly arrested and tortured for his writing, he detailed his prison experiences in *En mi jardin pastan los heroes*. See Ripell, *Harassing the Intellectuals*, p. 31.

139. Sevet Ziya Corakli, a writer and poet, lost the use of his left foot and hand as a result of repeated torture; Amnesty International, *Artists and the Urgent Action Network*, pp. 2–3.

140. *Index*, Vol. 16, no. 7, July 1987, p. 41. Khoja was arrested, along with 200 others, for membership in the Communist Party.

141. *Ibid.*, Vol. 9, no. 6, December 1980, p. 23.

142. *Ibid.*, Vol. 16, no. 10, November-December 1987, p. 22.

143. Amnesty International, "Malawi: Jack Mapanje, Imprisoned Malawain Poet," November 13, 1987, p. 1.

144. *Index*, Vol. 11, no. 6, December 1982, p. 47.

145. This, according to *Index* (Vol. 14, no. 5, October 1985, p. 16), was the Syrian government's motivation for arresting the poets Tadmus Trad and Wail Sawwah.

146. *Ibid.*, Vol. 1, no. 1, Spring 1972, pp. 89–90.

147. Article 19 Bulletin, Issue 3, August-September 1988, p. 2.

148. *Article 19*, pp. 254–259.

149. *Ibid.*, p. 253.

150. *Index*, Vol. 15, no. 4, April 1986, p. 11, and Vol. 14, no. 4, August 1985, p. 32.

151. *Article 19*, p. 35.

152. *Index*, Vol. 17, no. 2, February 1988, p. 22.

153. *Ibid.*, Vol. 10, no. 6, December 1981, p. 55.

154. Laye, the author of two important books, *The African Child* and *The Radiance of the King*, has lived in Senegal; see George Theiner, ed., *They Shoot Writers, Don't They?* (London and Boston: Faber and Faber, 1984), p. 86.

155. *Index*, Vol. 8, no. 2, April 1979, p. 18.

156. For example, the poet Dennis Brutus, who found asylum in the United States. *Ibid.*, Vol. 12, no. 6, December 1983, p. 17.

157. *Ibid.*, Vol. 10, no. 4, 1981, p. 44, and Vol. 11, no. 6, December 1982, p. 43.

158. *Ibid.*, Vol. 12, no. 4, August 1983, p. 7.

159. Ripell, *Harassing the Intellectuals*, p. 27, reports on the exile of poet José Mario as well as his friend Allen Ginsberg.

160. *Ibid.*, p. 36.

161. *Index*, Vol. 16, no. 6, June 1987, p. 28.

162. *Ibid.*, Vol. 12, no. 1, February 1983, p. 49.

163. Professor Mumtaz Soysal was exiled to a resort on the Aegean Sea, Kusadasi, for twenty-six months for including in his syllabuses books that contained references to Marx and Lenin; *ibid.*, Vol. 1, no. 1, Spring 1972, p. 90.

164. *Article 19*, pp. 254–255.

165. *Ibid.*, p. 253.

166. *Index*, Vol. 15, no. 9, October 1986, p. 24.

167. *Ibid.*, Vol. 18, no. 3, March 1989, p. 42.

168. See *ibid.*, Vol. 13, no. 4, August 1984, p. 37, for Esmail Khoi, "Khomeini Shoots Writers."

169. *Ibid.*

170. *Ibid.*, Vol. 18, no. 5, May-June 1989, p. 7; Amir Taheri, "Pandora's Box Forced Open."

171. *Article 19*, p. 258.

172. *Index*, Vol. 15, no. 2, February 1986, p. 29. For comprehensive analysis of the situation in Iraq, see *Freedom of Information and Expression in Iraq*.

173. Theiner, *They Shoot Writers*, p. 125; *Index*, Vol. 10, no. 2, April 1981, p. 3.

174. Amnesty International, *Artists and the Urgent Action Network*, p. 1.

175. *Index*, Vol. 18, no. 6-7, July-August 1989, p. 77.

176. *Ibid.*, Vol. 10, no. 6, December 1981, p. 26.

177. *Ibid.*, Vol. 8, no. 2, March-April 1979, p. 18.

178. *Article 19*, p. 35.

179. *Index*, Vol. 18, no. 6-7, June-August 1989, p. 80.

180. *Ibid.*, Vol. 14, no. 2, April 1985, pp. 56–57.

181. Report of the Writers in Prison Committee, 1975, p. 1.

182. *Index,* Vol. 10, no. 5, October 1981, p. 43, and Vol. 9, no. 2, April 1980, p. 49.

183. *Ibid.,* Vol. 12, no. 4, August 1983, p. 35.

184. *Ibid.,* Vol. 8, no. 2, March-April 1979, p. 64.

185. *Ibid.,* Vol. 6, no. 5, September-October, 1977, p. 65.

186. International PEN, Writers in Prison Committee, July 1988, pp. 10–11.

187. *Ibid.,* p. 11.

188. *Index,* Vol. 8, no. 2, March-April 1979, p. 19.

189. Ripell, *Harassing the Intellectuals,* p. 26.

190. *Index,* Vol. 17, no. 5, May 1988, p. 128.

191. *Ibid.,* Vol. 13, no. 4, August 1984, p. 43.

192. *Ibid.,* Vol. 10, no. 5, October 1981, p. 44.

193. *Freedom of Information and Expression in Iraq,* pp. 22–23.

194. *Index,* Vol. 8, no. 2, March-April 1979, p. 67.

195. *Freedom of Information and Expression in Trinidad and Tobago,* p. 7.

196. International PEN, Writers in Prison Committee Report, July 1988, p. 22.

197. *Index,* Vol. 12, no. 5, October 1983, p. 45.

198. *Freedom of Information and Expression in Iraq,* p. 31.

199. *Freedom of Information and Expression in Tunisia,* p. 14.

200. *Index,* Vol. 15, no. 9, October 1986, p. 6.

201. *Ibid.,* Vol. 14, no. 5, October 1985, p. 65.

202. *Ibid.,* Vol. 14, no. 2, April 1985, p. 53.

203. *Ibid.,* Vol. 15, no. 4, April 1986, p. 11.

204. Khoi, "Khomeini Shoots Writers," *ibid.,* Vol. 13, no. 4, August 1984, p. 37.

205. *Index,* Vol. 10, no. 1, February 1981, p. 71.

206. *Ibid.,* Vol. 8, no. 2, March-April 1979, p. 67.

207. *Ibid.,* Vol. 8, no. 6, July-August 1979, p. 5.

208. For general evaluation of the problem, see *Article 19,* p. 259.

209. *Index,* Vol. 16, no. 6, June 1987, pp. 27–28.

210. *Ibid.,* Vol. 15, no. 4, April 1986, p. 11.

211. *Ibid.,* Vol. 14, no. 4, August 1985, p. 83.

212. Amnesty International, *Artists and the Urgent Action Network,* pp. 2–3.

213. *Index,* Vol. 13, no. 2, April 1984, p. 49.

214. *Ibid.,* Vol. 11, no. 3, June 1982.

215. Ripell, *Harassing the Intellectuals,* p. 31.

216. Chairman's Half Year Report, Writers in Prison Committee, November 1975–May 1976, pp. 2–3.

217. *Article 19,* p. 45; *Newsweek,* Focus: Special Report on Censorship, p. 6.

218. *Article 19,* p. 132.

219. *Ibid.,* p. 269.

220. *Index,* Vol. 17, no. 2, February 1988, p. 39.

221. *Ibid.,* Vol. 15, no. 4, April 1986, p. 31.

222. *Freedom of Information and Expression in Tunisia,* p. 18.

223. Marzouki's book was among the six. See Article 19 Bulletin, Issue 4, December 1988, p. 2.

224. *Index,* Vol. 15, no. 4, April 1986, p. 31.

225. *Ibid.,* Vol. 12, no. 5, October 1983, p. 43.

226. *Ibid.,* Vol. 15, no. 7, July-August 1986, p. 46; see also *Violations of the Helsinki Accords: Turkey,* p. 24.

227. *Violations of the Helsinki Accords: Turkey,* p. 23.

228. *Index,* Vol. 6, no. 5, September-October 1977, p. 66.

229. *Article 19,* p. 45.

230. *Ibid.,* p. 275.

231. See *ibid.,* p. 143, regarding Indonesia. South Africa also uses the postpublication system.

232. *Index,* Vol. 16, no. 3, March 1987, p. 37.

233. *Ibid.,* Vol. 16, no. 8, September 1987, p. 36.

234. *Ibid.,* Vol. 9, no. 2, April 1980, p. 72.

235. *Ibid.,* Vol. 11, no. 4, August 1982, p. 46.

236. For fictional material, see, for example, *ibid.,* Vol. 17, no. 5, May 1988, pp. 130–131; for nonfictional material, see *State of Flux,* p. 25.

237. *Index,* Vol. 18, no. 3, March 1989.

238. *Ibid.,* Vol. 9, no. 2, April 1980, p. 70.

239. *Ibid.,* Vol. 11, no. 3, June 1982, p. 46.

240. *Ibid.,* Vol. 18, no. 2, February 1989, p. 39.

241. *Ibid.,* Vol. 17, no. 7, August 1988, p. 34.

242. *Article 19,* p. 151.

243. International PEN, Writers in Prison Committee Report, July 1988, pp. 3 and 12–13.

244. See, for example, a description of the Peruvian policy in *Index,* Vol. 11, no. 1, February 1982, p. 46.

245. *Freedom of Information and Expression in the Congo.*

246. Asia Watch, *Still Confined,* p. 5.

247. *Index,* Vol. 12, no. 6, December 1983, p. 43.

248. *Ibid.,* Vol. 7, no. 1, January-February 1978, p. 66 (Brazil).

249. *Ibid.,* Vol. 7, no. 3, May-June 1978, p. 64 (Indonesia).

250. *Ibid.,* Vol. 6, no. 4, July-August 1977, p. 67 (Argentina).

251. In 1977, a booklet entitled "Torture in South Africa," published by the Christian Institute, was banned as "undesirable." *Index,* Vol. 1, no. 4, July-August 1977, pp. 71–72.

252. *Index,* Vol. 17, no. 6, June-July 1988, p. 62.

253. Article 19 Bulletin, Issue 4, December 1988, p. 2.

254. *Index,* Vol. 10, no. 6, December 1981, p. 71.

255. *Ibid.,* Vol. 1, no. 1, Spring 1972, p. 82.

256. *Ibid.,* Vol. 10, no. 6, December 1981, p. 71.

257. *Ibid.,* Vol. 12, no. 4, August 1983, p. 41.

258. *Ibid.,* Vol. 9, no. 4, August 1980, p. 71.

259. *Ibid.,* Vol. 18, no. 6-7, July-August 1989, p. 77.

260. *Ibid.,* Vol. 18, no. 5, May-June 1989, p. 38.

261. *Ibid.,* Vol. 14, no. 3, June 1985, p. 37.

262. *Ibid.,* Vol. 15, no. 7, July-August 1986, p. 42.

263. *Ibid.,* Vol. 9, no. 1, February 1980, p. 73.

264. For a general analysis of this phenomenon, see *Encyclopedia of World Literature in the 20th Century,* rev. ed., Vol. 4 (1981–1984), "Society and Literature," pp. 255–264, esp. p. 263.

265. Charles Humana, *World Human Rights Guide* (New York: Facts on File, 1986).

266. *Article 19,* p. 12.

PART FOUR

Liberal Democratic Systems

9

Freedom of Expression in Western Europe: Law and Practice

Jan K. Dargel

Censorship is ubiquitous. It may be manifest in varying forms and in widely varying degrees, but it exists in every nation of the world, even in the democracies of Western Europe.

From a comparative perspective, Western Europe, with its history of intellectual enlightenment and the encouragement of an informed polity, as reflected in constitutions, bills of rights, and basic law, offers a high degree of protection for freedom of expression. Further, methods used to quell expression are generally of a tamer sort compared with methods employed in other parts of the world. Indeed, the expression may be allowed but later punished. However, this does not mean we may ignore the forms of censorship that do exist.

All legal action or threatened legal action against expression is a form of censorship because of the enormous "chilling effect" that results. Self-censorship is the response to these threats of legal action. Although government-imposed censorship may be much more frightening, we must also beware the proliferation of self-censorship, in all its manifestations. Therefore, all legal action against expression is important, as is the mechanism that is in place to supervise that legal action.

Many countries in Western Europe allow the courts only limited power to rule on the constitutionality or legitimacy of legislation or executive orders. For example, German judges may perform this task in the constitutional courts, but British and French judges are severely restricted in their authority to rule on the acts of the other two branches of government. This weakened role of "judicial review" results in censorial laws or orders being curtailed only by further legislation or by juries refusing to enforce them.[1] Of course, these laws perform a function even if not one case is brought to court, merely by encouraging self-censorship and restraint. Even a widely unpopular law will not create sufficient public demand for its repeal (the only other means of its demise) without a few celebrated "abuses" of the law; thus, these laws do their duty by remaining law and posing the threat of prosecution. When cases of censorship actually are litigated, these are only the tip of the iceberg.

There will obviously be different results when the legal policy of freedom of expression is less often in the hands of judges and more often left to public opinion or even legislators. One need look no further than the flag-burning debate and public opinion regarding censorship of news from the Persian Gulf war to find the answer. As judges in the United States realize every day, doing what is popular may not mean doing the right thing legally.

This reduced role of judicial review in Western Europe has resulted in very different substantive and procedural law governing freedom of expression. As discussed later, the European Court of Human Rights, with its authority to review any governmental action that may have violated a person's right to freedom of expression, has, in recent years, gained significantly in importance in Western Europe.

A question may then be asked: Is there developing a discernible pattern or jurisprudence of freedom of expression in Western Europe? Throughout Western Europe, there is a version of the constitutional balancing act used in the United States—namely, the mediation of the conflict between the rights of individuals to express themselves freely and the interests of the government in maintaining security, public morality, and the interests of other individuals. Also to be found are the legal means by which this delicate balance is to be drawn. It is important to examine these legal tools used by both sides—tools of protection used by individuals and tools of censorship used by governments.

Tools of Protection: Freedom of Expression in Law

Western Europe has an array of constitutions, bills of rights, basic law provisions, case law, and customs protecting the fundamental right of freedom of expression. These have culminated in the human rights convention, which nearly every country in Western Europe has now ratified.

One of the few countries in Western Europe without codified protection of freedom of expression is Great Britain. Ever since the debate over licensing of printers and newspapers, opposed so eloquently by John Milton in his *Areopagitica,* Britain has wrestled with the conflict between censorship and free expression. It addressed the issue in its Bill of Rights of 1688, but as true of so many of the early edicts on rights in Britain, this freedom protected only a small, elite group, in this case members of Parliament in their official debating role in that body. Although modern Britain has always recognized the concept of free speech, it has never codified the protection for its citizens as have most of the other countries of Western Europe.

Those European countries that have constitutional protections of freedom of expression are generally more expansive in their statements than those used in the United States. The celebrated First Amendment to the United States Constitution, ratified in 1791, states in extremely simplistic terms that "Congress shall make no law . . . abridging freedom of speech or of the press."[2]

In contrast, many constitutional provisions in Western Europe include one or two additional and paradoxical elements: first, a specific statement that there shall be no censorship and second, a declaration of the bases on which freedom of expression may legitimately be limited for the public good. The statements against censorship are clearly meant to prohibit what the American courts call "prior restraint," or censorship in advance, but not "subsequent punishment," or the imposition of a sanction after the expression. Discussed later is how effectively these schemes of subsequent punishment have been in limiting expression.

Sweden provides one of the earliest and most vigorous models of codified freedom of expression in its Freedom of the Press Act of 1766, which was made part of the country's Constitution. The current Constitution of 1975 also guarantees all Swedes a right to free expression as well as a right of access to information.[3] As a result of these documents and a statute of 1812, publications may not be censored in advance. In addition, these rights may not be abolished unless agreed to by two successive governments.[4]

Another early example of constitutional protection of speech is found in perhaps the second most well-known and celebrated bill of rights in the world, that of France. The seventeenth and eighteenth centuries brought a focus by legal scholars on the fundamental rights inherent in the concept of natural law. After the French Revolution, the Declaration of the Rights of Man and of the Citizen was drafted, Article 11 of which protects freedom of expression by providing that "the free communication of thought and of opinion is one of the most precious rights of man; every citizen then may speak, write and publish freely, but he is responsible for the abuse of that freedom in cases determined by law."[5]

This protection was born of the same influences impacting upon the U.S. Bill of Rights and resulted in revolutionary and broad protections for all citizens. Consecutive French constitutions have included this protection, and the current Constitution of 1958 makes specific reference to the Declaration in its preamble. However, its legal validity was not determined until a 1971 ruling by the Constitutional Council, a body established to review the constitutionality of legislation after it is drafted but before it is promulgated. In that year, the council ruled a law unconstitutional for violating a principle within the preamble to the Constitution.[6]

France's Declaration may be more subtle, but a clear example of the coalescence of a prohibition on censorship and a stated reason for limiting or forbidding expression can be found in Article 21 of Italy's Constitution:

> All are entitled freely to express their thoughts by word of mouth, in writing and by all other means of communication. No previous authorization shall be required of the press, and it shall not be subject to censorship. . . . Printed publications, spectacles and all other displays that offend against public decency are forbidden. The law will make adequate provisions to prevent and suppress such violations.[7]

Similarly, the Belgian Constitution states:

Freedom of worship and its public exercise, together with freedom to manifest personal opinions in every way, are guaranteed save for the punishment of offenses perpetrated in exercising those liberties.

The press is free; no form of censorship may ever be instituted; no cautionary deposit may be demanded from writers, publishers or printers.[8]

West Germany's Constitution also includes the paradox previously mentioned: As a review of the provision shows, the ban on censorship is clearly meant to provide further protection for the press, whereas the limits on expression in paragraph 2 are meant to apply to individual expression and are considered "post-censorship."[9] Article five, paragraphs 1 and 2, of the Basic Law, drafted in 1949, state:

Everyone shall have the right freely to express and disseminate his opinion by speech, writing and pictures and freely to inform himself from generally accessible sources.

Freedom of the press and freedom of reporting by means of broadcasts and film are guaranteed. There shall be no censorship.

These rights are limited only by the regulations of general law, legal regulations on the protection of juveniles and the rights of personal honor.[10]

There is a distinct hierarchy of basic rights in West Germany, with freedom of expression potentially limited by the concerns reflected in paragraph 2. However, unlike most codified fundamental rights, the first twenty articles of the Basic Law cannot be amended or abolished.

The last example of domestic constitutional protections of freedom of expression is found in Denmark. Its Constitution, perhaps more than any other, demonstrates the intent to retain the right to punish expression subsequently but to prohibit prior censorship. Article 77 of the 1953 Constitution states that "any person shall be entitled to publish their thoughts in printing, in writing, and in speech, provided that they may be held answerable in a court of justice. Censorship and other preventive measures shall never again be reintroduced."[11] It is clear that the Danes take their opposition to censorship seriously. In 1967 and 1969, the government abolished laws limiting obscenity in print and film.[12]

These varied and substantial forms of legal protection of expression leave one wondering why the countries of Western Europe felt the need to ratify yet another legal tool of protection in the form of a regional human rights convention. However, it may be to this regional document rather than domestic provisions that individuals increasingly look for protection.

After the United Nations adopted in 1948 the Universal Declaration of Human Rights, the newly formed Council of Europe drafted the European Convention for the Protection of Human Rights and Fundamental Freedoms (or, more commonly, the European Convention on Human Rights). Eventually, the twenty-one member nations of the Council of Europe signed and ratified the convention.[13] Ironically, the United Kingdom, without a bill of rights itself, played a large role in its drafting and was one of the first to sign the convention in 1950 and the first to ratify it in 1951. It then took effect in 1953 when the requisite ten member states had ratified the document.

This treaty established the European Commission on Human Rights (the Commission) and the European Court of Human Rights (the Court), both located in Strasbourg, France, with the other institutions of the Council of Europe. The convention covers a broad spectrum of civil, political, and human rights in its eighteen original articles and eight subsequent protocols, including a general tenet of freedom of expression in Article 10. Unlike the First Amendment to the United States Constitution and with even more specificity than domestic West European constitutions, Article 10 states both the general right to freedom of expression and the bases on which it may be legitimately abridged:

1. Everyone has the right to freedom of expression. This right shall include freedom to hold opinions and to receive and impart information and ideas without interference by public authority and regardless of frontiers. This Article shall not prevent States from requiring the licensing of broadcasting, television or cinema enterprises.
2. The Exercise of these freedoms, since it carries with it duties and responsibilities, may be subject to such formalities, conditions, restrictions or penalties as are prescribed by law and are necessary in a democratic society, in the interest of national security, territorial integrity or public safety, for the prevention of disorder or crime, for the protection of health or morals, for the protection of the reputation of rights of others, for preventing disclosure of information received in confidence, or for maintaining the authority and impartiality of the judiciary.[14]

Article 10 has been determined to protect not only the freedom to express ideas and information but also the right to receive information, with the general rule of free expression stated in the first paragraph and the exceptions outlined in the second. Predictably, it is the interpretation of these exceptions that causes the most difficulty.

Cases must result in a final decision from the domestic court of last resort before a petition may be filed, and all petitions go before the Commission first. Only those cases deemed admissible and that cannot be settled may be referred to the Court. If the Commission determines that the case does not merit referral to the Court, it is submitted to the Committee of Ministers. The Court has considered and issued opinions in approximately 130 cases since 1961; only about twenty of these have related in whole or in part to Article 10.[15]

Nations submit to the jurisdiction of these institutions and agree to abide by their decisions. However, only certain nations have incorporated the convention into their domestic law, but in a country that has taken this action, an individual may rely on the convention and its interpretation by the Commission and the Court as the basis of a lawsuit or a defense against the offending government in the appropriate domestic court of that country. Reliance on human rights protections under the convention then has the same status as any other legal argument in the domestic courts. In a country that has not incorporated the convention, the individual must rely on some other authority in the domestic body of law, argue that point through the hierarchy of domestic courts, and only when, and if, reaching Strasbourg legally rely on the convention. By the time cases have also passed through the two or three layers at Strasbourg, individuals have waited an average of six years for resolution of their claims of human rights violations.

As examples of incorporation, Austria has granted the substantive portion of the convention the status of constitutional law,[16] and the Netherlands has granted the convention supremacy over ordinary domestic statutes.[17] Most of the remaining nations, such as Denmark, have substantially the same protections in their domestic constitutions. The United Kingdom, which some argue could most benefit from incorporation, stands alone in having no bill of rights and declining to incorporate the convention.[18] Citizens are left to hope that laws will be passed and interpreted according to the convention.[19]

The most important caveat to this type of brief survey of some of the laws relating to freedom of expression is that no declarations, constitutions, or intellectual commitment to a free and open society will prevent governments from attempting to censor or punish expression they deem injurious to the nation's interests or, unfortunately, merely embarrassing to them. It is also clear that they have been extremely successful in doing so.

Tools of Censorship: Freedom of Expression in Practice

Examples of censorship are necessarily selective. The cases presented here have been chosen for their ability to demonstrate the substance, practice, and procedures of free-expression law in Western Europe, primarily through the Council of Europe and the European Convention of Human Rights.

Interestingly, one of the very few victories by the government of the United Kingdom before the European Court of Human Rights involved a case of censorship.[20] It was also one of the first Article 10 (freedom of expression) cases to come before the Court. In 1971, the United Kingdom had banned publication of the British translation of the Danish educational book *The Little Red Schoolbook*, arguing that its portion on sex violated the Obscene Publications Acts of 1959 and 1964. The book had been published in eleven other West European countries as well as Denmark, but the British courts fined Richard Handyside, the publisher of the British edition, and issued a forfeiture order for the destruction of the remaining books. A revised edition of the book was allowed to be published six months later.

In 1976, five years after the original action against the publisher, the Court upheld the actions of the British government. In determining whether there had been a breach of Article 10, the Court had to determine whether the alleged government action was (1) an actual interference "prescribed by law," (2) based on one of the legitimate aims listed in the second paragraph, and (3) "necessary in a democratic society" to fulfill that aim. This has remained the test for Article 10 cases, with the third and final determination continuing to be by far the most problematic and controversial for the Court.

In *Handyside*, the Court determined that the government's action was indeed "prescribed by law," by the Obscenity Acts, and that its purpose was one of those listed in paragraph 2, namely the "protection of morals." In determining whether suppression of the book was "necessary in a democratic society," as paragraph 2 further requires, the Court said much latitude and discretion must be given to states to determine their standard of morals and how best to protect them.

This case is a sample of the jurisprudence that would emerge from the Court in future freedom of expression cases. First, the Court stated categorically its view that this was one of the most important freedoms in a democratic society:

> Freedom of expression constitutes one of the essential foundations of such a society, one of the basic conditions for its progress and for the development of every man. Subject to paragraph 2 of Article 10, it is applicable not only to "information" or "ideas" that are favourably received or regarded as inoffensive or as a matter of indifference, but also to those that offend, shock or disturb the State or any sector of the population. Such are the demands of that pluralism, tolerance and broadmindedness without which there is no "democratic society." This means, amongst other things, that every "formality," "condition," "restriction" or "penalty" imposed in this sphere must be proportionate to the legitimate aim pursued.[21]

Second, the Court was quick to advise that it did not require, or even expect, the limitations in Article 10(2) to be defined universally by all of the twenty-one nations or to be applied identically in each case. The Court, specific to this case, said that "the requirements of morals varies from time to time and from place to place, especially in our era," and that "State authorities are in principle in a better position than the international judge to give an opinion on the exact content of these requirements as well as on the 'necessity' of a 'restriction' or 'penalty' intended to meet them."[22]

This is an example of the Court's doctrine of "margin of appreciation," or the degree of discretion allowed member nations in applying their standards of morality, security, and so on. This discretion is not unlimited, of course, and the margin of appreciation allowed will vary depending on the category of paragraph 2 at issue. For example, the Court has held that a greater margin will be allowed in cases involving the protection of morals than in those involving a "far more objective notion of the 'authority' of the judiciary."[23] This approach was certainly evident in the Commission's decision in *Case of Muller and Others,* in which it ruled that Switzerland's prosecution for display of obscene paintings was not a violation of the Convention.[24]

Third, the practices of other member nations of the Council of Europe are important in determining the necessity of a democratic society in a given case. For example, if an individual applicant is able to show that no other country practices the type of restriction that was applied, the person may well succeed in showing that it is not necessary in a democratic society. Conversely, the fact that all other member nations had legislation restricting obscenity was important to the Court in upholding the actions of the government of the United Kingdom in *Handyside.*

The British government was not as successful in a subsequent case of censorship using the domestic contempt-of-court laws. What became known as the *Sunday Times* case began with an article in the *Sunday Times of London* in 1972 about the pharmaceutical company Distillers and its distribution of the drug thalidomide as a tranquilizer for pregnant women in the 1950s and early 1960s. The company was, at that time, in litigation with families of children born with severe birth defects caused by the drug. The House of Lords unanimously ruled in favor of an injunction of a proposed follow-up article on the grounds that writing about the ongoing legal matter would constitute a contempt of court, a common-law criminal offense in Britain.

In 1979, the Court in Strasbourg applied the three-part test for alleged Article 10 violations and found that the injunction was prescribed by law, even though not in the form of a statute, and that it was based on a legitimate aim, namely maintaining the "authority of the judiciary." Again, the third part of the test proved to be the most difficult. By a narrow vote of eleven to nine, the Court held that there had indeed been a violation of Article 10; the suppression of these matters of great public concern was not proportionate to the legitimate aim and not necessary in a democratic society.[25] The opinion is noted not only for its eloquent defense of freedom of expression, particularly that belonging to the press, but also for the fact that it was contrary to the ruling by the Commission and, as mentioned, a unanimous ruling of the House of Lords.

Because the British law on contempt was generally considered defective in predetermining that all expression regarding ongoing legal matters would constitute contempt, the British government enacted the Contempt of Court Act 1981 to comply fully with the Strasbourg decision, pursuant to Article 53. The Committee of Ministers, responsible under Article 54 of the Convention for overseeing the execution of the Court's judgments, considered the obligation satisfied as soon as the British government introduced the new bill, even though the Committee had not yet seen a copy of it.[26]

If British cases seem to be overrepresented in this analysis of Court opinions, it is because the *Handyside* and *Sunday Times* cases have been particularly important in the development of the jurisdiction of European freedom of expression. It is also rather interesting, when determining the impact of the Convention, to examine cases from a country that lacks a competing or complementary bill of rights. The absence of a domestic bill of rights in Britain might be one explanation for the fact that more applications have been brought against it than any other signatory state. The Court has stated that the primary duty to uphold human rights rests with the domestic courts of the member nations. However, with no bill of rights and a myriad of customs, statutes and case law restricting freedom of expression, the balance between the rights of individuals and the interests of the government in Britain remains particularly one-sided.

This is not to suggest an absence of examples of suppression of speech in other nations with more substantial constitutional protections. Both the Commission and Court have been kept busy with Article 10 cases and have continued to apply the firm tests established in the *Handyside* and *Sunday Times* cases. In 1990, the Court had cause to reexamine the question of confidentiality of judicial proceedings. A Swiss journalist, who had filed a complaint against someone for defamation, allegedly released information about the judicial proceedings at a press conference. Despite the fact that the information had in essence already been disclosed, the journalist (Weber) was fined 300 Swiss francs under the Swiss cantonal law stating that "parties . . . shall be bound to maintain the confidentiality of an investigation."[27] As the trial judge concluded, it was "of little importance that the matter which was to be kept confidential was known to a limited or indefinite number of people because confidentiality had already been breached by a third party or by the same person."[28] A unanimous court of appeal agreed by ruling that it was "sufficient that the matters *should* be confidential in nature, without necessarily still being confidential"[29] (my emphasis).

This was the argument used by the British government in the *Spycatcher* case in which the government tried in vain to ban the sale and printed discussion of the book of the same name by the former British intelligence officer, Peter Wright. The government argued that despite the wide publication of the book in other countries and its availability illegally in Britain, it must be banned based on Wright's lifelong agreement to secrecy under the Official Secrets Act. The House of Lords finally ruled in 1987 that the ban could not stand because the material was already in the public domain.[30] Had it not been for Wright's residency in Australia, the government could have prosecuted him for his violation of the Official Secrets Act, but censorship of his material already known to the public was a different matter, according to the House of Lords. The question remains of whether precedent from the European Court of Human Rights and the possibility of a contrary ruling from Strasbourg influenced the House of Lords in its decision.

Regardless of the reasons, this ruling was far less censorial than that of the U.S. Supreme Court in the *Snepp* case of seven years earlier. The Supreme Court upheld an injunction on the sale of a book by former CIA officer Frank Snepp and even ruled that a constructive trust should be placed on profits already gleaned from sales.[31] Ignoring the freedom of expression implications and the fact that most of the information was already in the public domain, the Supreme Court ruled entirely on the basis of contract law. Snepp had also signed a lifelong secrecy and prepublication review agreement with the government. Limitations on and punishment of expression prohibited by law but already released to the public have proved to be a difficult issue for courts.

The European Court in *Weber,* however, unanimously overruled the court of appeal and held that the fine imposed had been a breach of Article 10. Because the information had already been disclosed, the action was no longer necessary to protect the authority of the judiciary. As the Court had said in the past, the margin of appreciation left to the member nations is considerably reduced when the aim pursued is the more objective notion of the judiciary's authority as opposed to protection of morals. The success of the applicants in both the *Sunday Times* and *Weber* cases may also stem from the Court's additional sensitivity to the need for open and public trial proceedings required by Article 6 of the Convention. Weber was also successful in his Article 6 claim before the Court.

The Court has also ruled on cases involving another type of expression on public matters—material that is allegedly defamatory—with sometimes surprising results. In 1986, it found unanimously in favor of an Austrian journalist who had written an article critical of the then federal chancellor, Bruno Kreisky, and had been fined for defamation. The Court pointed out in its opinion in *Lingens* that the protection under Article 10 should be considered broader in the realm of public discourse about a politician (as opposed to a private individual) due to the interest in free and open political debate.[32]

However, the Court seemed to contradict this doctrine of broader protection of political expression when it ruled in the *Barfod* case in 1989 that no breach of Article 10 had occurred.[33] In that case, a journalist had written an article implying that two lay judges on the High Court in Greenland had been influenced in their ruling in a tax case by their employment by the government, stating that the individuals "did their duty" in ruling as they did. He was convicted of defamation and fined.

As seen earlier, the Constitution of Denmark specifically prohibits censorship before publication, but pointedly permits subsequent punishment for expression contrary to the law. Defamation is a criminal offense under both the provisions of the Danish Penal Code[34] and the Greenland Penal Code. However, strict application of the precedent of *Lingens* would have resulted in a reversal of the conviction under the law of the convention. Indeed, although conceding that political expression must be strenuously protected, the Court seemed to go out of its way to find that the expression in question related more to the individual integrity of the lay judges than to their official role and did not therefore deserve greater protection. Judge Gölcüklü agreed with the ruling of the Commission in his dissenting opinion, reminding the Court that it had held in *Lingens* "that 'politicians' must be ready to accept more criticism than non-politicians."[35] Indeed, the ruling seemed completely contrary to the opinion of only three years previously in *Lingens*.

The court, like any other, is subject to changes in membership and styles of interpretation. It is faced with adjudicating cases from twenty-one different nations, each of them with its own body of freedom of expression law. Whether the Court has created a respected set of legal rules that will fundamentally change the way in which governments approach censorship remains to be seen.

Conclusion

Censorship and freedom of expression continue to be legislated and litigated throughout Western Europe. Europeans have divergent bodies of law on this subject, but perhaps they may one day be unified by a regional standard. The cases examined here are obviously only a portion of those decided by the European Court of Human Rights in its history. But these five cases, spanning fourteen years of the Court, have shown how domestic law on freedom of expression is interpreted and analyzed according to the principles of the European Convention of Human Rights.

A few conclusions may be drawn regarding the Court's views and, perhaps, about the new European jurisprudence of freedom of expression. The Court is obviously particularly protective of freedom of expression, considering it a cornerstone of democracy. In addition, unlike what appears in other bodies of free-expression law, there appears to be an admitted bias in favor of greater protection of political speech, or at least speech about public matters. Importantly, the Court is also willing to overrule a holding by a unanimous domestic court, as it did in the *Sunday Times* case.

Trends, though vitally important to analysts and scholars, are particularly difficult to determine in a court so young. However, it is a testament to the reverence with which so many view freedom of expression that the opinions of the European Court of Human Rights on this issue will continue to be viewed so closely in the future.

Notes

Research for this essay was made possible in part by a grant from the Dana Fund for Faculty Development at the University of Tampa.

1. An example of this was the jury acquittal in the trial of Clive Pointing, a British Ministry of Defense civil servant charged with violating section 2 of the Official Secrets Act by disclosing to Labour Party member of Parliament Tam Dalyell a report regarding the sinking of the Argentine ship *General Belgrano* during the Falklands war.

2. U.S. Constitution, First Amendment.

3. Albert P. Blaustein and Gisbert H. Flanz, *Constitutions of the Countries of the World,* Vol. 17 (New York: Oceana Publications, 1985), Sweden: Instrument of Government, Chapter 2, Fundamental Freedoms and Rights, Article 1, p. 11.

4. Jonathan Green, *Encyclopedia of Censorship* (New York: Facts on File, 1990), p. 307.

5. Declaration of the Rights of Man and of the Citizen, as quoted in Roger Errera, "The Freedom of the Press: The United States, France, and Other European Countries," in Pnina Lahav, ed., *Press Law in Modern Democracies* (New York: Longman, 1985).

6. Vernon Bogdanor, *Constitutions in Democratic Politics* (Aldershot: Gower 1988), p. 248.

7. As quoted in Mauro Cappelletti et al., *The Italian Legal System* (Stanford, CA: Stanford University Press, 1967), p. 285.

8. Blaustein and Flanz, *Constitutions,* Vol. 2, 1989, Belgium: The Belgians and Their Rights, Heading 2, Articles 14 and 18, pp. 2–3.

9. Ulrich Karpen, "Freedom of Expression as a Basic Right: A German View," 37 *American Journal of Comparative Law,* p. 395 (1989).

10. Basic Law of the Federal Republic of Germany, as quoted in *ibid.*

11. Green, *Encyclopedia of Censorship,* p. 78.

12. *Ibid.*

13. Not all nations immediately accepted the right of individual petition, the right of individuals to petition for a redress of grievances and to bring a nation to the European Commission on Human Rights or the European Court of Human Rights. For example, the United Kingdom signed the convention in 1951, but it allowed only individual petition in 1966, and one nation, Cyprus, has yet to do so.

14. As quoted in Vincent Berger, *Caselaw of the European Court of Human Rights* (Sarasota: UNIFO Publishers, 1989), p. 415.

15. *Ibid.*

16. Peter Leuprecht, "Making Human Rights and Human Rights Information More Accessible: The Documentation Centre for Human Rights in Strasbourg," in Jacob Sundberg, ed., *Laws, Rights and the European Convention on Human Rights* (Littleton, CO: Rothman, 1986).

17. Douwe Korff, "The Guarantee of Freedom of Expression Under Article 10 of the European Convention on Human Rights," *Media Law and Practice* (December 1988).

18. There have been attempts to incorporate. Lord Wade's proposed Bill of Rights legislation received a third reading in the House of Lords in 1979.

19. There has been gradual change in this regard, an example being a statement by Lord Denning, then Master of the Rolls: "The courts could and should take the Convention into account in interpreting a statute. An Act of Parliament should be construed so as to conform with the Convention." *Birdi* v. *Secretary of State for Home Affairs* 3 W.L.R. 225 (1975).

20. European Court H. R., *Handyside* judgment of December 7, 1976, Series A, no. 24.

21. *Handyside*, para. 49.

22. *Ibid.*, para. 48.

23. European Court H. R., *Sunday Times* judgment of April 26, 1979, Series A, no. 30.

24. Mark W. Janis and Richard S. Kay, *European Human Rights Law* (Storrs: University of Connecticut Law School Foundation Press, 1990), p. 254.

25. European Court H. R., *Sunday Times* judgment of April 26, 1979, Series A, no. 30.

26. N. V. Lowe, "The English Law of Contempt of Court and Article 10 of the European Convention on Human Rights," in M. P. Furmston, ed., *The Effect on English Law of Membership of the European Communities and Ratification of the European Convention on Human Rights* (Boston: Kluwer, 1983), p. 339.

27. European Court H. R., *Weber* judgment of May 22, 1990, Series A, no. 177.

28. *Weber*, para. 16.

29. *Ibid.*, para 17.

30. *Attorney-General* v. *Guardian Newspapers and Others, Observer Ltd. and Others, Times Newspapers and Another*, 1 W.L.R. 1248 (1987).

31. *Snepp* v. *United States*, 444 U.S. 507 (1980).

32. European Court H. R., *Lingens* judgment of July 8, 1986, Series A, no. 103.

33. European Court H. R., *Barfod* judgment of February 22, 1989, Series A, no. 149.

34. Green, *Encyclopedia of Censorship*, p. 78.

35. *Barfod*, Judge Gölcüklü dissenting, para. 3.

10

The American System of Censorship and Free Expression

J. M. Balkin

The United States is well known for having one of the most speech-protective regimes in the world. Its record is by no means perfect, however; American history is full of examples of government officials using their power to punish political opponents and dissenting groups. Nevertheless, the most egregious forms of censorship have largely been eradicated in the past twenty-five years. The basic guarantees of free-speech protection that human rights advocates now struggle for in other countries have been realized in the United States. To a considerable degree, the street corner speaker with unpopular views, the government critic, and the radical political activist are protected in this country. They will not be arrested and tortured for their beliefs, nor will they be sent to a mental institution or to a "reeducation camp." The institutional press is largely free and unregulated and is generally subject less to the government's whim than to its own lapses of judgment and its insatiable drive for profits.

At least in its basic outlines, modern American law is quite protective of free speech. Persons who can afford most means of communication (other than radio and television) are generally free to acquire or use them. However, there is an elaborate regulatory apparatus for the distribution of broadcast franchises.[1] Content-based regulation of the broadcast media is still permissible under some circumstances,[2] although such censorship is more likely to be directed at sexually explicit expression than anything else. Outside of the broadcast media, content-based restrictions are strongly frowned upon,[3] but such restrictions are permitted to regulate obscenity and so-called fighting words—words that by their very nature tend to provoke an immediate breach of the peace.[4] Pornography involving minors is subject to regulation regardless of whether it would be legally obscene if it involved adult actors.[5] Political criticism (at least material not viewed as falling into one of the previous categories of regulated speech) receives strong protection. Even advocacy of lawless activity is protected unless it is directed toward inciting imminent lawless action and is likely to produce such action.[6] Criticisms of public officials or other figures in the public eye cannot be punished either civilly or criminally unless such statements are knowingly false or made with reckless disregard of their falsity.[7] Statements of opinion about such public figures are absolutely protected from liability for defamation unless they imply false statements of fact that are known to be false or made with reckless disregard of their falsity.[8] Government officials are generally not permitted to impose prior restraints on speech based upon its actual or supposed content and must instead rely on subsequent civil actions for libel.[9] However, prior restraints are permitted for sexually oriented films to determine their obscenity, as long as such determinations are made promptly and with adequate opportunity for judicial review.[10]

There is perhaps no better symbol of the American commitment to free speech than two recent cases in which the United States Supreme Court held that burning the American flag as a form of political protest was constitutionally protected under the guarantee of free speech embodied in the First Amendment to the U.S. Constitution. The two cases, *Texas* v. *Johnson*[11] and *United States* v. *Eichmann*,[12] were decided by a 5-4 margin in the U.S. Supreme Court. The first case, *Texas* v. *Johnson,* struck down a Texas statute that prohibited desecration of a "venerated object."[13] The decision created great controversy throughout the country. Immediate calls were made to amend the Constitution to reverse the decision. The Democratic Party, which has traditionally had stronger ties to civil liberties issues and which controlled both houses of Congress, tried to slow the momentum for amendment by offering a federal flag-burning statute that party leaders claimed addressed the deficiencies of the Texas statute in *Johnson.* After the Supreme Court struck this law down in the second case, *United States* v. *Eichmann,* the Congress took a formal vote on amendment. The proposal gained a majority in Congress, but failed to win the two-thirds vote necessary to submit the measure to the states for ratification.

The most interesting feature of the flag-burning cases is not that the antiregulation forces so narrowly won. Nor is it unusual that most Americans would react to flag burning viscerally as a threat to their sense of national dignity. Rather, it is an indication of the degree to which the values of free speech have been assimilated in American culture that in almost no other country would the question of whether a nation may prohibit the burning of its flag even be thought a close one. The libertarian strain in American thought is also clear from the way the debate was carried on, both in the arguments of the opponents and the proponents of regulation of flag burning. Those who supported the constitutionality of prohibitions on flag burning and a flag-burning amendment did not argue that highly offensive forms of political dissent could be regulated simply because of their extremely offensive character. Rather, they argued that the country's flag was a special case—a unique national symbol for which a special exception could and should be carved out. Opponents of the constitutionality of regulation and of the flag-burning amendment countered that this one exception would destroy the entire edifice of free speech in America: Once the simplicity of the principle of free speech was altered by exceptions, it would be easier to create new exceptions in the future. It is likely that from the standpoint of most other countries, the latter argument would have seemed implausible if not ridiculous, and the terms of the entire debate heavily weighted in favor of the opponents of regulation.

As the flag-burning cases suggest, the American ideal of freedom of speech is basically libertarian, even if the actual system of regulation has never been truly libertarian at all. The American conception of free speech is based on a notion of government *noninterference* with individual liberty, whether this principle is in fact honored in the breach or in the observance. Thus, even when federal and state legislatures pass statutes regulating speech, they work on the assumption that passing statutes involves regulation of speech, that not passing statutes involves nonregulation, and that the latter is more protective of individual liberty. This equation of government inaction with individual liberty is what I mean by the libertarian ideal in American free-speech law. When coupled with the ingrained American distrust of regulation in general and regulation of free speech in particular, the result is a relatively unregulated sphere that is thought to be highly protective of individual liberty.

One can divide criticisms of the American system of free expression into two basic types. First are criticisms that American free speech has not lived up to its libertarian ideals. A good example of this perspective would be that content-based regulation of broadcasting is incompatible with a robust system of free expression.[14] The other type of criticism is somewhat more complicated; it involves the view that the libertarian association of government inaction with individual liberty is flawed and incomplete. The discussion that follows focuses on both elements. I discuss areas in which there is too much regulation of speech, using regulation in the sense of the libertarian model. However, I also focus on ways in which American experience has demonstrated that the libertarian model is too simplistic. In other words, I describe how the assumption that the government is not "interfering" with freedom of expression when it does not pass statutes specifically touching on speech inevitably produces a number of defects in a system of free expression. This second type of criticism will probably raise little concern among human rights activists in countries where the government has not abstained from the grossest forms of political censorship and where intimidation, arrest, and even torture and assassination of dissidents are still commonplace. One might well argue that from the standpoint of these regimes, complaints about the libertarian model are mere cavils. At the same time, countries seeking to emulate American constitutional freedoms should be well aware of the costs of a libertarian model as they have developed in this country. As I argue, the defects of the libertarian model may have deleterious consequences for the health of American democracy itself.

Governmental Control of Speech Through Content-Neutral Regulation

Although Americans generally believe they have considerable freedom to speak whenever and wherever they wish, federal and state governments in fact regulate speech extensively. They do so by restricting access to government property for expression and by imposing content-neutral time, place, and manner restrictions on those places where expression is permitted. Any protester who has been arrested for failing to obtain a demonstration permit quickly learns that the right of free speech is fraught with many unexpected regulatory hurdles. Indeed, most Americans are quite unaware of the remarkable degree to which spontaneous demonstrations against government policies are effectively restricted by traffic laws, permit requirements, parade insurance regulations, and other elements of municipal bureaucracy.

In most cases, American free-speech law makes a distinction between content-based regulations and time, place, and manner regulations. Government officials are given much greater latitude to restrict expressive conduct in the latter case than in the former. The flag-burning cases are a good example of this. The Supreme Court struck down the Texas statute in *Johnson* because it believed Texas wished to punish Johnson for actions that conveyed a message of disrespect for the American flag. However, there would have been no constitutional barrier had Texas prosecuted Johnson for destroying the property of the government or that of another private individual. This would have been viewed as a content-neutral restriction on expression, designed to prevent harms unrelated to the content of the message conveyed. In fact, the *Johnson* case involved the burning of a flag that had been stolen from a government building. Clearly Johnson could have been convicted of destruction of government property, and there would have been no constitutional impediment to his punishment under such a statute. The fact that Texas chose to prosecute him instead for desecrating a venerated object, regardless of its ownership, supported the Court's claim that the prosecution stemmed from disagreement with Johnson's message and the strong emotional effect his act had on his audience rather than the protection of property or public safety. Thus, fears that the right protected in *Johnson* also would permit protesters to deface the Washington Monument are quite unfounded. The government has strong content-neutral reasons for protecting the integrity of government buildings and other government property, and content-neutral statutes preventing their destruction are clearly constitutional.

Nevertheless, even content-neutral restrictions on speech may lead to inappropriate degrees of censorship. A major difficulty stems from the fact that the U.S. Supreme Court has directed lower courts to engage in increasingly less judicial scrutiny of content-neutral restrictions on speech or restrictions of access to government property for expressive purposes. Although courts have recognized that traditional public forums like streets and parks must remain open for public demonstrations, they have been increasingly willing in recent years to allow the government to close off virtually any other type of government property as a public forum for expressive conduct.[15] Public demonstrations and less disruptive forms of protest (for example, the distribution of literature) often are more effective on government property other than in streets and parks. For example, protesters might wish to engage in a silent vigil in a segregated library,[16] gather outside a public prison to protest a politically motivated arrest,[17] or distribute literature in a public airport or a public hospital lobby.[18] Of course, the government should always be allowed to show that expressive conduct would interfere with the lawful purposes for which the property is dedicated. Loud protests in a hospital lobby might interfere with the work of health care, for example. But if the government could not show a serious incompatibility with these or other forms of political expression—for example, silent vigils or the distribution of handbills—it should be required to provide access, subject always to reasonable restrictions on time, place, and manner.

However, American courts, led by the Supreme Court, have increasingly rejected such an approach in recent years. Instead, they have allowed governmental officials merely to state that they do not consider government property a public forum and thus an appropriate place to permit public protest of any kind.[19] This approach leaves great discretion in the hands of public officials and leads to fewer and fewer outlets for protest. Moreover, even in places designated as public forums, courts in the United States have increasingly required government officials to show only that their regulations of time, place, and manner have some rational purpose that is not related to the content of speech. They have not required government officials to show that their regulations are no more restrictive of speech than is necessary to achieve legitimate governmental purposes.[20]

One might wonder why these developments pose a significant problem for free speech, as long as restrictions and regulations of speech on government property are content-neutral. The reason is that restrictions and regulations that reduce the total amount of expression in society on a content-neutral basis can sometimes be just as harmful as those that single out particular groups or ideas. Moreover, content-neutral regulations rarely have the same impact on all ideas. Usually restrictions on access to streets, parks, and other government property affect those persons who cannot afford to purchase means of communication in the marketplace (print and broadcast advertising, for example) or whose views are sufficiently controversial or unpalatable that these individuals and groups will face great difficulty convincing others to sell them access. In other words, although content-neutral restrictions in theory affect everyone equally, in practice they affect poor people and unpopular or controversial groups more than any others.

Governmental Control of Speech Through Selective Subsidy

The preceding criticism of content-neutral regulation can be made purely on libertarian grounds. Nevertheless, the libertarian equation of individual liberty with government noninterference is itself ill-equipped for other problems that arise in the modern regulatory and welfare state. Much governmental intervention today does not arise from direct restrictions on conduct. Rather, government affects and controls our lives through subsidies, spending grants, licenses and tax benefits, and other forms of governmental largess. Governments may then attempt to withdraw these subsidies unless individuals restrict their expressive rights or exercise them in particular ways that are to the government's liking. If failures to subsidize are seen as mere government inaction, then such selective funding policies would not be considered as censorship at all. The difficulty with this conclusion is that American life has become increasingly dependent upon these forms of subsidies, and they can no longer be seen merely as privileges that the government may withdraw for any reason. Thus, even if the government is not required to engage in certain types of subsidy programs, one might argue it may not selectively withdraw subsidies in such a way as to affect fundamental rights like speech. For example, in *Speiser* v. *Randall*,[21] the United States Supreme Court argued that California could not make property tax rebates for veterans contingent on their signing loyalty oaths. Even though California did not have to offer the rebates in the first place, it could not put veterans to the choice of taking the rebate or making a statement inconsistent with their consciences. In American constitutional law, the problem of when government may or may not modify behavior through selective subsidization is called the problem of unconstitutional conditions. It is one of the most perplexing and difficult areas of legal scholarship today—and one of the most important. Unless clear restraints are placed on the government's use of its fiscal powers, it may be able to achieve indirectly through selective subsidies what it could not achieve through direct regulation.

A particularly chilling example of the dangers of government power to censor through selective subsidy is the Supreme Court's recent decision in *Rust* v. *Sullivan*.[22] In 1988, the Reagan administration promulgated regulations providing that family planning clinics receiving federal funds could not counsel pregnant women about the possibility of abortion, mention the existence of abortion as an alternative to pregnancy, lobby in favor of more liberal abortion laws, disseminate proabortion information, or engage in any activity designed to make abortions easier to obtain. Moreover, such funded clinics were also required to refer all pregnant women to prenatal care services and forbidden from referring a pregnant woman to an abortion provider, even if the woman specifically requested such a referral. If asked about abortion, health-care providers were required to state that they did not consider abortion an appropriate method of family planning and, therefore, did not counsel or refer patients for abortions.

Doctors and other health-care providers have strongly criticized these regulations for intervening in their relationships with their patients. They have argued that forcing doctors to withhold relevant therapeutic information and substitute a statement disapproving of abortion forces them to breach ethical duties to their patients. If Congress directly prohibited private doctors or family-planning clinics from discussing these issues, or if it required them to make statements disapproving of abortion, few would doubt that serious free-speech concerns would arise—indeed, most scholars would consider such regulations blatantly unconstitutional. Nevertheless, in the *Rust* 5-4 decision, the Supreme Court held that because private health-care providers were not required to accept federal funds, the regulations on speech about abortion were constitutional.

It seems clear that the decision in *Rust* rested in part on the undisguised hostility of five members of the Supreme Court to *Roe* v. *Wade*,[23] the case that made constitutional the right of abortion in America. Nevertheless, the implications of *Rust* potentially extend much further than speech about abortion. If the government can constitutionally withdraw grants, licenses, tax subsidies, and other forms of government benefits, which most Americans have come to depend on, from those individuals who do not parrot the government's preferred political beliefs or who do not remain silent about information the government would not like others to hear, the First Amendment and the principles for which it stands are indeed threatened. In this light, *Rust* portends new possibilities for government control of free expression—not with direct regulation but with threats disguised as offers, penalties disguised as subsidies, and sticks disguised as carrots.

Perhaps the most noteworthy example of the problem of unconstitutional conditions in recent times is the current controversy surrounding the National Endowment for the Arts (NEA), which awards funding to promising artists and musicians. In the past few years, members of Congress have objected to funding of works with homoerotic or other themes they find offensive, arguing that the government should not be in the business of subsidizing such art. They have further argued that withdrawal of funds to art with homoerotic themes or other content they find objectionable does not constitute censorship, because the government has no obligation to fund art in the first place.

Unlike in *Rust,* the NEA controversy is not a pure problem of unconstitutional conditions because it intersects with another very difficult issue in modern free-speech theory—the problem of the government as speaker.[24] When the government dedicates its property as a public forum, it may not make content-based distinctions. However, when the government itself acts as a speaker—for example, when it commissions a presidential monument or music for an inaugural concert—it may make content-based judgments just as any other speaker can. One might view the NEA controversy merely as an uncontroversial question of government speech: The government offers a certain amount of money to create interesting artistic works and, as any connoisseur or patron is entitled to do, is permitted to select those it likes from those it does not. Nevertheless, the system of government funding for the arts is partly analogous to the government's dedication of its property as a public forum, albeit one limited to artistic expression. The government, believing that it is important to promote the arts, sets a certain amount of money aside to support artistic projects of various types. Once it has so designated this money, it may not then withdraw support for artists simply because their work offends particular sensibilities or is politically controversial. What complicates the NEA controversy even further is that even under this scenario, the government does engage in at least one form of content-based judgment—it delegates to a panel of experts decisions concerning artistic quality, which are inevitably content-based.

Nevertheless, not all forms of content-based decisionmaking raise equal dangers for free-speech values. It is one thing to delegate to a panel of experienced critics the question of which artistic works are meritorious, even if political and social issues cannot be eradicated from these debates. It is quite another thing to allow Congress to award and deny particular grants to make political points. The most sensible solution, then, appears to be one that offers the agency distributing the grants a large degree of control from content-based restrictions by Congress, but that nevertheless allows the agency to make its own content-based judgments of artistic merit. Although plausible, this solution does not fit easily into the forms of analysis provided by a libertarian conception of free speech. I suggest that this is so precisely because government speech and issues of unconstitutional conditions require a fundamentally different framework for analysis.

Private Censorship

Perhaps the most important blindness of the libertarian conception of free speech is the very premise that government inaction necessarily increases individual freedom. Often the government's decision to deregulate an area of social life simply relegates individuals to the vicissitudes of private power, which may be as onerous as that of the government and much less accountable because it is not democratically controllable. The history of the American experience with economic regulation is a good analogy. Laissez-faire policies in labor regulation in the late nineteenth century did not necessarily enhance the freedom of Americans. Rather, they left them at the mercy of increasingly powerful industrial organizations. One legacy of the Great Depression and the New Deal is the recognition that public welfare and public freedom are increased by prudent regulation of the private sphere in the public's interest. Even the partial return to freer markets in the 1980s did not undo the basic principles of the American regulatory state. Indeed, if anything, the current fiscal crisis brought on by the alarming lack of government oversight of savings and loans institutions during the Reagan era demonstrates that a careful mix of free markets with sensible regulatory measures is as important as ever to the nation's continued economic health.

In an assessment of the benefits and defects of the libertarian approach, it is important always to remember that what is generally called "nonregulation" or "deregulation" is also a regulatory choice. In the absence of any form of governmental intervention (i.e., no government at all), it is possible to speak of a truly nonregulated regime. But once the government begins the process of allocating property rights, contract rights, and other rights of individuals vis-à-vis each other, it has embarked upon a scheme of regulation. At this point, there are no unregulated regimes, only regimes with different forms of regulation. The question then becomes how to allocate public and private power so as to maximize human freedom and best serve human needs.

Thus, a system of regulation (which includes what is commonly called nonregulation) is a system that allocates both public and private power. When the government establishes the rights of individuals against itself, it simultaneously demarcates the rights of other individuals. Conversely, the line separating the competing rights of individuals is always a line drawn by government regulation. Thus, a system of private rights to speak and government rights to regulate speech is simultaneously a system of private rights to speak and to prevent others from speaking.

Strong protection of individual speech rights against the government does not eliminate all forms of censorship. Rather, it establishes an alternative system of private censorship in place of direct governmental censorship. Indeed, one of the most revealing ways to understand the American system of free speech is as a system of private censorship. Because the government stays out of the business of directly telling individuals what they can and cannot say, the most important censor in American life today is not government but private parties. Private parties can act as censors because they also have rights of freedom of speech and conscience and, more important, they possess economic rights to control various means of communication. To communicate effectively in America, it is increasingly important to have access to newspapers, radio, television, and all other forms of mass communication. However, access to such means of communication costs money. One needs money either to own the means of communication outright or to purchase access to it.

Thus, because of technological innovations, the right of free speech in this country has become increasingly tied to the rights of private property. Because property rights include the right to exclude others from use unless access is purchased, the system of economic rights is an important method by which private parties can keep other private parties from access to the media or other means of communication. For example, television networks can refuse to sell airtime to individuals with controversial views that might offend viewers and cut into ratings. Newspapers can refuse to run political advertisements. Advertisers can threaten to withdraw support from the media if they discuss controversial or offensive topics. Publishers can refuse to publish controversial or offensive manuscripts. It is too often forgotten that much of the censorship of the Joseph McCarthy era took place through acts of private parties. For example, the blacklisting of actors, writers, directors, and producers in Hollywood was the result of private employment decisions by powerful persons in the entertainment industry and not the product of direct government control.

Ironically, under a strictly libertarian conception of free-speech rights, none of the preceding situations involves either a violation of the constitutional right to free speech or unconstitutional censorship. In each case, the denial of access is not the result of direct governmental action but rather of economic rights created by the government and held by private parties. Private parties can wield these rights over others and prevent certain types of expressive conduct from occurring.

By defining censorship exclusively as government censorship, the proponent of the libertarian conception misses the many ways in which private parties can effectively hinder or even prevent widespread dissemination of information or unpopular political views. In addition, the system of so-called government nonregulation actually ties free-speech rights to the rights of private property. If these rights are heavily skewed in a country, as they are in America, there is a strong potential for a comparable skewing of the rights of effective expression. To vary Anatole France's famous aphorism slightly, rich and poor alike are free to purchase thirty-second spots on prime-time television.

The analysis here is hardly novel; its basic contours were worked out by the analytical jurist Wesley Hohfeld at the beginning of this century.[25] However, they have only rarely been applied to the problems of speech.[26] Hohfeld's argument is that a system of rights that creates immunities for some persons simultaneously creates exposures for others. Thus, in any system of rights between the government and private individuals on the one hand, or between private individuals on the other, there will be a set of corresponding and interlocking legal relations. Expanding on Hohfeld's work, Duncan Kennedy and Frank Michelman have postulated a "law of conservation of exposures" in systems of legal rights.[27] Their law of conservation of exposures promises that no matter how legal rights are allocated, exposures to harm from the actions of others cannot be eliminated, for they are the concomitant of any system of rights. In the realm of free expression, this means simply that any system of free expression will also be a system of censorship. The only question is the extent to which the censorship will be exercised by governmental actors rather than by private parties. Therefore, the task should be to discover the mix of public and private power that best accommodates human freedom. If the power of censorship must rest somewhere, the goal should be to choose the mix that does the least damage and the most good. There is no reason to expect that the maximally free solution is one that eliminates government power as much as possible and leaves individuals most at the liberty of their fellow citizens. Just as history teaches that a sensible mix of that form of regulation called "free markets" and other regulatory regimes best furthers human freedom, so too is some mixture of public and private censorial power likely to produce the best results in the area of freedom of expression.

All things being equal, it is usually better to leave the power of censorship in private hands because the power of government is so large and so concentrated and because governments have long histories of abusing the power of censorship. Nevertheless, there may be situations in which private concentrations of power are so great and so pervasive that private censorship inhibits free speech just as much or even more than government censorship would. Concentrated private economic power may so dominate debate that it skews the democratic process. In such cases, disproportionate private power can threaten the integrity of the political system itself. These are the most appropriate cases for departing from the libertarian model.

Nevertheless, in ameliorating a system of private censorship, governments need not simply reinstitute their forms of censorship. Governments can counteract the problems produced by unequal distributions of property by subsidizing access to means of communication or by providing forums for mass communication that are open to all or whose ownership is shifted on a rotating basis. Redistributional measures such as these can increase opportunities for effective speech without forcing particular individuals or business organizations to bear a disproportionate share of the costs.

The preceding comments are an equality critique of free-speech doctrine. Nor should this be surprising. Once the formal liberty of speech has been guaranteed, the greatest problems concern not liberty but equality. Significant inequalities in the effective ability to communicate between rich and poor, or between groups in the political center and those with dissenting views, ultimately call into question the extent to which substantive liberty has been truly guaranteed. These problems are serious, but it is always important to keep them in perspective; they pale in comparison to the denials of even a formal liberty to speak that the populace must suffer in other countries. The current problems in the United States are in an important sense the product of American success in guaranteeing basic formal liberties of conscience and political participation.

Regulation of Racist and Sexist Speech

Problems of equality intersect with free speech in another way. Expressive conduct can conflict with the goal of eradicating discrimination against women and ethnic minorities. This is not a claim of inequality of access to means of communication. Rather, it is a claim that what passes for free speech is actually the furtherance of sexism or racism and therefore should not be protected. It is worth noting in this light that many Western democracies have laws restricting or prohibiting group vilification based on ethnicity or race. Although the Supreme Court upheld a group libel statute in 1952,[28] it is likely that such statutes would be thought to violate the First Amendment, or at least raise serious constitutional concerns. Thus, the conflict between racial equality and free speech in America, as in the case of so many other important issues, has become one of constitutional proportions.

The conflict between free speech and egalitarian principles has arisen in a number of contexts in recent years. An important example concerns employment law. When private employers discriminate against minorities and women, they often do so through speech. In some cases, no serious problem is presented. When an employer says "I'm not hiring X because he is black," the mere fact that the employer has discriminated by speaking does not immunize the act of discrimination. A difficulty arises because an important way employers can discriminate against workers is through the creation of a "hostile environment." The employer and coworkers may leave insulting messages for the worker, place racist posters or pornographic magazines around the workplace, and engage in a system of sexual and racial harassment and abuse. Some of these acts outside the workplace might be considered protected speech, but in the workplace, they are the means by which employment discrimination is carried out. An analogy is that false statements spoken in some contexts are fully protected by the Constitution; in other contexts, they constitute fraud or perjury and can be criminally punished.

Racist and sexist speech in the workplace should also be treated differently from speech outside the workplace, because the nature of the workplace restricts how employees can respond to a hostile work environment. In the case of offensive speech in ordinary public places, individuals are free to avert their eyes or go to another place. However, avoidance of the workplace is not a viable solution for most employees. In the language of First Amendment doctrine, employees subjected to hostile work environments are a captive audience. Thus, because of the special nature of the workplace, racial and sexual harassment should enjoy no more First Amendment protection than the speech that occurs in securities fraud or perjury.

When the context is not the workplace, the problems of regulating racist and sexist speech become increasingly difficult. One of the most interesting political alliances of recent years is that between religious fundamentalists and radical feminists, both of whom wish to enforce stronger regulations of sexually explicit movies and books. However, the feminist opposition to pornography is not based on concerns about family values or a desire to preserve social or religious orthodoxy. Their argument is that pornography, especially violent pornography, contributes to the subordination of women. This subordination occurs in three ways. First, women who perform in pornographic productions are subjected to physical and emotional abuse so that their performances are coerced. Second, pornography contributes to a general system of patriarchy in which women are viewed as sexual objects whose primary purpose is to serve men's sexual pleasure. Pornography, in other words, reinforces gender roles that contribute to women's physical, political, and economic subordination. Third, because pornography convinces men that women are sexual objects who desire and deserve sexual subordination, it leads men to ignore or devalue what women have to say. In the words of feminist theory, pornography silences women. It makes counterspeech by women ineffective because it produces a world in which women's views are not taken seriously.

In recent years, the feminist critique of pornography has generated considerable controversy. Some feminists who oppose pornography have, nevertheless, also opposed increased legal prohibitions against pornography because of concerns about civil liberties. They have instead used their own free-speech rights to picket pornographic cinemas and bookstores and to raise the public's awareness of the dangers of pornography. This strategy is a classic example of how a system of free-speech rights also works as a system of private censorship. Through the use of private power (itself constitutionally protected), feminists seek to remove pornographic materials from bookshelves and movie theaters or to persuade people not to read or view the materials.

Other feminists have concluded that political protest, economic coercion, and moral suasion will be ineffective and believe direct legal regulation of pornography is necessary. Instead of using only private power to control pornography, they seek to employ public power as well.[29] In response to their lobbying efforts, the city of Indianapolis passed an ordinance that permitted civil lawsuits against persons who publish portrayals of women in sexually submissive situations or present women as objects to be beaten, tortured, or physically abused. A federal court of appeals struck down this statute as unconstitutional under the First Amendment, and this opinion was summarily affirmed by the United States Supreme Court.[30]

From one perspective, the feminist argument for increased civil and criminal regulation of pornography flounders on the same shoals as the argument for criminalizing the burning of the American flag. It is clearly content-based regulation that attempts to prevent harms caused by the persuasive, cognitive, and emotional effects the prohibited expression produces. One may object to this comparison on the grounds that, unlike flag burning, pornography helps create sexual roles and sustain them on a societywide scale. The major difficulty with this argument is that pornography (defined in a conventional sense as including X-rated movies, but not mainstream cinema) is probably only the tip of the iceberg. It is likely that the entire culture of this country—including perfume ads, television, movies, music, and books—creates and sustains the image of women as sexual objects. Given that few men and women in this country view X-rated movies and books, but that most are inundated with sexist messages every day, the systemic argument may prove unconvincing unless one is equally committed to prohibiting a massive amount of everyday expression as well.

The feminist argument might be strengthened in a number of ways. It might limit its concerns to protecting women who appear in pornographic films and draw the analogy to workplace regulations that prevent overreaching by employers and that keep workers from working in unsafe environments or taking hazardous job assignments. It might narrow its focus from regulation of all forms of sexual objectification of women to specific restrictions on violent pornography. Nevertheless, even in this case, it would be important to demonstrate that the combinations of violence and sex widely viewed on mainstream television and cinema are less likely to generate similar violent behavior against women than is the violent pornography viewed by a small fraction of the citizenry.

The recent increase in reported incidents of racial harassment on college campuses has given rise to calls for university policies to ban racial harassment as well as racist speech on campus. It is clear that harassment in the form of destruction of property and physical abuse presents no constitutional difficulties; universities may discipline such actions, at least in the rare instances when the persons involved can be located and their involvement proved. However, students have also asked for regulation of taunting, name calling, and other acts that do not involve physical abuse of persons or destruction of property. It is possible (and unfortunate) that students now demand restrictions on such speech precisely because persons who engage in racist or sexist taunts are more easily identified than vandals and thugs, who currently terrorize students but who generally escape identification and thus punishment.

Nevertheless, university policies regulating racist and sexist speech raise a number of difficult First Amendment issues that are not involved in the regulation of vandalism and physical abuse. One must first distinguish state institutions from private institutions—only the former are legally subject to First Amendment controls over state regulation. This distinction is yet another example of how the American system of free expression simultaneously establishes and protects a system of private censorship. In theory at least, private educational institutions may exercise the right of private censorship guaranteed by the American system of free speech with impunity. Nevertheless, debates about racial harassment at private universities have largely tracked those at public universities because both types of institutions as universities share a commitment to the free exchange of ideas.

The types of strategies employed at public universities have varied widely. The University of Michigan enacted a fairly broad policy, which prohibited remarks that stigmatized or denigrated members of a considerable variety of groups, extending not only to blacks, women, and gays, but even to veterans of the Vietnam War. A federal district court struck down this regulation as overbroad and unduly vague.[31] It is likely that most federal courts would find student expression protected even if it stigmatized or denigrated members of a particular religious or ethnic minority on the grounds that merely offensive speech, without more, is not subject to regulation. Indeed, in his opinion in the *Eichmann* flag-burning case, Justice Brennan seemed to go out of his way to announce that even if "desecration of the flag is deeply offensive to many . . . the same might be said of virulent ethnic and religious epithets" and that a "bedrock principle underlying the First Amendment . . . is that the government may not prohibit the expression of any idea simply because society finds the idea itself offensive or disagreeable."[32]

Given this background, university officials have offered a number of alternative theories for regulation of verbal racial harassment. One approach is to make use of the "fighting words" doctrine in First Amendment law and argue that racial epithets can be punished if they are of the kind that would provoke an immediate breach of the peace. There are two difficulties with this approach: First, the flag-burning cases teach that the government may not assume a priori that "an audience that takes serious offense at particular expression is necessarily likely to disturb the peace."[33] Thus, content-based classifications of fighting words are unlikely to be held constitutional after *Texas* v. *Johnson* and *United States* v. *Eichmann*. A second difficulty is that the fighting-words doctrine does not really grapple with the problem of harassment itself. It assumes that racial, sexist, or homophobic epithets will cause people to fight. However, racial minorities, women, and gays are just as likely to shrink from a challenge offered by a group of rowdy students. Indeed, their major complaint is that such harassment makes them feel isolated, unwanted, and powerless. Of course, one can redefine "fighting words" to include situations in which harassment silences or humiliates victims rather than provokes them to open combat. However, this semantic solution does not solve the constitutional difficulty, for now the university may no longer make use of the fighting-words doctrine to justify its regulations.

Another approach in the law to the problem of racial harassment is to employ the tort of intentional infliction of emotional distress. The University of Texas policy allows for discipline of racial epithets directed at specific individuals that are intended to produce and do produce severe emotional distress. Because the Texas policy is based on an existing tort cause of action, there is a good chance that it is constitutional. Nevertheless, precisely because it is restricted to a very narrow set of situations, it is unlikely to cover many situations of racial harassment. For example, if individuals who engage in racial harassment state they did not understand that racist epithets are deeply offensive and likely to cause severe emotional distress (for example, if they viewed their comments as witty or as a joke), or if they do not direct them to a particular individual, their expressions may not be covered by the policy. Moreover, by its own terms, the Texas policy does not deal with harassment based on sex or sexual orientation.

"Political Correctness" and the Problem of Private Power

The demand for regulation of sexist and racist speech on college campuses is often linked with a complaint from a quite different part of the political spectrum. Persons within and outside the university community have complained that because of concerns about racism and sexism on college campuses, a pall of orthodoxy has descended on academic discussions. It is claimed that students, faculty, and administrators are afraid to discuss issues that might show them to be insensitive to egalitarian positions because they will be severely criticized by other students. This phenomenon has been called the enforcement of "political correctness." Many faculty members report horror stories of conversations and lectures being taken out of context by radical students who demand public apologies or even censure and discipline by university administrators. In language strikingly similar to that of antipornography feminists, conservative student groups now claim they are silenced by a left-wing consensus about issues of race, sex, and sexual orientation.

One must treat claims of a left-wing consensus on college campuses with some skepticism. For one thing, they are somewhat inconsistent with the voting patterns of eighteen- to twenty-five-year-olds in the past decade, patterns that have helped place both Ronald Reagan and George Bush in the White House. It is perhaps more correct to say that the so-called pall of orthodoxy complained of is the result of a small group of students who are quite willing to complain loudly against any threat, real or perceived, to their egalitarian vision. These students are not strongly resisted by academics who themselves tend to be much more liberal than the political mainstream and are, therefore, particularly sensitive to accusations of insensitivity.

Whether the actual phenomenon is overstated or not, the furor over political correctness on university campuses is an excellent example of the American system of private censorship at work. Moreover, it produces theoretical difficulties for both the Left and Right sides of the political spectrum and suggests ways in which both sides can learn something from the other's concerns. To the extent that political correctness is enforced on college campuses, it is enforced through acts of private power. Students shun or criticize faculty, administrators, and other students who make remarks deemed insufficiently sensitive. Yet all of these acts of complaint, protest, and shunning are protected acts of speech, and the atmosphere created by their exercise is, ironically, an atmosphere created and sustained by rights of free speech. Nevertheless, it is important to recall that free-speech rights sustain a system of private censorship that operates both within *and* without the academy. Thus, the advertiser who withdraws support from a controversial television program and the campus radical who decries fellow students' insensitivity have more in common than either would like to recognize.

Thus, the orthodoxy in the academy that conservatives now complain of is merely a miniature of the system of private censorship that operates in mainstream American political culture. It is perceived as an undesirable orthodoxy only because the political views enforced are different from those in the mainstream, which are no less orthodox but considerably more conservative. By studying the cultural phenomenon called "political correctness," we can begin to understand generally the analogous phenomenon in American culture. The mainstream imposes—and always has imposed—its standards of political correctness outside the academy, in diverse ways ranging from small group social interaction to large-scale economic clout. Indeed, one can understand the attacks on political correctness launched from outside the academy as in part manifesting a deep hostility toward the only public institution that has resisted the rightward drift of American politics in the last two decades and has become a haven for radicals and dissenters. From this perspective, it is quite unclear which group—the proponents or the opponents of the left-wing academy—are engaging in inappropriate bullying tactics.

It follows from this analysis that it is hardly fair for political conservatives to defend the system of private censorship in the country as a whole and then complain about a different system of private censorship within the limited bastions of the academy. If conservatives feel that the deck is stacked against them in universities and that they are afraid to make provocative and challenging statements against the status quo for fear of social disapproval by their peers, they should consider transferring these observations to mainstream discourse in America, because they have just produced an excellent portrait of what it is like to be a member of a dissenting group or a holder of unpopular views in mainstream America. Perhaps, if they understand what it is like to be silenced in a relatively minor area of social life, they will have increased sympathy for claims by women and minorities that they are silenced in the larger world outside the academy.

Nevertheless, this analysis of private censorship has equal and opposite difficulties for theorists on the Left side of the political spectrum. It will do no good for radical students to complain that mainstream thought acts to enforce political hegemony through private censorship if they too seek to control the political climate on campuses through acts of private power. Political radicals, as well as feminists and members of minority groups who seek social change, must always remember that a system of private censorship is not only potentially debilitating but also potentially empowering. The purpose of boycotts, protests, and other forms of moral and political suasion is to use private power to cause others to modify their beliefs and behavior. If methods of private censorship were curtailed generally, the most effective forms of activity available to dissenting groups would also be curtailed. Thus, one cannot attack the system of private censorship in this country simply because it is private, powerful, and effective. Grants of the right of private censorship, ironically, are the flip side of grants of political freedom. One must rather criticize particular instances of the private power to censor as fundamentally unfair or as destructive of democratic institutions. Moreover, it is not enough to say that existing institutions are fundamentally unfair or undemocratic simply because one's views do not carry the day. Rather, one must make a much more nuanced claim about substantive liberty that rests on guarantees of effective communication—but not necessarily guarantees of success.

Conclusion

It should now be clear why this chapter is titled as it is. Free speech and censorship must always exist together as a system. To create one is simultaneously to create the other in a different aspect of social life. Therefore, it is unrealistic to think that one can create an absolute freedom of speech in both public and private spheres. Protection of free-speech rights is always an allocation of public and private power to control what is said and under what conditions. The great success of American free-speech law has been its recognition of the dangers of public censorship. Its achievements in this respect are worthy of pride. Nevertheless, the United States cannot rest content with past accomplishments. It has won this victory only at the cost of ignoring the issue of private power. The challenge for American free speech in the next century will be to recognize the dangers posed by private as well as public censorship—and at the same time to recognize that the two are, and always must be, inextricably intertwined.

Notes

My thanks to Doug Laycock, Sanford Levinson, and Scot Powe for their comments on an earlier draft of this chapter.

1. Federal Communications Act of 1934, 47 U.S.C. § 151 et seq.
2. *FCC* v. *Pacifica Foundation*, 438 U.S 726 (1978).
3. *Boos* v. *Barry*, S. Ct. 1157 (1988).
4. *Chaplinsky* v. *New Hampshire*, 315 U.S. 568 (1942).
5. *New York* v. Ferber, 458 U.S. 747 (1982).
6. *Brandenburg* v. *Ohio*, 395 U.S. 444 (1969).
7. *New York Times Co.* v. *Sullivan*, 376 U.S. 254 (1964); *Curtis Publishing Co.* v. *Butts*, 388 U.S. 130 (1967); *Gertz* v. *Robert Welch, Inc.*, 418 U.S. 323 (1974).
8. *Milkovich* v. *Lorrain Journal Co.*, 110 S. Ct. 2695 (1990).
9. *Near* v. *Minnesota*, 283 U.S. 697 (1931).
10. *Freedman* v. *Maryland*, 380 U.S. 51 (1965).
11. *Texas* v. *Johnson*, 109 S. Ct. 2533 (1989).
12. *United States* v. *Eichmann*, 110 S. Ct. 2404 (1990).
13. 109 S. Ct. at 2537.
14. Lucas A. Powe, Jr., *American Broadcasting and the First Amendment* (Berkeley: Uniersity of California Press, 1987).
15. E.g., *Perry Educational Association* v. *Perry Local Educators Association*, 460 U.S. 37 (1983); *Cornelius* v. *NAACP Legal Defense and Education Fund, Inc.*, 437 U.S. 788 (1985).
16. *Brown* v. *Louisiana*, U.S. 131 (1966).
17. See *Adderley* v. *Florida*, 385 U.S. 39 (1966)
18. *Board of Airport Commissioners of Los Angeles* v. *Jews for Jesus, Inc.*, 482 U.S. 569 (1987).

19. *Perry Educational Association* v. *Perry Local Educators Association,* 460 U.S. 37 (1983); *Cornelius* v. *NAACP Legal Defense and Education Fund, Inc.,* 437 U.S. 788 (1985).

20. *Ward* v. *Rock Against Racism,* 109 S. Ct. 2746 (1989).

21. *Speiser* v. *Randall,* 357 U.S. 513 (1958).

22. *Rust* v. *Sullivan,* 1991 Lexis 2980 (May 23, 1991).

23. 410 U.S. 113 (1973).

24. On the problem generally, see Mark Yudof, *When Government Speaks: Politics, Law, and Government Expression in America* (Berkeley: University of California, 1983).

25. Wesley Newcomb Hohfeld, "Some Fundamental Legal Conceptions as Applied to Judicial Decisionmaking," *Yale Law Journal,* Vol. 23 (1913), pp. 16–59.

26. For a fuller discussion, see J. M. Balkin, "Some Realism About Pluralism: Legal Realist Approaches to the First Amendment," *Duke Law Journal,* Vol. 1990 (1990), pp. 375–430.

27. Duncan M. Kennedy and Frank Michelman, "Are Contract and Property Efficient?" *Hofstra Law Review,* Vol. 8 (1980), pp. 711–770.

28. *Beauharnais* v. *Illinois,* 343 U.S. 250 (1952).

29. See Catharine A. MacKinnon, *Feminism Unmodified: Discourses on Life and Law* (Cambridge, MA: Harvard University Press, 1987).

30. *American Booksellers Association* v. *Hudnut,* 771 F.2d 323 (7th Cir. 1985), *affirmed* 475 U.S. 1001 (1986).

31. *Doe* v. *University of Michigan,* 721 F. Supp. 852 (E.D. Mich. 1989).

32. *United States* v. *Eichmann,* 110 S. Ct. at 2410.

33. *Texas* v. *Johnson,* 109 S. Ct. at 2541.

11

Censorship in Israel

Gary J. Jacobsohn

The unique features of the constitutional system of Israel must serve as the point of departure for any examination of that country's experience with censorship. Foremost among these is the absence of a formal, comprehensive written constitution (or any document, for that matter) that includes explicit guarantees against infringements of free speech. This constitutional reality is a reflection of the Israeli political culture; indeed, the same factors that explain the absence of a formal constitution have also shaped the nation's policies on censorship. The most obvious of these is the unique security situation existing in Israel since the inception of the state, but nearly as important (and perhaps more theoretically interesting)is the country's complex approach to democratic political development. Thus, it is obvious that a country in a perpetual state of war with its neighbors will develop positions on censorship that differ in significant ways from those of comparable nations that are not in a confrontational position. Perhaps less clear are the contrasting implications for censorship that flow from alternative conceptions of democratic politics, and it is this point that is the principal concern of this chapter.

Constitutional Considerations

The absence of a written constitution has been a perennial concern in Israeli politics, one that in recent years has been the occasion for mass demonstrations. Those seeking constitutional reform inevitably appeal to Israel's Declaration of Independence, which contains a specific commitment to "a Constitution to be drawn up by the Constituent Assembly." Resistance to the immediate adoption of such a document quickly emerged; however, the effort was postponed in favor of a Knesset-passed compromise resolution that prescribes a process of incremental accumulation of individual chapters—or basic laws—that when terminated will together form the state constitution. Known as the Harari Resolution, this vaguely worded legislation left unclear the status of the basic laws, just as it was silent about a timetable for completion of the constitution.[1] As a result, there exists in Israel what can perhaps best be described as an evolving constitution—an incremental series of basic laws (to date nine such laws have been designated by the Knesset)—that would appear to possess superior status to ordinary law but that coexist uneasily with the Israeli practice of parliamentary supremacy.[2] Conspicuously lacking in this list of basic laws are two items of special importance to censorship policy—a bill of rights and a provision for the exercise of judicial review by the courts.

This is not to say that individual rights are left unprotected in Israel or that the judiciary is not a critical actor in their enforcement. Indeed, the urgency of passing a formal constitutional enumeration of rights is mitigated considerably by the success the Supreme Court has had in creating a "judicial bill of rights." This has been accomplished principally as a result of a determined policy of interpreting statutes in a manner consistent with an expansive view of individual liberties. Although the Court has been reluctant to challenge the lawmaking supremacy of the Knesset, it has become increasingly vigorous in reviewing the actions of those whose responsibility it is to administer the law. Just as the Israeli Declaration of Independence provides the major textual source for advocates of constitutional codification, it has also become the spirit behind the judicial defense of individual rights. As one of the present justices has expressed it, in the face of statutory language that is ambiguous or open-ended, the Court is expected to decide "according to the articles of faith of the nation, as these found expression in the Declaration of Independence."[3]

The most important precedent for this view is also arguably the most significant decision ever handed down by the Israeli Supreme Court, the censorship case of *Kol Ha'am* v. *Minister of Interior*. It was in this landmark decision that the Court, speaking through Justice Shimon Agranat, cited the "well-known axiom that the law of a people must be studied in the light of its national way of life."[4] Inasmuch as that way of life was revealed in the language of the declaration, the document should, he argued, play a vital role in the constitutional law of Israel. In the case at hand, involving the minister of interior's decision to suspend two newspapers because their publication was likely to endanger the public peace, the Court ruled that this action violated the principle of freedom of expression, a principle intrinsic to the democratic regime envisioned in the Declaration of Independence.

But the Israeli way of life, as projected in the declaration, is a complex matter, as is quite apparent when one contrasts this document with its American counterpart. Unlike in the Israeli charter, the opening line in the U.S. document speaks of universalistic terms in the abstract language of natural right, whereas the Israeli declaration commences with a simple affirmation of particularity: "The land of Israel was the birthplace of the Jewish people." The American document mentions self-evident truths bearing directly upon the status of *individuals;* the Israeli declaration stipulates that "It is the self-evident right of the Jewish people to be a nation, like all other nations, in its own sovereign state." Among the freedoms it guarantees is that of "culture," and when it indicates what needs to be "safeguard[ed]," it refers to the "sanctity and inviolability of all religions." It also affirms the "social and political equality of all its citizens," but it is clear in a way that simply does not pertain in the American case—the rights of Israelis are in important and, perhaps, contradictory ways tied to the organic nature of the political community and its constituent parts. Thus, the state provides official recognition for limited cultural autonomy, a practice manifested most strikingly in the substantial authority granted the various religions over matters of personal status.[5] If the ethos of individualism provides definition to the American constitutional order, in Israel it is significantly muted by principled commitments to respect the integrity of communal life.

In *Kol Ha'am*, for example, Justice Agranat, though eloquently affirming the importance of free expression, was careful to establish the limits to its exercise. Predictably, "state security" was designated as the most important interest that could legitimately constrain free expression, but he also listed "the prevention of outrage to religious feelings,"[6] an interest that, as is discussed in connection with censorship policy, reveals the constitutional dynamic of a pluralist regime that acknowledges groups as more than collections of individuals but as units whose corporate identity carries with it certain claims upon the state for specific entitlement. The Israeli polity is composed of sharply divided populations— "others" to each other—whose coexistence within the state depends upon a mutual willingness to accept the realities of their differences. The extent of the differences vary in intensity from those that in time are likely to disappear (Ashkenazi and Sephardic Jews) to those that are in principle irreconcilable (secular and religious Jews) to those that in their tribal fury (Arab and Jew) transcend the normal ethnic rivalry present in most Western democracies. What seems clear is that unlike in the United States, where a respectable debate over the possibilities of a melting-pot society can still be heard, in Israel such talk possesses the quality of fantasy. As one observer has noted, "[T]here has been a de facto recognition of cultural pluralism."[7]

Understanding the actual practice of censorship in Israel requires bearing in mind three points from the preceding discussion: First, the Supreme Court has emerged as the primary institutional support for a free-speech principle that stands in opposition to the implementation of censorship. Second, the substance of the free-speech principle is affected by the historical and philosophical commitments of the polity, which means that the limits imposed by the Court and the Knesset are related to perceptions of the underlying pluralist reality of democratic politics in Israel. Third, the Court's power to impose its will upon those responsible for the various kinds of censorship is necessarily constrained by doubts concerning the legitimacy of its exercise of judicial review in the absence of a written constitution.

Patterns of Censorship

National Security

The law concerning censorship in Israel is suffused in irony. It is rooted in Britain's Palestine Mandate legislation that once was the special target of outrage and contempt from those in Palestine who had been engaged in the struggle to establish an independent Jewish state. That it should now be the principal legal basis for censoring expression designated a threat to the postindependence public order is a matter of great controversy and not a little soul-searching.

Two inheritances from the British Mandate are at the center of concern: the 1945 Defense Regulations and the 1933 Press Ordinance Law. Military censorship is traceable to the 1945 legislation, which includes this stipulation: "The censor may by order prohibit generally or specially the publishing of matters the publishing of which, in his opinion, would be, or be likely to be or become, prejudicial to the defense of Palestine or to the public safety or to public order."[8] Under the Mandate, the censor was appointed by the high commissioner, but since independence, the power to censor has been exercised under the authority of the minister of defense. Although the censoring power falls clearly within the jurisdiction of the military, the reference to public safety and public order in the authorizing language of the regulations suggests that the jurisdiction of the censor is not confined to the publication of sensitive military secrets. Concerns expressed very early on in the life of the state about the breadth of this power and its potential danger led to an effort to abandon the regulations in favor of a less sweeping censorship mandate that would be narrowly confined to security matters. This effort was dropped after the formalization of an agreement between a committee of editors (representing Israel Radio and the major Hebrew newspapers) and the minister of defense, in which they promised not to exercise the authority of the military censor against news carriers that were members of the committee.[9] This meant that an expansive censorship regime could continue against the nonestablishment press, a reality that in the present circumstances has had its greatest impact upon the Arabic-language newspapers in East Jerusalem. Indeed, these papers are occasionally prevented from publishing material that has already found its way into the Hebrew press.

Under the Press Ordinance Law of 1933, censorship may assume a more drastic form: The minister of interior (the high commissioner under the Mandate) is given the authority to revoke or refuse to grant a license to operate a newspaper. Thus, "if any matter appearing in a newspaper is, in the opinion of the [minister of interior], likely to endanger the public peace," the minister may "suspend the publication of the newspaper for such period as he may think fit."[10] Although the *Kol Ha'am* decision did much to defang this law, the recent case of the Hebrew newspaper *Hadashot* graphically reveals what may still happen to enterprising journalists. When, in 1984, Palestinian hijackers of a bus filled with Israelis were killed by members of the Israeli security services, the initial report by the government that the killings had occurred in battle turned out to be a fabrication. A huge public scandal ensued after it was revealed that they had in fact been executed after their capture. For its role in reporting on this extremely embarrassing story (a breach of security according to the authorities), *Hadashot's* license to publish was suspended for four days, the first closure of a daily newspaper for censorship violations in thirty years. The suspension was upheld by the Supreme Court, which could very easily have employed respected precedent to rule otherwise.

Even though outcomes are heavily influenced by the particular judges constituting the panel, one should not discount the fact that this case was directly concerned with terrorism, an issue that more than any other underlines the omnipresent Israeli sensitivity about questions of security. As Judith Karp, Israel's deputy attorney general, has pointed out, "[Israel's] entire democratic tradition has evolved alongside its security crisis."[11] She goes on: "The accumulation of years of security struggles leaves its psychological impact on the agencies of the state and the population, making it even harder to yield to abstract values."[12] Indeed, even when the Supreme Court has been eloquent in affirming the unique and intrinsic importance of these values, its acute awareness of the less abstract interest in the existence of the state and the continuity of the Jewish people has always been a prominent presence in its adjudicative calculations.

Thus in *Kol Ha'am*, for example, Justice Agranat borrowed freely from the rich free-speech jurisprudential tradition of the United States, but when it came to formulating a specific doctrinal position for interpreting the Press Ordinance Law's language regarding publications "likely" to "[endanger] the public peace," he parted company with his ideological U.S. cousins, Oliver Wendell Holmes and Louis Brandeis. Rather than insisting "that the danger to the public peace created in consequence of the publication is . . . proximate in time," Justice Agranat advanced the less "extreme" standard of "probability," which, even though it represented a significant move away from the "bad tendency" test employed by the British during the Mandate, reveals a greater deference to security considerations than one is likely to find among liberal American judges. In the course of his opinion, he offered some unsolicited advice to the minister of interior—namely, "pay attention" to the general principles espoused by Holmes and Brandeis—but in the end, it was deemed unnecessary that the minister abide by the very demanding libertarian standard to which these principles had led the aforementioned jurists. To be sure, the *Dennis* case, which involved the application of the probable-danger test by a deeply divided Supreme Court, had only recently been decided in the United States; but whereas *Kol Ha'am* has always been viewed as a progressive, visionary decision in Israel, *Dennis* was from the moment of its announcement roundly condemned in American legal circles as a retrograde capitulation to anticommunist hysteria. This reflects more than the fact that unlike in *Kol Ha'am*, the probability standard was employed to uphold a conviction; rather, it is suggestive that Israel as a political culture attaches much greater legitimacy to the claim of national security.

The 1988 case of *Schnitzer* v. *Chief Military Censor* represents the most far-reaching effort by the Court to limit the power to censor under the 1945 Defense Regulations. It is too early to say how significant a precedent the decision is, but it certainly bears scrutiny as demarcating the current outer limits of the free-speech principle in the context of national security considerations. The case also vividly illustrates the interpretive process through which the Supreme Court has come to be regarded as the main bulwark of protection for individual rights in Israel.

A Tel Aviv newspaper that was not a member of the editors committee sought to publish an article critical of the head of the intelligence organization Mossad. According to the military censor, the article was prejudicial to the operational capability of the organization. Justice Aharon Barak's opinion for the Court is noteworthy for several things, not the least of which is its attempt to place the power to censor directly within a democratic political context. To accomplish this, it was necessary for him to establish in *Schnitzer* that the Defense Regulations emerged in a colonial setting antithetical to the animating principles of the subsequent independent polity: "The interpretation to be given to the Defense Regulations in the State of Israel is not identical to the interpretation which was appropriate in the period of the Mandate. The Defense Regulations today are among the laws of a democratic state. They need to be interpreted on the basis of the fundamental principles of Israeli law."[13] Because Article 11 of the Transition Law of 1948 establishes that the law existing in the country on the day of independence will remain in force "subject to the changes emanating from the establishment of the State and its rights,"[14] Justice Barak could appeal to these "changes" as the basis for constructing a more enlightened set of guidelines to govern the activities of the military censor.

To determine the fundamental values (in other words, what has changed) that will provide the context for balancing the interests in free expression and national security, the Supreme Court must have recourse to "basic principles of equality, freedom and justice, which are the property of all developed and enlightened nations."[15] This highlights the fact that for those judges like Justice Barak who wish to tighten restrictions against the use of the censorship power, the strategy is to deemphasize the unique aspects of Israeli statehood in favor of those universal principles to which progressive liberal democratic states are or should be committed. In applying this approach, the Court went on to declare "that a reasonable censor, acting in a democratic state, is obliged to strike a balance between security and freedom of expression, and would not have reached the conclusion reached by the respondent."[16] What might have been declared had the Court addressed the actions of a reasonable censor acting in a Jewish state surrounded by unremittingly hostile Arab neighbors is, of course, highly speculative. For many, including perhaps Justice Barak, there is no conflict between the concepts of a democratic state and a Jewish state; therefore, a divergent result would and should not follow from the posing of an alternative conceptualization of the censorship question. After all, the particular security interests of Israel were taken into account by the Court in its balancing exercise; hence, there should be no grounds for anticipating an outcome other than what was achieved by emphasizing the democratic nature of the polity.

This analysis is all quite reasonable, except that it may obscure the fact that the manner in which competing interests are balanced is a function of the weight assigned to each interest. Justice Barak drew inspiration from the democratic commitments of the declaration, but it is easy to imagine a different panel of justices placing the censorship issue more centrally within the spirit of those passages in the document that emphasize the tragic history of the Jewish people and their consequent need to be secure in a state of their own. In the *Schnitzer* case, the Court's understanding of the problem led it to announce the following standard: "The question in each case is, whether a reasonable censor is entitled to reach the conclusion that, on the basis of assessment of the given facts, publication is likely to cause—i.e., there exists a near-certainty that publication will cause—severe or substantial damage to the security of the State."[17] This, as Justice Barak points out, is a less severe standard than the American prior-restraint rule (again reflecting a more urgent sense of physical insecurity than exists in the United States). In the end, it must be seen as a potentially significant doctrinal support for the cause of press freedom.

This cause cannot be served unless there is a sufficiently broad scope for judicial review to cover the authority of statutory agencies operating under the Defense Regulations. The limited nature of the Court's powers in this respect had been established early on. At least as important as its doctrinal contribution to prior-restraint law was clear affirmation in *Schnitzer* of a judicial role in reviewing administrative actions undertaken in a security context: "[S]ecurity considerations enjoy no special status."[18] Following evolving standards of judicial review in Great Britain, Justice Barak left no doubt that judicial deference in these matters was a thing of the past: "Regarding the scope of our intervention, there is one rule for all governmental authorities. They are all subject to the instructions of the law and they are all subject to review by the court, according to the normal and accepted occasions of review which reflect the legal requirements of administrative jurisdiction."[19] Thus, although the Supreme Court has no real choice but to accept the validity of all of the statutory authorizations for censorship, it now has considerable leeway to affect, through interpretation, the actual course and extent of censorship in the sphere of national security. This has as yet not affected the exercise of censorship in the occupied territories, a factor that has led some to express legitimate concerns that attitudes about what is permissible outside the Green Line will corrupt mainstream Israeli thinking on the dangers of censorship, but there is no denying the fact that a legal basis for heightened scrutiny has been clearly established.[20]

Offensive Speech

Another Israeli institution that has survived the transition from Mandate status to state is the Film and Theater Censorship Board, established by the British in 1927. Giving offense to religious sensibilities was an offense under Ottoman rule and remained so under the British administration in Palestine. After independence, the board came under the jurisdiction of the Ministry of Interior, where the issue has continued to be controversial—just how controversial may be gleaned from a relatively recent decision of the board that attracted international attention.

The decision involved the banning of the American film *The Last Temptation of Christ*. To many people, the ruling seemed bizarre—after all, countries with Christian majorities had permitted the film to be shown, albeit in the face of considerable protest. In an interview with me, the chairman of the board defended the decision in terms of the uniqueness of the Israeli social and historical predicament.[21] Thus, Israel and, in particular, Jerusalem hold a special significance for Christians as well as for Jews. Therefore, it was especially important, he claimed, that public authority be cognizant of the various communities for whom the region meant so much. He also argued that the unique historical suffering of the Jewish people should make them acutely sensitive to material that (in the view of the board) deeply offends the core beliefs of a religious minority. He acknowledged that in the United States, these arguments would carry much less weight, but in Israel, a credible claim can and should be made for the state to guarantee that the public space exhibit respect for each of the varying cultures that compose the overall society. In touching on two significant bases (cultural integrity and the poignant history of the Jewish people), the chairman was implicitly drawing upon themes given prominence in the Declaration of Independence—themes, however, that do not necessarily produce liberal constitutional results. Indeed, this cultural pluralist perspective, in a sense, justifies censorship, whereas in the United States, the dominant model of liberal or individualist pluralism requires that the public space be available for essentially unconstrained verbal free-for-all, even if this may result in unfair and perhaps tasteless attacks upon one's most treasured affiliations.[22]

The chairman's claim did not impress the Supreme Court, which could see no logic in the fact that a film that had been screened widely in Christian countries should be banned in Israel because it had been deemed offensive to Christian sensibilities. It overturned the board's ruling on the ground that there was no evidence of a "near certainty" of a serious impairment of the public order. This is not to say, according to the Court, that the board acted improperly in seeking to protect religious sensibilities; there was, after all, a section of the Penal Law that made it a crime to offend religious feelings. However, the justices in their various opinions agreed that a restriction on free speech could not proceed absent clear evidence of likely damage to a legitimate countervailing public interest.

This decision was followed in a matter of weeks by a further constriction of the powers of the Censorship Board. The Knesset eliminated (for a two-year trial period that is likely to remain permanent) the board's authority to censor plays, a move that is perhaps best understood as a concession to the legal realities created by previous Supreme Court decisions in support of freedom of expression. In the leading case of *Laor* v. *Film and Theatre Censorship Board*, decided in 1986, the Court succeeded in convincing many in the legal and artistic communities that theater censorship had become a practical impossibility. In this, they were following the lead of the justices themselves; as one of them said of the principal opinion of Justice Barak, "[I]t raises the question whether there is any point any more for the existence of censorship on plays, and perhaps the legislature should consider this."[23]

Now that the legislature has considered censorship of the arts, it is fair to say that this type of censorship is no longer very significant. The dominant issue raised in the arts arena—the liability that can appropriately be attached to offensive expression—extends well beyond the domain of creative expression. In democratic polities, the protective ambit of the free-speech principle is most assiduously employed to shield political speech, and it is here that the question of offensive or abusive expression is especially important to understanding the Israeli experience with censorship. That experience is closely bound up with the question of how far a constitutional order must go in tolerating expressive activities that have as their principal purpose the vilification of particular groups in the society. The Supreme Court has confronted the question in a number of settings and cases—the common denominator in which has almost always bee the late Rabbi Meir Kahane, whose racist agenda was usually accompanied by highly provocative acts directed toward Arabs in Israel and the territories. One such case involved the appeal of a ruling by the Israel Broadcasting Authority (IBA) to ban Kahane from the airwaves.

The ruling was overturned by the Court in an opinion by Justice Barak that contained this observation: "A near certainty that the feelings of a religious or ethnic minority be really and harshly hurt, by publication of a deviant speech, is enough to justify limiting that speech. Therefore . . . it would be justified to prevent a demonstration of Petitioners, if it intends to pass through Arab populated areas, and a near certainty of a real injury exists because of the racist content of Petitioners' message."[24] To appreciate the implications of this remark, it may be instructive to contrast it with an observation from the *Skokie* case, in which a United States district court ruled on the rights of a group of Nazis to march through a Jewish neighborhood: "We live in a society that is very conscious of racial and religious differences, in which open discussion of important public issues will often require reference to racial and religious groups, often in terms which members of those groups, and others would consider insulting and degrading." And a later U.S. court decision pointed out that "the [Supreme] Court has made it clear that speech may not be punished merely because it offends."[25]

What are the alternative perspectives indicated in these excerpts? The district court opinion acknowledges the heterogeneous character of American society and, following Supreme Court precedent, concludes in effect that this very heterogeneity precludes punishment of speech that may be offensive to particular groups. To protect discussion of public issues, it is necessary to tolerate insulting and degrading speech because it is the inevitable by-product of public discourse in a diverse and open society. The decision is designed to safeguard the interests of both the individual (in this case the Nazi Frank Collin)and the society as a whole, the latter being the beneficiary of an unrestricted, uninhibited discussion of matters affecting the public interest. However, groups are not recognized as having a corporate interest that commands judicial or constitutional consideration.[26]

Justice Barak's opinion in the *Broadcasting* case also acknowledges social heterogeneity, but for him Israeli law appears to entail a different result from this reality. Thus, the sensitivities of minority groups are a factor to consider in any final assessment of the free-speech interests involved in a given case. In this particular instance, such sensitivities were arguably not implicated, but in Justice Barak's hypothetical of a Kahane-led demonstration through Arab-populated areas, it is suggested that the Court would be justified in limiting speech if there was a near certainty that the racist content of the speech might cause real injury. The acknowledgment of group diversity is accompanied by a respect for the communal integrity of minorities to the extent that it could call for the trumping of the individual's right of free expression.

The *Skokie* opinion is fully consonant with the prevailing orthodoxy of American free-speech jurisprudence, specifically the doctrine of content or viewpoint neutrality. Thus, "the first amendment gives speech and related forms of expression virtually absolute protection against restriction based upon the dangerous character of the worlds."[27] Furthermore, "the decision not to allow free speech protection to turn on the point of view adopted by the speaker goes to the epistemological and political cores of free speech theory."[28] Indeed, so strong is the American antipathy to prohibition on the basis of content that the United States, at international conventions on racial discrimination, has refused to accept any agreements that would require it to ban racist speech in contravention of the First Amendment. In contrast, Israel's approach is in this respect much more similar to that of most Western European countries in having laws against incitement to racial hatred. There is, for example, an Israeli law stipulating that (1) whoever publishes anything, intending to incite to racism, shall serve five years in prison, and (2) it does not matter if the publication led to racism or whether it was true or not.[29] In addition, an amendment to the basic law on the Knesset now bans any political party from participating in elections to the Knesset if that party advocates as part of its program incitement to racism.[30]

The criminal law against racist incitement was well known to the IBA, which had ample reason to believe that given the opportunity to disseminate his views through the airwaves, Kahane would engage in illegal speech and that it too might then be susceptible to criminal liability. Where the IBA erred was in its blanket exclusion of Kahane (not including news coverage of his activities), so that even in the unlikely event that he might be interested in airing a perfectly legitimate message, he would not be permitted to have that opportunity. All three justices agreed that this exceeded the IBA's authority, but as an editorial in the *Jerusalem Post* put it, the Court left "the central issue unresolved: is enunciation of racist doctrine itself sufficient ground for denial of access to the state media, or must it pass a pragmatic test of its likely baneful impact in every instance before it is so declared?"[31]

On this critical matter, there was division on the Court—a division that speaks to the current state of uncertainty about the limits of political censorship in Israel. To the extent that the Court follows the American approach, in which the racist content of someone's speech does not, standing alone, render it unprotected, the prior-restraint censorship of an institution like the IBA is illegitimate. Thus, it is noteworthy that Justice Barak, who maintained that the IBA could not impose a policy of excluding the broadcast of racist views and sentiments on the basis of content alone, cited eighteen American cases and fourteen scholarly works. His position was criticized by Justice Gabriel Bach, usually a jurisprudential ally, who was perplexed by his colleague's "near certainty" test for racist speech. "Can racist incitement somehow *not injure* the feelings of the public, or at least that part of the public, it is levelled at? And that not just with 'near certainty,' which would be enough to ban it, but with *absolute certainty?* Therefore, it seems to me that including publication of racial incitement in the list of topics protected by the principle of freedom of expression is unjustified and artificial" (emphasis added).[32] In short, according to Justice Bach, the type of racist speech Kahane was known for should be categorized as unprotected speech.

In the United States, even an absolute certainty that injury would occur to the public's feelings would not justify a restriction on speech. It has already been argued that Justice Barak's recognition of this sort of constitutionally significant injury is reflective of differences in the respective pluralist visions embodied in the America and Israeli regimes. Justice Bach's criticism then amounts to this: Given the legislative determination that racist incitement is criminal behavior (even if it does not lead to racism), it follows that in Israeli law, such expression falls outside the protective reach of the free-speech principle. This means that censorship on the basis of racist content is not only permissible but may actually be consistent with the will of the Knesset, the only legitimate lawmaking authority. Therefore, the Supreme Court has an obligation to enforce the understanding of free expression (and its implications for censorship) mandated by the legislature, not the Court's set of principles. In short, the resolution of the debate over this kind of censorship is inescapably entwined in another unresolved debate, the extent of the Court's rulemaking power in exercising judicial review.

Justice Barak's opinion does not explicitly challenge the principle of legislative supremacy; in fact he rather straightforwardly accepts it: "[N]o constitutional provision determining the permissible limits on freedom of speech has yet been enacted. Therefore, every law limiting freedom of speech is constitutionally valid."[33] But as Justice Bach's opinion makes clear, the law on racist incitement clearly places public authority in a position in which it cannot help but restrict expression on the basis of content. In other words it blatantly challenges the doctrine of viewpoint neutrality. Some may see the law as a violation of the spirit of Israeli democracy—particularly because the prohibition does not specify a need to demonstrate a near certainty of a danger to the public order—but the law is as valid as any other legislation that might be thought to embody the essence of that spirit. Justice Barak's strategy is not to attack the validity of this law but to argue that the IBA cannot hide behind it to justify a policy of prior restraint. It is bound only by its specific grant of authority.

The Israel Broadcasting Authority operates under a statutory mandate enacted by the Knesset in 1965. Among the roles prescribed for it is furthering "the aims of public education," which include the advancement of "a society based on liberty, equality, tolerance, mutual aid and love of neighbors."[34] However, another section affirms that "the authority will ensure that the broadcasts will properly reflect the various views and opinions prevailing in the public and broadcast trustworthy information." What, then, is the obligation of the IBA with regard to the opinions of those who express an ugly hatred of their neighbors? For Justice Barak this ambiguity can be resolved only through an inquiry into the basic principles of the legal system, beginning with Justice Agranat's premise in *Kol Ha'am* that Israel is a democratic state. From this it follows, according to the justice, that a society based on liberty must accord a special place to freedom of speech and that a society that values equality and tolerance must be tolerant of views that promote intolerance.

"Democracy is based on tolerance."[35] As we have seen, this can mean either that such a regime must tolerate all opinions or that it must do something about opinions that are intolerant. The choice depends upon what we mean by democracy. Justice Barak is correct in seeking clarification of the IBA's mandate in the principles of the polity, but the answer to this question is itself not unrelated to the question of judicial review. It is one thing for Justice Barak to determine on the basis of democratic theory that "deviant speech, namely speech that annoys and hurts, spreads hatred and anger, based on racial and national/ethnic origin—is included within freedom of speech."[36] Does it follow that these assumptions regarding democratic theory are shared by the legislature, which has passed laws pertaining to the permissible limits of speech that are quite clear in excluding deviant speech—in this instance speech with a racist content—from the scope of the free-speech principle? Might this not indicate that the principles of the polity are in an important sense contestable and that their characterization by the Court in a given case may be at odds with the prevailing understanding of the legislature?

That this should be the case is perfectly understandable and to be expected in light of the tension embodied in the Israeli Declaration of Independence. In a 1972 film-censorship case, Justice Moshe Landau wrote: "[U]nder Israeli law even a playwright is not absolved of the duty not to hurt the feelings of others. This duty stems directly from the reciprocal obligation of tolerance among free citizens of different creeds without which a pluralist democratic society like ours cannot survive. So important is this obligation, that even the basic principle of free expression must be withdrawn."[37] Justice Landau was one of the justices who had joined in Justice Agranat's *Kol Ha'am* opinion. Presumably, his views on censorship were written in the belief that they were consistent with the Declaration of Independence. That would be the case only if the interpretation of that document embraced a conception of pluralist democracy in which the interest in communal integrity was of such importance that it might justify governmental suppression of speech. In a subsequent case, Justice Landau pointedly disavowed the characteristically American approach taken in the *Skokie* decision.[38] Pertinent to understanding this rejection are the passages in the declaration that describe the Jewish people's history of persecution, culminating in the nightmare of the Holocaust. Among the lessons to be learned from this history are that tolerance of intolerance is not necessarily a political virtue and that public indifference to the vilification of minorities may entail an enormous price. The criminalization of speech on the basis of its racist content may then represent a considered judgment regarding the social prerequisites of pluralist democracy. Much of the debate over censorship in Israel is directed to the merits of this judgment.

Conclusion

This chapter has placed Israeli censorship within a context whose parameters are set out in the commitments of the nation's founding document. Israel's Declaration of Independence prescribes that Israel is to be the sovereign state of the Jewish people. That the founders of the state understood this affirmation of the raison d'être of the state to entail serious risks for the nation's future security is suggested by the declaration's "call upon the Arab inhabitants of the State of Israel to return to the ways of peace," and its "offer [of] peace and amity to all the neighboring States and their peoples." This is an invitation to harmonious relations that expresses more than an understandable yearning for a safe neighborhood; it is in addition a gentle reminder that the state was born into a hostile world of both internal and external threats.

A nation that is acutely aware of its status as an alien presence in its part of the world is unlikely to surprise observers when it institutes a censorship regimen that does not conform to all of the expectations associated with a democratic polity. It is not only the physical existence of the state that is relevant to the issue of censorship; as we have seen, it is also its existence as a Jewish state. However, unlike in the case of some of its neighbors (for example, Saudi Arabia and Iran), censorship is not a tool of theocracy. Instead, the Jewishness of the state is, according to the Declaration of Independence, not incompatible with democratic aspirations. Some may wonder whether such a reconciliation is, in the end, realizable, but the effort to achieve it nevertheless has important implications for understanding the Israeli experience with censorship. Thus, the establishment of a nontheocratic Jewish state involved the retention of limited communal autonomy for Jews and non-Jews alike. Such autonomy, it can be argued, supports political stability by providing nondominant groups with mechanisms that enable them to minimize the effects of their inferior position in the larger society.[39] It also renders acceptable, in ways that may be less apparent in other democratic settings, constitutional outcomes that limit freedom of expression in the interests of civility and group sensibilities. The protection of religious and ethnic feelings from outrage and insult acquires greater legitimacy in a pluralist environment, where groups are accorded a certain measure of constitutional autonomy.

What is also clear is that these theoretical and practical rationales for particular types of censorship are easily abused. National security may become an excuse for restricting embarrassing political revelations, and tolerance of cultural diversity can be applied in an uneven fashion to silence the expressive provocations of only certain groups. The Jewish character of the state might lead the censor to be appropriately vigilant with respect to minority sensibilities, but the censor could just as well (although this has not been a significant problem to this point) provide sanction for protecting the dominant culture against verbal assaults directed at it by an aggrieved minority. As David Kretzmer has pointed out, the Israeli commitment to a Jewish state entails the use of a concept of security that encompasses broader considerations than direct threats to the physical security of the state: "Acts that strengthen the Jewish collective are perceived as acts that promote security. On the other hand, acts that tend to strengthen Arab nationalist aspirations among Israeli Arabs are regarded as threatening to the Jewish collective. They are seen as acts that ultimately affect the security of the state, even if they take the form of political expression."[40] The presence in Israel of a highly respected judiciary, whose members find the more libertarian aspirations of the Declaration of Independence of critical importance, is essential to the development and preservation of a robust democratic political tradition. Moreover, the absence of a comprehensive written constitution that includes specific guarantees for freedom of expression underscores the centrality of the Supreme Court's role in striking a sensible balance among the various commitments of the declaration—commitments that taken together define the unique character of the Israeli polity.

Notes

1. The resolution reads: "The Knesset charges the Constitutional Legislative and Judicial Committee with the duty to prepare a draft Constitution for the State. The Constitution shall be composed of individual chapters in such a manner that each of them shall constitute a basic law in itself. The chapters shall be brought before the Knesset to the extent which the Committee will terminate its work and all chapters together will form the State Constitution." 5 Knesset Protocols.

2. For helpful discussions of this history, see Jeffrey M. Albert, "Constitutional Adjudication Without a Constitution: The Case of Israel," *Harvard Law Review,* vol. 82, pp. 1245–1265 (1969); and Amos Shapira, "Judicial Review Without a Constitution: The Israeli Paradox," *Temple Law Quarterly,* vol. 56, pp. 405–462 (1983).

3. Aharon Barak, *Judicial Discretion* (New Haven: Yale University Press, 1989), p. 266. This is a sentiment also expressed by Justice Bara in a number of his judicial opinions.

4. *Kol Ha'am* v. *Minister of Interior,* 7 P.D. 871 (1953). The citation here is to 1 *Selected Judgments of the Supreme Court of Israel* 90 (1948–1953), at 105.

5. This practice has its roots in the Ottoman Empire's *millet* system, in which those who did not belong to the dominant religion of Islam were granted authority, under ecclesiastical aegis, to administer their own communal affairs. This extended through the period of Britain's Palestine Mandate, with Jews exercising considerable control over the internal affairs of their community. See, in particular, Dan Horowitz, "Before the State: Communal Politics in Palestine Under the Mandate," in Baruch Kimmerling, *The Israeli State and Society: Boundaries and Frontiers* (Albany: State University of New York Press, 1989); and S. Zalmon Abramov, *Perpetual Dilemma: Jewish Religion in the Jewish State* (Rutherford, NJ: Fairleigh Dickinson University Press, 1976).

6. *Kol Ha'am* v. *Minister of Interior,* in *Selected Judgments,* at 98.

7. Moshe Lissack, "Pluralism in Israeli Society," in Michael Curtis and Mordechai Chertoff, eds., *Israel: Social Structure and Change* (New Brunswick, NJ: Transaction, 1973), p. 364.

8. Defense Regulations, Section 8, Regulation 87(1).

9. The editors committee has also supported voluntary censorship, a practice in which members (by unanimous consent only) agree not to publish information that government officials maintain would be damaging to the national interest. For this, they gain access to information that the government withholds from the nonestablishment press.

10. Press Ordinance, Section 19(2)(a).

11. Judith Karp, "Finding an Equilibrium," *Israeli Democracy,* Fall 1990, p. 29.

12. *Ibid.,* p. 29.

13. *Schnitzer* v. *Chief Military Censor*, 42(4) P.D. 617, p. 628 (1989). The citations in the text to this case are from a translation by Philip Simpson.

14. *Ibid.*, p. 625.

15. *Ibid.*, p. 627 (quoting from Justice Haim Cohn's opinion in *Street* v. *Chief Rabbi of Israel*, 18(1) P.D. 598, p. 612 (1963)).

16. *Schnitzer*, p. 645.

17. *Ibid.*, p. 636.

18. *Ibid.*, p. 639.

19. *Ibid.*, p. 640.

20. for an example of these concerns, see Pnina Lahav, "The Press and National Security," *Israeli Democracy*, Winter 1989, pp. 28–32.

21. Interview with the author, Jerusalem, December 1988.

22. For example, the work of John Hart Ely suggests the message of the prevailing constitutional orthodoxy: "The original Constitution's . . . strategy . . . can be loosely styled a strategy of pluralism." John Hart Ely, *Democracy and Distrust: A Theory of Judicial Review* (Cambridge: Harvard University Press, 1981), p. 80. From this reading of American pluralism, Ely points out (p. 116) that the system entails the following: "Allowing people to assault our eardrums with outrageous and overdrawn denunciations of institutions we treasure will inconvenience, annoy, and infuriate us on occasion, even set us to wondering about the stability of our society; that's exactly what such messages are meant to do, and exactly the price we shouldn't think twice about paying."

23. *Laor* v. *Film and Play Supervisory Board*, 41 P.D. 421 (1986), p. 444. Another Justice thought it best to abolish censorship entirely because "the rigid tests [of the Court] render the entire business of censoring plays (and films) a farce." 41 P.D. 421, p. 445.

24. *Kahane* v. *Broadcasting Authority*, 41(3) P.D. 255 (1986), pp. 295–296.

25. *Collin* v. *Smith*, 447 F. Supp. 676, at 691, 697 (1978).

26. On this point, see Ronald Garet, "Community and Existence: The Rights of Groups," *Southern California Law Review*, vol. 56, pp. 1001–1075 (1983); and Owen M. Fiss, "Groups and the Equal Protection Clause." *Philosophy and Public Affairs*, vol. 5, pp. 107–177 (1976).

27. Archibald Cox, *Freedom of Expression* (Cambridge: Harvard University Press, 1981), p. 48.

28. Frederick Schauer, "Categories and the First Amendment: A Play In Three Acts," *Vanderbilt Law Review*, vol. 34, pp. 265–307 (1981), at 284.

29. Section 144(b) of the Penal Act of Israel.

30. Basic Law: the Knesset (Amendment No. 9), 1985.

31. *Jerusalem Post*, July 30, 1987.

32. *Kahane* v. *Broadcasting Authority*, 41 P.D. 255, p. 312.

33. *Ibid.*, p. 283.

34. *Ibid.*, p. 265.

35. *Ibid.*, p. 277.

36. *Ibid.*, p. 285.

37. *Keynan* v. *Cinematic Review Board*, 26(2) P.D. 811, at 814 (1972).

38. *Electric Co.* v. *Ha'aretz Publishing Co.*, 32(3) P.D. 337, at 344 (1977).

39. This factor has been cited as an explanation for the greater stability of Israel in comparison with Thailand, both of which have had to wrestle with the acute problems associated with the presence of an important ethnoreligious minority. See Erik Cohen, "Citizenship, Nationality, and Religion in Israel and Thailand," in

Baruch Kimmerling, ed., *The Israeli State and Society: Boundaries and Frontiers* (Albany: State University of New York Press, 1989), p. 84.

40. David Kretzmer, *The Legal Status of the Arabs in Israel* (Boulder, CO: Westview, 1990), p. 136.

12

The Censor's New Clothes:
Censorship in Liberal Societies

Sue Curry Jansen

In *Censorship: The Knot That Binds Power and Knowledge,*[1] I undertook an encyclopedic survey of censorial processes and practices in the West from antiquity to the present to place current forms of state, market, and theocratic censorships within historical perspectives. This survey convinced me that censorship is an enduring feature of all human communities, including Western democracies.

Although this exercise in historical analysis established the ubiquity and intractability of censorship, it was not intended to serve as an apology for censorship. To the contrary, my ultimate objective was—and is—to try to identify the social conditions and institutional arrangements that maximize opportunities for expression of the widest range of opinion and minimize opportunities for imposition of arbitrary forms of censorship.

In the brief period that has elapsed since publication of that book, the world has changed dramatically. International power relations are undergoing the most profound transformations that have occurred since the dawn of the Enlightenment more than 200 years ago. As a result of these changes, issues related to censorship, freedom of expression, and transnational information flows are now widely discussed in both domestic and international forums. The many-layered manifestations of political and military censorships that have come under the media spotlight as a result of the U.S.-led war in the Persian Gulf, the former Soviet Union's embrace of and subsequent retreat from the principles of glasnost and perestroika, the events in Tiananmen Square, the Salman Rushdie affair, and the resurgence and intensification of ethnic and religious conflicts in many nations throughout the world raise profound questions about the conditions and limitations of flows of information and ideas in a world wired for instantaneous international communications.

I identify and explore some of these questions by (1) briefly defining the contexts, terms, and dynamics of censorships in the West, and the global implications of these dynamics, (2) replaying the "end of liberalism" argument in light of the new inflections it has acquired as a result of globalization and privatization of information resources and apparatuses, and (3) examining some of the implications of the controversies about the nature and limits of press freedom that have been raised by the wars in the Falkland Islands, Grenada, Panama, and the Persian Gulf.

Censorship and Enlightenment:
Western Traditions and Contradictions

According to conventional histories of censorship, the West solved "the problem" of censorship during the eighteenth century when the great figures of the Enlightenment (Voltaire, Diderot, D'Alembert, Franklin, Jefferson, and Madison) confiscated the domestic stamps of church and state censors. These histories valorize the abolition of censorship as the decisive achievement of the Enlightenment.

This position is so widely accepted and deeply entrenched within the canons of liberal thought that standard dictionaries define "enlightenment" as "the free use of reason," the exercise of reason unfettered by external constraints (*Webster's New Collegiate Dictionary*). For liberals, power knowledge assumes that the Enlightenment set thought free from the distortions of church and state censorship and patronage and thereby made free inquiry, scientific progress, and objectivity possible. In short, it supports the claim that the Enlightenment severed the knot that had always bound power and knowledge.

The hubris of this claim has been systematically exposed and challenged by feminist, postcolonialist and postmodernist critics for nearly two decades.[2] These critics regard this assumption as a distinctive conceit—perhaps even a definitive principle—of white, Western, patriarchal and bourgeois privilege.[3] They claim that the "reason" empowered by the Age of Reason is a peculiar form of reason: one that carries distinctive cultural, class, racial, and perhaps gender-specific markers. According to the critics of liberalism, this Europocentric form of reason became the universal standard and measure of all rationality because the West became the dominant political and economic force in the modern world as a result of colonial, capitalist, and military expansionism. In short, these critics explode "enlightened reason's" claims to objectivity and neutrality by exposing the interests it protects when it systematically marginalizes—and, when necessary, censors—the knowledges, interests, and voices of members of "other" cultures, races, genders, and classes.

These critics affirm that Western thought—including the forms of thought that have provided the auspices for the West's great scientific and technological achievements—is very much like the thought of other cultures. In this view, the models of reason embraced by the Western Enlightenment, like all forms of human reason, are cultural artifacts: socially constructed, embodied, and situated in human interests, values, priorities, and aspirations. Like their historical antecedents and non-Western counterparts, these models organize, focus, and clarify our vision by narrowing its range.

The epistemological advance and the recent critiques of instrumental rationality have opened some Western eyes to the richness and diversity of the world's cultures. This approach has provided support for greater tolerance and new approaches to cross-cultural understanding, and it may even enhance global communication. However, it also renders traditional liberal rationales for free expression (and protections against censorship) largely untenable. It exposes them as, at least in part, instruments of Western patriarchy, colonialism, and capitalism.

For this reason, social constructivist epistemologies pose profound dilemmas for those who remain committed to democratic values and to discovering ways of creating free, diverse, tolerant, and just environments in which basic human needs can be met without communities destroying one another. These observers force us to recognize that all politics and all systems of knowledge are secured by "strategic closures" of debate.[4] These epistemologies require us to confront the ubiquity and necessity of both "constitutive" and "regulative" censorships and to begin to try to articulate rational warrants for censorships that are firmly secured in—and dedicated to— the preservation of democratic values.[5] They take away the comforts of Promethean myths of transcendence and burden us with the very difficult and very human work of becoming self-conscious and self-critical about what we do when we posit claims to truth and justice, marginalize alternative claims, suspend debates, and secure systems of social order.

These epistemologies require those of us who retain democratic commitments to work toward creation of new institutional structures. They challenge us to develop ongoing forums for identifying, monitoring, challenging, debating, and, where warranted, legitimating forms of organized censorship that operate within states secured by democratic covenants. This democratic work is difficult and inefficient, full of conceptual hazards and fraught with contradiction. It neither offers refuge for epistemological purists nor provides any sure rules for conducting legitimating discourses or guaranteeing just outcomes of debates.[6]

The alternative to the difficult work of democracy is a blind surrender to the will of power. Such surrender marks a dramatic retreat from the founding principles of liberal democracy. It relinquishes citizens' rights and obligations to participate in democratic debates and decisionmaking processes and allows those who control governments, corporations, and information media to decide *en cachette* what the public should know.

This alternative is becoming increasingly common in Western liberal or postliberal democracies. The abdication of democratic responsibility and accountability that it licenses has come about as a result of a long, sustained and more or less systematic structural process, which began early in the twentieth century and accelerated rapidly in the 1970s and 1980s—a process that has affected massive transfers of cultural capital and power from public to private resources bases.[7] This transfer of resources has transformed the liberal state into a corporate state; it also changed the venue of censors' operations from courtrooms to boardrooms.

These structural transformations have been so thorough and successful that the "free market" has replaced the "free society" as the conceptual centerpiece of late twentieth-century Euro-American political rhetoric. Declarations of war can now be articulated without heavy ideological covers, and fair exchange rates for blood and oil can be determined within the new commodity-based calculus of power.

In civilian sectors, cultural products—ideas, books, newspapers, magazines, artworks, music, drama, programming, software, and so on—have all become subject to the profit principle. Economies of scale determine what cultural commodities can meet the test of the marketplace. Under this economic discipline, diversity of ownership and of commodity design constricts. Information that will not generate a profit is not produced.[8] For example, in Margaret Thatcher's Britain, privatization of knowledge eliminated poverty statistics.[9] In the United States, economies of scale have produced highly concentrated and centralized ownership patterns in information industries, electronics, telecommunications, and publishing, as well as in those sectors of the economy that supply the raw materials, control the distribution networks, and operate retail outlets for information and cultural products.[10] Moreover, privatization and concentration of ownership of information industries are a global trend.[11] This pattern is not only restructuring information systems in Western Europe; it is also providing the template for organizing newly privatized information sources in Eastern Europe.

In sum, the transfer of censorial powers from public to private trusts has profoundly altered the nature and warrants of power knowledge in liberal societies. As a result, market censorship has become the most pervasive, if still largely invisible, form of censorship operating in the late twentieth century.[12]

In the next section, I examine some of the features of emerging structures of power knowledge by briefly (1) comparing democratic and corporate approaches to social order, information resources, and censorship; (2) identifying the tensions and contradictions in classic liberalism that provided openings to development of the modern corporate state; and (3) examining the mythic dimensions of the "new world order" and its approach to resolving the contradictions of liberalism.

"End of History," End of Democracy: A New World Order?

Although liberalism has always promised more democratic participation than it has delivered, it nevertheless offers the most comprehensive and fully developed ideological justification for freedom of expression and against theocratic and state censorship. This is why it has bee the essential point of departure and prime target for all post-Enlightenment social and philosophical movements in the West that have sought to extend, equalize, universalize, reform, or restrict freedom of expression. For example, Marx crafted his position, in part, as a critique of liberalism's subordination of free expression to principles of trade and conservatism that emerged in the eighteenth century to some extent as a reaction against liberalism's empowerment of the masses.[13] Similarly, advocacy of a new international information order by nonaligned

Third World nations sought to require the West to make good on the guarantees of universal rights to free expression it promised in the founding covenant of the United Nations.

From its inception, liberalism has contained an essential tension, some would even say contradiction: a dual embrace of freedom and equality. Johann Goethe identified this contradiction in the eighteenth century when he pointed out that equality requires submission to a general norm, whereas freedom "strives toward the unconditional." He maintained that "legislators or revolutionaries who promise at the same time equality and freedom are fantasts or charlatans."[14]

This tension or contradiction is manifest in American approaches to First Amendment law. The concept of a "free-market of ideas," valorized by Justice Oliver Wendell Holmes, has frequently been interpreted in ways that conflate freedom and ownership and thereby has given credence to A. J. Leibling's[15] cynical assertion that freedom of the press applies only to the person who owns one.[16] This approach has occasionally been tempered, if not checked, by legislators and judges who have embraced the countervailing Madisonian principle of diversity and have intervened to protect the rights of minorities, including rights of access to media.

Privatization resolves this contradiction by subjecting virtually all mass-media messages to the test of the marketplace. As a result, it renders arguments for public accountability and minority access largely moot. It reduces definitions of freedom to market terms and conflates the concepts of democracy and capitalism.

Architects of this solution may not be "charlatans or fantasts," but neither are they democrats or equalitarians in the classic liberal sense. As Samuel Bowles and Herbert Gintis succinctly point out, democracy and capitalism have contrasting agendas:

> The central problems of democracy are: insuring the maximal participation of the majority in decision-making; protecting minorities against the prejudices of the majority; and protecting the majority from any undue influence on the part of a unrepresentative minority. . . .
>
> Making U.S. capitalism work involves: insuring the minimal participation in decision-making by the majority (the workers); protecting a single minority (capitalists and managers) against the wills of a majority; and subjecting the majority to the maximal influence of this single unrepresentative minority.[17]

Privatization is an instrument of the capitalist agenda and a very successful one. Not only has it transformed structures of power in the liberal democracies of the West, but it also has assumed ascendancy in the nations of the Pacific Rim and is now a powerful force in Eastern Europe and the republics of the former Soviet Union.

The recent successes of capitalism have, however, undermined the resonance of liberal's old rhetorics of power knowledge. Threats of "the Red menace" had served as a rallying point and organizing principle for Western, especially U.S., political rhetorics since their first appearance during the French Revolution.[18] The collapse of communism vacated this space and in the process, it produced a profound ideological crisis for U.S. power and information brokers.[19] It radically subverted the narrative structures, languages, and logics that had provided the auspices for Western expansionism for most of the twentieth century. This historical inversion forces those who would preserve the simplicity, predictability, and hierarchical relations of the present world order to innovate—to find new narrative frames for explaining and containing events that were, by definition, impossible under the terms of the old rhetorical and ideological structures.

Some tentative moves now under way to meet this ideological and rhetorical crisis are, in my judgment, likely to remove the last vestiges of the agendas of classic liberalism—and perhaps participatory democracy—from Western structures of power knowledge. The most successful of these rhetorical moves to date has been President Bush's articulation of the concept of a "new world order" as the centerpiece of his Persian Gulf policy. Although the particulars of this order remain vague, its philosophical and ideological rationales have been rather fully developed in an article entitled "The End of History?" which appeared in *The National Interest* in summer 1989. The author, a relatively obscure defense analyst named Frances Fukuyama, became an instant, intellectual cause célèbre. Subsequently the subject of a long article in *The New York Times Sunday Magazine* Fukuyama's piece explores the possibility that "we" (the United States, the West, the world—in that order) have reached the end—terminus and telos—of history. He constructs his argument by returning to what he sees as the root of the problems of the modern world: Karl Marx's inversion of Georg Hegel's idealism. Fukuyama rights this wrong by recovering Hegelian idealism and stripping it of its dialectical complexity. Fukuyama restores ideas, particularly the Hegelian concept of evolution, to the center of the historical process. Within this reconstruction of historical immanence, communists are no longer conceived as the gravediggers of capitalism. To the contrary, communism is recast as a regressive move in the inevitable march of historical progress—a march set in motion by the quest for individual and commercial freedom. This quest reaches its apogee and terminus with the development of a global network of free-market economies. According to Fukuyama, the "end" of history produces "a universal homogeneous state" characterized by "liberal democracy in the political sphere combined with easy access to VCR's and stereos in the economic."[20]

The "fantastic" element (in Goethe's sense) within this scheme is the assumption of autonomy in the political sphere. It is rendered plausible only by (1) negating or, more accurately, neglecting Marx's arguments and the results of most forms of modern scholarly research that document homology or structural integration of the various spheres of cultural activity; (2) ignoring global trends toward concentration and privatization of material and information resources; and (3) ignoring the fact that "liberal democracy" presupposes the presence of a public sphere that includes public resources, forums, spaces, and access. The effect of this phantasm, this mythmaking, is to provide full ideological and historical legitimacy for market-based tests for freedom of expression. It transmutes rights of citizenship into consumer rights and thereby completes the transition from the liberal state to the corporate state.

By securing the mythic groundings for the vision of the new world order within an evolutionary logic, Fukuyama hangs history on an extremely narrow hinge. Following Barthes's[21] myth can be conceived as an essential constituent of all systems of knowledge, not simply as a "big old lie."[22] Its "imperative, buttonholing character" can then be appreciated: Myth tells me, its addressee, as much about myself as it does about the world. It is speech that possesses a profoundly subjective character in spite of its apparent lack of specific marks of personal or direct address. In short, it tells me who I am and how I fit into the scheme of history.[23] Fukuyama's mythic rereading of evolutionary logic tells me that I am riding the crest of history—that all history was mere preparation for this epic moment. This logic positions my nation and my time—and by extension me—at the center of history. The enemy "other" of this mythic system consists of all forces, domestic and foreign, that reside outside of the discipline of the marketplace because these forces are by definition inferior, lower, and regressive. Like democracy, they are difficult, slow, messy, inefficient, full of conceptual hazards, and fraught with contradiction. Eliminating these forces is not only logical within the terms of an evolutionary system but also natural and inevitable. In sum, Fukuyama's solution to the crisis restores America's position at the center of history by making the United States the architect and heir of the new world order; it also renews the U.S. warrant for economic and military expansionism by affirming its agency in achieving the "manifest destiny" of global capitalism.

Social evolutionary interpretations of history are not, of course, new. They have had a long and undistinguished career in the annals of sociological theory. Charles Darwin actually borrowed the idea from the sociologist Herbert Spencer, who used it to explain the development of laissez-faire economics. The eighteenth-century French sociologist Auguste Comte, who also wanted to create a new world order in the wake of the French Revolution, developed a Hegelianized evolutionary interpretation of history that bears remarkable similarity to Fukuyama's scheme. Critique of the teleological, tautological, and racialist assumptions of social evolutionary theory has been part of the "canon" of sociology for over sixty years.[24] The role of social evolutionary assumptions in American conservative thought, as well as in the advance of racialist and imperialist ideologies, has been carefully documented by historian Richard Hofstadter and by Stephen Gould.[25] In sum, the wheel Fukuyama has reinvented is, in fact, a familiar and, in some of its previous incarnations in mythic systems, a very dangerous one.

Contrary to the position of current U.S. strategic thinking, the new world order is not a natural or inevitable outcome of the ideological crisis posed by the disintegration of communism. It is a logical outcome for a corporate state secured by a "permanent war economy" and committed to preserving and expanding its global investments.[26] It remains to be seen whether it will prove to be a viable outcome.

Censorship and War in Postliberal America

In his state of the union address (January 21, 1991), President Bush framed the U.S.-led coalition action in the Persian Gulf as marking the inauguration of a "new world order." In an acidic counterrhetorical move, poet and peace activist Robert Bly described the Persian Gulf war as "the war to make the world safe for war." Bly's poetic license notwithstanding, that war does appear to mark a radical break with historical precedents at several levels. The remainder of this chapter focuses on one of those levels—one that is, in my judgment, especially telling. I review some of the practices and controversies that have developed around the issue of war censorship, or as Walter Cronkite dubbed it, "pre-censorship."[27]

Liberal democracies have always permitted censorship in wartime and in situations involving national security. Within U.S. First Amendment law, however, military censorship has been constructed narrowly. It has authorized restrictions on information about troop movements, battle plans, and other sensitive information. These restrictions have usually been enforced for limited time periods, usually no more than a few days. During World War II, the United States developed a censorship system that screened all dispatches, film, and tape leaving battle areas; it even monitored letters the troops sent home to their families. However, it was a rational system with clearly articulated rules and procedures. The officers in charge of the system were trained as lawyers in civilian life, and their decisions were open to appeal. By most accounts, it was a system that journalists found workable.[28]

The Vietnam War has been called "the uncensored war." Although there was no formal censorship bureaucracy during the Vietnam war, there were military secrets as well as press guidelines; and as David Halberstam and other journalists have repeatedly emphasized, there is no evidence that American journalists ever breached military secrecy in Vietnam.[29] In response to very damaging postwar revelations, such as accounts of the Mai Lai incident and the Gulf of Tonkin affair, that exposed inhumane and/or illegal actions by the U.S. government and its military, the Pentagon developed a profound, albeit understandable animosity toward the press. This animosity led to the creation and widespread acceptance of the myth by the Pentagon that press coverage was responsible for turning the American people against the Vietnam War—the only war the U.S. military has ever lost.[30]

Since Vietnam, the military bureaucracy has had different and much more adversarial relationships with the press. When the United States invaded Grenada, the press was not allowed to cover the action. For the U.S. invasion of Panama, a larger action that could not be kept entirely under wraps until it was a fait accompli, a pool system for press coverage was put in place. The inequities of this system and the frankly political nature of the pool process triggered widespread, if relatively ineffective, criticism in journalistic circles. As Christopher Hitchens has pointed out, the Pentagon spent a lot more time in the post-Vietnam era studying the press than the press spent studying the Pentagon.[31] Therefore, the Pentagon was well prepared for and quite facile in meeting and deflecting press criticism of its information (and sometimes disinformation) policy. For example, the military claimed that the guidelines it issued for coverage of the war in the Persian Gulf were based upon the recommendations of the Sidle commission, a commission of inquiry set up after the Grenada invasion. The commission, which met in 1984, was chaired by retired Major General Winant Sidle, who had been chief of U.S. Army information in South Vietnam. According to A. J. Langguth, a member of the Sidle commission:

> The panel's report very specifically limited any future pool arrangements to the first hours of an operation, when it might be unrealistic for the military to accommodate every reporter who wanted to take part. Otherwise, the panel endorsed the degree of freedom that the press had enjoyed in Vietnam.
> General Sidle recalled that only two reporters had violated the sensible guidelines that the military had established during the long war in Vietnam. Both violations were inadvertent; neither caused any casualties.
> Politicians and the Pentagon clearly have reasons for the onerous new restrictions they have put on the press, but they should not invoke the Sidle commission. Our aim was to promote unfettered access for reporters during wartime.[32]

In announcing the guidelines for press coverage before the beginning of the war, the Pentagon did not conceal the fact that they had been developed in response to what it regarded as "the lessons of the Vietnam War." Reinforcing the myth about the media's role in the defeat in Vietnam, the Pentagon protocols restricted battlefield access to a small pool of reporters, required these reporters to travel with military escorts, barred interviews of troops without an officer present, and subjected all battlefield dispatches and photographs to "security review." These rules barred photographing of bodies being returned from the war zone to the U.S. Military Mortuary in Dover, Delaware; they proscribed official estimates of Iraqi casualties that U.S. Field Commander General H. Norman Schwartzkopf dismissed as "not productive"; and they permitted total news blackouts such as the one put in place during the early stages of the ground war. The pool process was used to bar two publications that were highly critical of the Vietnam War and that are critical of current U.S. policy in the Middle East, *The Nation* and the *Village Voice*.

The Pentagon rules were also used to justify explicit propagandistic interventions in editorial processes. For example, a reporter from the *Detroit Free Press* was required to change his description of the mood of the first pilots returning from bombing missions from "giddy" to "proud." The lessons of Vietnam also provided the impetus for proactive, public-relations initiatives by the Pentagon to try to ensure favorable press coverage of the war. Thus, before the commencement of hostilities, Hometown Media Travel Program, a program paid for by the Pentagon, flew selected reporters to the Gulf for four-day stays with the troops from their hometowns. Similarly, the Pentagon provided the media, especially television, with extraordinary, if highly selected, visuals: dramatic video shots of U.S. missiles entering the doors of a targeted Iraqi building, spectacular video displays of Patriot antiballistic missiles intercepting Scuds over Israel and Saudi Arabia, and awesome displays of night skies exploding in deadly fireworks over Baghdad. The Pentagon also produced extensive video footage and profiles of the latest in military technology, materials that bore remarkable resemblances to television advertisements and marketing videos. In addition, it devised a highly sanitized language for describing war—for example, "collateral damage," "surgical strikes," "friendly fire," missiles falling "harmlessly" into the desert—a language that is a public-relations representative's dream and a journalist's nightmare.[33]

Predictably, most major U.S. media organizations registered complaints about the Pentagon restrictions. Cronkite, who favored implementing the kind of military censorship that operated during World War II, labeled the Pentagon practice as "political censorship." He claimed that "the fact that we don't know, the fact that the military apparently feels there is something it must hide can only lead eventually to a breakdown in home-front confidence and the very echoes from Vietnam that the Pentagon fears most."[34] Greg English, an Associated Press photographer on duty in the Gulf said, "The last time I had so much trouble taking pictures was in South Africa."[35] *Harper's, The Nation,* the *Village Voice, Mother Jones,* the *Progressive,* and authors William Styron and E. L. Doctorow and *Newsday* columnist Sidney Schanberg did not merely object: Barred from the pools, these left-leaning magazines and writers and their supporters sued the Pentagon on First Amendment grounds, a suit that some constitutional lawyers fear will further damage U.S. press freedom if the current conservative U.S. Supreme Court finds for the Pentagon and broadens the legal warrant for military censorship.

Murray Frompson claims that the prime lesson of Vietnam learned by President Bush, director of the Central Intelligence Agency during the post-Vietnam military malaise, is that "There will be no bad news from the White House."[36] There was, indeed, no bad news about the war from the president, and there was very little from the Pentagon. Contrary to Cronkite's prediction, this political censorship did not lead to a "breakdown in homefront confidence"—far from it. During the war, President Bush enjoyed the highest approval rating (81 percent) of any American president.[37] Moreover, the polls conducted during the war by *Times Mirror* and *The Washington Post* showed that although Americans were closely following the war in the media, they nevertheless strongly approved of the Pentagon system of prior censorship. The *Times Mirror* poll indicated that 57 percent wanted more censorship, and 78 percent said the military was not hiding any embarrassing information about the conduct of the war. Only 34 percent thought editorial decisions should be left entirely to journalists. In the *Post* poll, 85 percent expressed confidence in the military; in contrast, only 33 percent and 29 percent of the respondents in this poll expressed the same levels of confidence in television and newspapers, respectively. In spite of this low confidence rating, 72 percent called press coverage "objective," and 61 percent described it as "accurate."[38]

Clearly, the Pentagon is winning the war against press freedom. The public wants good news during a crisis. The president and the Pentagon are prepared to provide it, and criticism by the press of the way they do it invite charges of negativism at best, treachery at worst.

Conclusion

What may be most revealing about the controversies surrounding the Pentagon press restrictions are the grounds of the arguments used to frame and debate the issues. Except for old-line liberals like Cronkite, Schanberg, and Styron and left-leaning publications such as *The Nation*, few opponents of the press restrictions invoked First Amendment principles or classic liberal arguments for press liberty. Most arguments for freer access were articulated on pragmatic grounds; they were framed as arguments about competitiveness and unfair monopolies of information. The major television networks wartime infighting with the Cable News Network was, in large part, an argument about Peter Arnett's exclusive access to information and the viewers and revenues that access took away from network news—access made possible by Iraq, not the United States, because of CNN's smart business practices prior to the war.

The Pentagon has a monopoly over a valuable commodity: information about and access to war. The pools make it possible to deny or permit access on an ad hoc basis. Friendly reporters can be taken to interesting places; hostile ones can be left cooling their heels or can even be expelled from the pools. Favorable news reports can be processed rapidly, and unfavorable reports can be delayed long enough to render them unmarketable. As Tom Brokaw noted, it is good business not to aggressively challenge press restrictions in situations in which censorship prevails.[39] Within the context of a corporate state, these market-based arguments are the best, most convincing arguments against censorship. Classic liberal positions like Patrick Henry's "Give me liberty or give me death" do not have the same resonance. Indeed, one suspects that many of the Americans who so enthusiastically supported the war and favored prior censorship by the military would today greet that patriot's statement as a bulletin from the lunatic fringe.

The most disturbing aspect of these developments is not the Persian Gulf war censorship per se. It is not even the blank spaces in history books that will result from the media's absence from significant events. The war has ended, and the American public will grow weary of war stories. The media are already pursuing more lucrative profit centers.[40] What is disturbing is that this war is being represented to the American people and to the populations of the nations of the allied coalition (most of them Western democracies) as the cornerstone of a new world order, and yet the most restrictive form of military censorship the United States has ever experienced is a constituent feature of that order. Indeed, this new world order is secured by a fateful alliance of market and military forces.

In my judgment, the new world order does not mar the triumph of liberal democracy, as its apologists claim. It marks the final demise of any meaningful use of the term "liberalism," and it raises profound questions about the viability of democracy.[41] Moreover, these new moves come at a time when traditional arguments for free expression have been profoundly weakened.

The political and philosophical challenges these moves pose to those who continue to believe in the possibility of democracy are daunting. They require nothing less than a new enlightenment.

Notes

1. Sue Curry Jansen, *Censorship: The Knot That Binds Power and Knowledge* (New York: Oxford University Press, 1988).

2. Marx was, of course, the earliest and most thorough critic of the hidden commercial dimensions of Enlightenment philosophies. See Karl Marx, *On Freedom of the Press and Censorship,* Saul K. Padover (ed.), Karl Marx Library, Vol. 4 (New York: McGraw-Hill, 1974); and Karl Marx and Frederick Engels, *The German Ideology* (New York: International Publishers, 1970).

3. Examples of this are Franz Fanon, *The Wretched of the Earth* (New York: Grove, 1968); Carolyn Merchant, *The Death of Nature: Women, Ecology, and the Scientific Revolution* (New York: Harper & Row, 1980); Chandra Mohanty, "Under Western Eyes," *Boundary* 11 (1984) 2/3, pp 333–358; Donnar Haraway, "Situated Knowledge: The Science Question in Feminism and the Privilege of Partial Perspectives," *Feminist Studies,* Vol. 14 (1988) (3), pp. 575–599; and Sandra Harding, *The Science Question in Feminism* (Ithaca, NY: Cornell University Press, 1986).

4. Stuart Hall, "Cultural Studies and Its Theoretical Legacies," Cultural Studies Conference at the University of Illinois at Champaign-Urbana, 1990.

5. The concepts of "constitutive" and "regulative" censorship are borrowed from Jonathan Miller, *Censorship and the Limits of Permission* (London: Oxford University Press, 1962). The first refers to fundamental forms of censorship that make social order possible. This existential censorship operates at the level of founding premises; it is a pervasive feature of all systems of social order. Regulative censorship refers to specific canons of censorship; these vary in time, space, and severity. They can be amended revised, or revolutionized, but constitutive censorship provides their precedent and anchor. See also Jansen, *Censorship,* for fuller development of these concepts.

6. One of the best hopes in this approach may lie in the work of those who are seeking to develop "rational" and equitable rules for conducting legitimating debates. See Jurgen Habermas, *Legitimation Crisis* (Boston: Beacon, 1975); Jurgen Habermas, "Why More Philosophy?," *Social Research,* II Vol. 38 (1971), p. 4; and Jurgen Habermas, "Towards a Theory of Communicative Behavior," in *Recent Sociology, Vol. 2: Patterns of Communicative Behavior,* Hans P. Dreitzel (ed.) (New York: Macmillan, 1970), pp. 114–148.

7. J. W. Freiberg, *The French Press: Class, State, and Ideology* (New York: Praeger, 1981); Herbert I. Schiller, *Culture, Inc.* (New York: Oxford University Press, 1989); and Philip Elliott, "Intellectuals, the 'Information Society' and the Disappearance of the Public Sphere," in *Mass Communication Review Yearbook,* Ellen Wartella, D. Charles Whitney, and Swen Windahl (eds.), Vol. 4 (Beverly Hills, CA: Sage, 1983).

8. Schiller, *Culture, Inc.*

9. Elliott, "Intellectuals."

10. Jansen, *Censorship.*

11. Freiberg, *The French Press;* and Schiller, *Culture, Inc.*

12. A sadly ironic manifestation of this process took place in the former Soviet Union where the KGB was once invested with the authority to inspect shopkeepers' currency and accounts.

13. Marx, *On Freedom;* and Karl Mannheim, *The Sociology of Knowledge* (Boston: Routledge & Kegan Paul, 1952).

14. Quoted in Georg Simmel, *The Sociology of Georg Simmel,* Kurt H. Wolff (ed.) (Glencoe, IL: Free Press, 1950), p. 66.

15. A. J. Liebling, *The Press* (New York: Pantheon, 1981).

16. Champions of Holmes maintain that this is a crude reading of his work. They cite passages' in his writings and decisions that demonstrate that he resisted reduction of freedom to market considerations; however, the crude reading is the interpretation that has prevailed in discussions of free speech and censorship.

17. Samuel Bowles and Herbert Gintis, *Schooling in Capitalist America: Educational Reform and the Contradictions of Economic Life* (New York: Basic Books, 1976), p. 56.

18. Even Abraham Lincoln's alliances with the laboring classes fell under suspicion for this reason during his presidential campaign.

19. Julian Hallidan, Sue Curry Jansen, and James Schneider, "The Threat of Peace: Framing the Crisis in Eastern Europe" in *Media, Crisis and Democracy*, Marc Raboy and Marc Dagenais (eds.) (Beverly Hills, CA: Sage, 1991).

20. Frances Fukuyama, "The End of History?," *The National Interest* (Summer 1989), p. 8.

21. Roland Barthes, *Mythologies* (New York: Hill and Wang, 1972).

22. Zora Neale Hurston, *Dust Tracks on a Road* (Urbana and Chicago: University of Illinois Press, 1984).

23. Halliday, Jansen, and Schneider, "The Threat of Peace."

24. Critique of social evolutionary perspectives was already well developed by 1927 when Pitirim Sorokin completed *Contemporary Sociological Theories: Through the First Quarter of the Twentieth Century* (New York: Harper & Row, 1928). It was part of the taken-for-granted assumptions of the field by the time standard theoretical reference works appeared at mid-century. See Nicholas Timasheff, *Sociological Theory: Its Nature and Growth* (New York: Random House, 1955); Llewellyn Z. Gross, *Symposium on Sociological Theory* (New York: Harper & Row, 1959); and Don Martindale, *The Nature and Types of Sociological Theory* (Boston: Houghton Mifflin, 1960). In the wake of the horrors that social evolutionary–based theories of Aryan racial supremacy had wrought during World War II, the term had very limited currency in social theory during the peak of the cold war, although its stepchild, modernization theory, retained many of its assumptions. The leading figure behind modernization theory, Talcott Parsons, did reclaim the term in *Societies: Evolutionary and Comparative Perspectives* (Englewood Cliffs, NJ: Prentice-Hall, 1966). In Parson's version, cybernetic metaphors replaced their biological antecedents. There has been a renewal of interest in neo-Parsonian, cybernetic-based incarnations of evolutionary theory among some social scientists in recent years. See James Beniger, *The Control Revolution* (Cambridge, MA: Harvard University Press, 1986).

25. Richard Hofstadter, *Social Darwinism in American Thought* (Boston: Beacon, 1944); and Stephen J. Gould, *The Mismeasure of Man* (New York: W. W. Norton, 1981).

26. Jansen, *Censorship.*

27. Walter Cronkite, "What Is There to Hide?" *Newsweek,* February 26, 1991.

28. *Ibid.*

29. "The Press Goes to War," Cable Network News, January 26, 1991.

30. Casualties, not the press, turned Americans against the war. See William Hammond, *Public Affairs: The Military and the Media 1962–1968* (New York: Gordon, 1988).

31. Christopher Hitchens, "Lies in the Sand," lecture at Muhlenberg College, Allentown, PA, March 10, 1991.

32. A. J. Langguth, letter to *The New York Times Magazine,* March 31, 1991.

33. Indeed, one of the prime architects of the Pentagon's plan for handling the press, Pete Williams, assistant secretary of defense for public relations, was a television reporter and cameraman for KTWO-TV in Casper, Wyoming.

34. Cronkite, "What Is There to Hide?"

35. Greg English, *Philadelphia Inquirer,* February 10, 1991.

36. Murray Frompson, "Marketplace," National Public Radio, January 29, 1991.

37. "All Things Considered," National Public Radio.

38. *Philadelphia Inquirer,* February 3, 1991.

39. Tom Brokaw, "Dangerous Assignment," PBS, February 25, 1991.

40. One of the major lessons of the Persian Gulf war for major media organizations has been that war coverage is not profitable. Advertising is, of course, the primary source of revenue for commercial media, and those revenues fell precipitously during the war. As a result, the news divisions of the major U.S. television networks are not operating in the red and are, as a result, cutting back on operations. It is reasonable to assume that this lesson will affect how they allocate personnel and resources during the next major international crisis.

41. Democracy, as a market concept, is of course flourishing. Consumer sovereignty, the right to choose freely from a wide array of commodities, including commodities produced by information industries is, however, an emaciated concept of democratic decisionmaking. See Dallas Smythe, *Dependency Road: Communications, Capitalism, Consciousness, and Canada* (Norwood, NJ: Ablex, 1981).

PART FIVE

Conclusion

13

Trends of Censorship and Freedom of Expression

Ilan Peleg

In the post–World War II era, the right to free expression of one's opinions, ideas, and thoughts has become a fundamental, generally recognized human rights. Moreover, changes in the world's political landscape over the past few years have further enhanced this basic right even in countries lacking any liberal tradition. Nevertheless, even today one does not have to look deep and far to identify severe violations of the right to free expression. Even though many governments formally recognize the right of free expression, attempts, successful or not, to impose censorship and deny freedom of expression to individuals and even classes of people are not as rare as one might think. There is an interesting, persistent paradox between the willingness of governments to express their commitment to free expression and their actual behavior toward those who oppose them. It is important to examine this paradox in our changing world.

The objective of the authors of this book has been to assess the status of free expression in today's world, a world that has seen unprecedented political changes in numerous countries and even in the overall character of international politics. The authors see censorship as primarily a political act and hypothesize that censorship, in general, ought to be affected by political revisions and trends. Censorship is often so tightly linked to the central political institutions of a country that not only is it affected by changes in such institutions, but also it provides a sensitive measure—a litmus test—of the very character of the regime that employs it.

Specifically, this chapter dwells on a few tasks. First, a theoretical framework introduced elsewhere[1] is reviewed, albeit briefly, in an attempt to give the present chapter a broader theoretical significance and place the analysis within a more comprehensive context. Second, general comments about relevant changes in world politics and in numerous societies are reviewed in order to place censorship trends within their appropriate historical context. Third and most important, censorship practices in a few contemporary societies are assessed empirically and in a detailed examination of the hypothesized link between politics and freedom of expression in a variety of regime types. Finally, as I evaluate the dynamics of censorship trends in today's world, I look into the future of free expression, my macrohypothesis being, again, that the general complexion of the political scene—the regime character—will continue to determine the nature of the constraints imposed on free speech by different polities. Although I use a significant number of examples, the breadth of the analysis makes it, necessarily, abstract at times.

Censorship Trends: An Analytical Framework

The essence of censorship is political: It is the systematic control of the contents of communication by governments (and sometimes by others) through the use of various means.[2] Although limitations on free expression exist everywhere, the intensity and comprehensiveness of the censorship effort vary, often significantly, from country to country and from one regime type to another. Although case studies in censorship are instructive,[3] I as an analyst am interested in identifying patterns of censorship and characterizing different societies, not individual cases and incidents of censorship.

If censorship is perceived as a political tool designed to preserve and enhance power—in fact, as a mere extension of the physical power in the hands of governments—it could be hypothesized that there will always be a strong link between the overall nature of the regime in power and its tendency to use censorship for promoting its political goals. Thus, a highly centralized, ideologically motivated regime (of the type sometimes called "totalitarian") would tend to use censorship extensively and intensively by instituting comprehensive prepublication restraints on freedom of expression and by establishing an elaborate censorship bureaucracy. A liberal democracy, in contrast, is more likely to employ relatively modest means to restrain free expression, to define causes for such restraint in a narrower fashion (limiting them, for example, to issues of national security, defamation, and pornography), and to insist that controls of free expression must be reviewed by judicial institutions.

A fruitful way of approaching censorship as a political tool is to look at it through the prism of regime types. This prism is broad and flexible enough to allow the analyst to focus not only on governmental restraints on free expression but on societal restraints as well.

If the regime-type perspective is adopted, an extremely useful differentiation is that drawn among totalitarian, authoritarian, and liberal democratic regimes. Although this is, surely, only one out of many possible classficatory schemes, it is useful for dealing not only with censorship in general but specifically with the objectives and methods of censorship in today's world.[4] Thus, regime types should be recognized as social and political environments that determine many of the parameters of censorship: its form, intensity (how obtrusive it is), comprehensiveness, harshness, and so forth. In the final analysis, the usefulness of adopting the regime-type classificatory scheme offered here is that it demonstrates that when it comes to censorship, different regimes behave differently. I believe this is indeed the case, particularly in today's world.

A New World Order for Censorship?

A series of dramatic, unprecedented, and on occasion even astonishing changes have occurred in the world over the last few years. These changes have affected dramatically the character of the international system, particularly as it relates to the long-term East-West dispute, as well as the nature of the political order in many states, the vast majority of them in Eastern Europe. The political earthquakes and their aftershocks caused some analysts not only to adopt abstract Hegelian concepts in an effort to explain the unfolding events but even to proclaim, prematurely, the "end of history."[5]

Despite the enormous changes, it is not entirely clear if, how, and to what extent they have changed the role of censorship in various societies. The function of this chapter is to explore this relationship between the emergence of a post–cold war world and limitations on free expression in a number of countries representing all three regime types. The idea that the world departure from the practices of the cold war has resulted in the decline of censorship as a worldwide phenomenon can be treated at this stage only as a hypothesis.

It is not my goal here to review at great length the fundamental changes in contemporary world politics; rather, my focus is on revisions in free speech and the way it is treated in various societies. Nevertheless, I offer a brief review to place the analysis of censorship in its appropriate historical context.

Internationally, a series of events in the former Soviet Union, Germany, and Europe brought about the termination of the Cold War in the early 1990s. Some of the most profound consequences of World War II were reversed almost overnight—and with no bloodshed. In a quick process, the Berlin Wall was opened and then destroyed; East and West Germany were united within the North Atlantic Treaty Organization. Simultaneously, communist regimes collapsed, not only in East Germany but also in a number of other East European states. Dramatic, seemingly irreversible changes resulted in dissolution of the Soviet Union. The Warsaw Pact withered.

Along with the realignment of forces in the East, Western Europe continued to move toward growing economic and possibly even political unity. Before the USSR collapsed, the Soviets accepted this reality, desiring even a possible role for themselves in this new "European House." Furthermore, the former Soviet regime bowed to German unification and agreed to negotiate with the West a troop reduction in Europe. This new attitude, inconceivable only a few years before, reflected changes within the Soviet Union itself, some going even deeper than Gorbachev's twin policies of perestroika and glasnost. The Soviet attitude deeply affected all East European countries. Although some world problems, such as the military situation in Europe, seemed to disappear, other issues, such as the Iraqi invasion of Kuwait, kept the attention of the public in a seemingly less dangerous, post-cold war era.

Censorship Trends in the Contemporary World

The impact of these changes on the practice of censorship in various parts of the world ought to be empirically studied; it cannot be assumed. This is the function of this section, which deals with specific cases as representatives of regime types.

On the whole, it seems that the political and geostrategic changes brought with them considerable changes in the way censorship is applied in numerous societies. Nevertheless, the changes have been rather uneven. Some totalitarian regimes collapsed, bringing down with them the entire censorship facade carefully built over decades, but other totalitarian regimes have remained on course in preventing any liberalization in the area of free expression. In the case of China, after years of economic and political liberalization, the government has cracked down on democratic forces all over the land and reinstituted tough censorship. In both authoritarian and democratic regimes, developments have been significantly less dramatic.

Totalitarian Regimes

Totalitarian regimes are characterized by an all-encompassing governmental control, often through party organs, over all aspects of societal life. Totalitarianism is committed, by ideology and self-interest alike, to monopolistic control over all means of mass communication, including the written and electronic media; the monopoly is maintained in the hands of one ruler or a small political elite. In every totalitarian regime, political and artistic censorship tends to be systematic, comprehensive, and rigidly imposed from above and directly tied to the central political organs governing the society. The goals of the censorship are, almost invariably, not only to eliminate all direct political opposition to those in power but also to suppress all free expression perceived as even remotely unsupportive of the official political and social philosophy. Since totalitarian regimes claim possession over absolute truth, any challenge to that truth, or to them as representing it, is severely punished.

Recent events in world politics have influenced totalitarian regimes more than any other type. One area in which this influence has been considered is the place of censorship within the political system. However, the impact has been extremely uneven. Some totalitarian systems have gone through extremely dramatic revision of their censorship policies, others have instituted relatively moderate changes, and yet others have remained essentially unchanged.

Hungary is an example of a Communist regime that collapsed under the combined pressure of world events and domestic disturbances. The fall of the regime led to the demise of its censorship apparatus and the emergence of a new freedom of expression previously unknown to Hungarians.[6] The end of the Communist era brought with it total press freedom, with restrictions applied only to the propagation of racial hatred and antidemocratic incitement. The right of establishing a newspaper was given to all, which resulted in a large field of publications.

Despite these positive developments, the current government in Hungary is now trying to establish its own newspapers and to control the electronic media.

Notwithstanding the press freedom, the difficult market conditions make it extremely hard to publish either books or magazines. Similar conditions affect the film and theater industries. We may see in Hungary the emergence of a liberal democracy that could entail some of the problems censorship meets in the West.

The former Soviet Union is an example of a totalitarian Communist regime in which changes in its overall character had some effects on censorship but where governmental control over free expression was still substantial. The Soviet case is of special importance because of the prominent position the country held in the world and the deep historical roots of censorship in Russia. Russian and Soviet political cultures had always accepted censorship as a legitimate political tool. In fact, Lenin and his associates learned from and improved upon tsarist censorship techniques. These techniques were crafted by subsequent Soviet leaders, especially Stalin, and they remained unchallenged until Gorbachev assumed the leadership in 1985.[7]

After the rise of Gorbachev, the elaborate censorship system was shaken significantly, but not discarded altogether. The Law on Press Freedom, adopted on June 12, 1990, is especially instructive in this context. Although censorship of the press was directly forbidden, as was political interference in the media, in practice both continued. Vladimir Wozniuk found that censorship continued to be imposed "whenever it suited the government and the party apparatus," and that this control was supplemented by powerful self-censorship.[8]

In general, it seems that although Soviet censorship weakened considerably in the late 1980s, it remained a frequently used control mechanism. Gorbachev and other glasnost supporters worked for the relaxation of censorship, but the more conservative elements within the government and the party resisted their pressure. Unknown now is how the former Soviet republics will handle the censorship situation.

The case of Cuba is quite different from that of Hungary, where changes in censorship have been rather dramatic, or that of the former Soviet Union, where liberalization was significant, if incomplete. The three societies are extremely interesting to compare because, on the one hand, they represent a similar type of political system (or regime), totalitarian communism but, on the other hand, have rather different histories. Even though censorship in Cuba was applied in the same fashion as in the Soviet Union and Hungary, the Castro regime has not been affected by the geopolitical forces that have relaxed censorship in other totalitarian states. In fact, the Cuban government seems to have intensified its control over free expression. The trend is toward more, rather than less, censorship, possibly due to the fear of popular opposition on the part of the Castro regime.

The communications industry as a whole continues to be owned, controlled, and closely supervised by the Cuban government. Moreover, the government controls the livelihood of writers and has not shown restraint in using the penalty system against those it perceives as its opponents. Castro's crisp position—"Within the Revolution, everything; against the Revolution, nothing!"[9]—is as much a part of Cuba's political reality today as it has been for over thirty years. There can be no question that the revolution, as defined by the Cuban government and, finally, by Castro himself, continues to be much more important than free expression. The Cuban Communist Party continues to be committed to the creation of a new type of individual. The control over all means of communication is an instrument to bring about this all-encompassing vision.

Not only the objectives but also the methods of censorship in Cuba have remained quite stable and inflexible. Monopoly over all the media is the cornerstone of Castro's censorship regime, as is the sure and severe punishment of all violators of restrictions on free expression. The poet Tania Diaz, an organizer of a human rights group in Cuba, was arrested in March 1990 and forced to confess on television that she had been manipulated by American diplomats.[10]

Roger Reed concludes that "the campaign against dissent in Cuba shows no sign of abating."[11] In his chapter, he documented a series of cases indicating that Cuban courts continue to impose stiff sentences on those who dare break the censorship laws. Yet, Reed notes, journalists and writers have not been assassinated in Cuba (unlike in other Latin American countries such as Colombia, El Salvador, and Peru).

One method by which Castro's regime controls information is to deny all Cubans access to foreign newspapers, magazines, and books that might challenge the official line. In fact, the ban on the circulation of periodicals has been expanded over the past few years: it even included a few former Soviet periodicals. On the whole, Havana did not follow Moscow's liberalization, let alone the Hungarian model.

Authoritarian Systems

In general, there has been much less activity in the area of free expression in countries ruled by authoritarian regimes than in countries governed by totalitarianism or liberal democracy. The reasons for this conclusion are not immediately clear, but it seems they relate to the very essence of the regime in question and to the place of free expression in that regime. In a liberal democracy, free expression is a sacred principle. Yet it is a fundamental right constantly challenged because it is in competition with other rights, societal values and needs, and even constitutional principles. Thus, free expression is often constrained by the need (or perceived need) for national security, protection of individuals' reputations, moral considerations, and so forth. The right of free expression in liberal society is so absolute and is used so widely (and, if you will, boldly) that it is bound to be under constant public scrutiny.

In totalitarian regimes of the type that prevailed in the former USSR and in Eastern Europe, free expression is also intimately linked to the very essence of the political system; the regime cannot survive without comprehensive censorship on an ongoing basis. Therefore, once the regime is shaken—as has happened in most communist states over the last few years—censorship, including its character and its bounds, becomes a major bone of contention. Thus, there is a high level of activity related to free expression.

In many authoritarian countries (although not in all), censorship is a more subtle, built-in component of the political as well as the social structure. The majority of the Arab countries are good examples for that mostly subtle existence of censorship.[12] In the Arab Middle East, several issues simply are not to be discussed by journalists or writers: Self-censorship often takes over, and direct censorship is relegated to a secondary, peripheral role.

Yet this is not always the case. In some countries, such as Syria and Iraq, writers are carefully watched by the authorities. Some use pseudonyms even when they already live in exile. Executions and disappearances of writers are not unusual. A report by the Arab Organization of Human Rights noted in 1988 that "hardly anything in Syria escapes the censor's attention . . . all media are subjected to the very strictest censorship."[13]

In most of the Arab countries, not only publication of material is controlled but distribution is also. In Algeria, many writers have difficulties not only with the censor but also with the state-owned distribution agency.[14]

It must be emphasized that even a great reputation abroad cannot save a writer from the heavy hand of the censor. A short time after he had received the Nobel Prize for literature, Najib Mahfuz became, once again, a victim of censorship in his land when the sheikh of Al-Azar published a decree reconfirming the ban on the *Children of Gebelawi*.[15] Although Egypt is not a harsh authoritarian state, governmental and nongovernmental censorship is quite common.

The situation in regard to censorship in many other Third World countries is quite similar.[16] Despite the formal commitment to free expression, writers are often the target of censorship, harassment, or even violence and assassination in authoritarian Third World countries. Although censorship in such authoritarian countries is often less systematic than in totalitarian countries and its objectives are narrower, the methods are often more arbitrary and violent.

Liberal Democracies

As a regime type, liberal democracies are significantly more committed to free expression than either totalitarian or authoritarian governments. Nevertheless, limitations on free expression are not uncommon even in liberal democracies despite the principled commitment to keep censorship to a minimum. Ironically, over the last few years, censorship occurred in some of the least expected places in the liberal democratic world, demonstrating clearly that the issue of free expression and its limits are far from being resolved.

In view of the well-established American commitment to the principle of free expression and the leadership position of the United States in the world, the U.S. case is of special importance as a barometer for free expression among liberal democracies (and in the world at large). The American reputation for protecting free speech was recently strengthened when the Supreme Court held that the burning of an American flag, as a form of political protest, was constitutionally protected free speech, embodied in the First Amendment to the U.S. Constitution.[17]

Despite this remarkable decision, the American system of free expression has seen a number of important setbacks for and challenges to free speech as of late:

(1) U.S. courts have been increasingly willing to allow governmental agencies to close off any type of government property as a place for expressive conduct;[18] (2) in recent years, significant pressure has been put on the National Endowment for the Arts not to fund certain types of art; (3) some people on college campuses have argued forcefully that they cannot freely express their views and that there is a demand for them to be "politically correct" or remain silent; and (4) during recent military conflicts, many limitations were put on journalists covering the events, as occurred during the Persian Gulf war and the previous conflicts in Grenada and Panama.

The tension between a traditional commitment to free expression, on the one hand, and its full-fledged applicability in real life, on the other hand, has plagued not only the United States but also Israel. The Israeli case is also an interesting one, because Israel lacks a written constitution and has a particularly difficult security dilemma. These features could result in a significant censorship problem, and indeed, Israel has had its share of difficulties over the past few years.

In 1984, the Israeli newspaper *Hadashot* revealed that three Palestinians captured by the security services in a terrorist incident were executed after their capture, despite the government's report that the killing occurred in battle. As a result of this report, defined by the authorities as a breach of security, *Hadashot's* license to publish was suspended for four days, a decision upheld by the Israeli Supreme Court. This action, the first closing of a daily newspaper for censorship violation in thirty years, could be seen as a clear warning to journalists and publishers.

Nevertheless, the direction of decisions on free expression has not been necessarily toward more restraint; often it has been in the direction of a more liberal stance. In a 1988 case, *Schnitzer* v. *Chief Military Censor,* Israel's High Court of Justice tried to limit the censor's power under the 1945 Defense Regulations. In its ruling, the Court emphasized that "a reasonable censor, acting in a democratic state, is obliged to strike a balance between security and freedom of expression," which, according to the Court, was not done in this case.[19] The Court stated that the banning of a publication must be based on a reasonable assertion that the publication of the report is likely to cause severe or substantial damage to the security of the state. Gary Jacobsohn interprets the Court's decision as indicating that it now has "considerable leeway to affect, through interpretation, the actual course and extent of censorship in the sphere of national security," even though the Court "has no real choice but to accept all statutory authorizations for censorship."[20]

In the sphere of offensive speech, the development has been similar. Since the Mandate era, Israel has had a Film and Theater Supervisory Board. A number of years ago, the board banned the showing of the American film *The Last Temptation of Christ.* The High Court overturned the ruling, stating that there was no evidence that the showing of the film would constitute a serious impairment of the public order. A few months later, the Knesset eliminated completely the board's authority to censor any theatrical productions, thus significantly enhancing artistic freedom in Israel.

Insofar as free expression in liberal democracies is concerned, Western

Europe is also an interesting region, especially because developments there are not merely (or even mainly) domestic in nature but international in scope. Because judicial review is not as powerful in West European countries as it is in the United States, the role of the European Court of Human Rights in reviewing cases has become crucial. The Court has dealt with a number of cases in which governmental action may have violated a person's right to free expression.[21] The West European model is of particular interest because it constitutes the emergence of a new mechanism for protecting human rights of all types, including that of free expression. Although one can never assume that the European Court would necessarily overturn a ruling by a national court, the judicial review process itself is a powerful tool for protection of human rights in Europe.

A number of recent cases demonstrate the enormous potency of this new instrument. In 1990, a Swiss case, in which a person was convicted for releasing confidential information about court proceedings, was brought before the European Court.[22] Although the release of the information was illegal, the Court found that since the information had already been disclosed, the action of the Swiss court was no longer necessary. Thus, the European Court decided in favor of free expression.

Similarly, the Court in 1986 found in favor of an Austrian journalist who had written a critical article about Chancellor Bruno Kreisky and was fined by an Austrian court for defamation. In *Lingens* v. *Austria,* the European Court overturned the decision, demonstrating that it sees in free expression an essential cornerstone of democracy.[23] Through the years, the Court has been protective particularly of political speech.

Conclusion

Even a casual, quick review of different societies and different regime types demonstrates that, in one way or another, they all apply some sort of limitation on free expression. The widely held belief that the Enlightenment and the establishment of liberal democracy have found once and for all a permanent, satisfactory solution to the issue of censorship is challenged by a growing number of scholars.[24] The American approach to free speech, which prohibits the government from interfering with freedom of expression, seems to some scholars to allow the control of the market of ideas by private interests. The libertarian equation of individual liberty with government noninterference remains unconvincing to many.

What is crucial to understand is that in any regime there is some regulation of free speech. In no system is everything stated publicly and openly, in no country does everyone in society have equal access to the media, and in no regime is limitation on expression completely absent.

Regime types differ in many ways, but one of the most meaningful ways in regard to free expression is in the distribution of governmental and private power. One of the crucial questions is the extent to which such distribution allows human freedom, including free expression. A distribution of power that leaves all or most of the power in the government's hands may lead to draconian censorship policies, but a distribution that leaves all or most power in the hands of private interests may lead to a grossly unequal opportunity to use the media and to many biases in the use of the media. Private censorship could, and often does, replace governmental censorship; it then reflects the distribution of economic power within a society.[25]

In an effort to maximize freedom of expression for all of its citizens, each society should look for a reasonable mixture of control, some given to the public and another part to private interest. By and large, overconcentration of power in the hands of governments has proved to be highly dangerous for free expression. Yet private interests should not be allowed to control such a large segment of the media as practically to dominate and monopolize the marketplace of ideas.

Notes

1. See Chapter 1.

2. Michael Scammell, "Censorship and Its History: A Personal View," in Kevin Doyle, ed., *Article 19: Information, Freedom, and Censorship (World Report 1988)* (New York: Times Books, 1988), p. 10.

3. Roger Reed, "The Evolution of Cultural Policy in Cuba: From the Fall of Batista to the Padilla Case," Ph.D. thesis, University of Geneva, 1989.

4. See Chapter 1.

5. Francis Fukuyama, a U.S. Department of State analyst, is among those adopting this perspective. See his "The End of History?" *The National Interest,* Summer 1989, pp. 3–18.

6. See Chapter 4.

7. See Chapter 3.

8. *Ibid.*

9. See Chapter 5.

10. *New York Times,* March 13, 1990, p. A3.

11. See Chapter 5.

12. See Chapter 7.

13. Arab Organization for Human Rights, Report for 1988, Cairo, 1988, p. 95.

14. *Index on Censorship,* Vol. 18, no. 1, January 1989, p. 18.

15. *Index on Censorship,* Vol. 18, no. 3, March 1989, p. 36.

16. See Chapter 8.

17. *Texas* v. *Johnson,* 109 S. Ct. 2533 (1989).

18. *Cornelius* v. *NAACP Legal Defense and Education Fund, Inc.,* 473 U.S. 788 (1985).

19. Israeli High Court of Justice 88/680 (1989).

20. See Chapter 11.

21. See Chapter 9.

22. *Weber* v. *Switzerland,* 12 E.H.R.R. (1990), pp. 508–515.

23. *Lingens* v. *Austria,* 8 E.H.R.R. (1986), p. 103.

24. Sue Curry Jansen, *Censorship: The Knot That Binds Power and Knowledge* (New York: Oxford University Press, 1988).

25. See Chapter 10.

About the Book and Editor

From "political correctness" on U.S. college campuses to political imprisonment of writers in Latin America, censorship remains a pervasive and persistent political force in nations the world over. This collection of essays explores the many faces of censorship, placing them in a theoretical and comparative context. The contributors—who include lawyers, scholars, and an author who has chosen to remain anonymous for fear of government reprisals—show how censorship is used in totalitarian regimes to promote an official ideology and exert party control, in authoritarian regimes to restrict or eliminate civil liberties, and in liberal democracies to limit the freedom of expression. Whether accomplished through torture and execution of dissidents or more subtly through laws, regulations, or tacit threats, there is no doubt that censorship is a potent instrument of power and a political tool that both affects and is affected by the national and international political climate. *Patterns of Censorship Around the World* presents a clear and sobering picture of the ways in which one of our most fundamental human rights is curbed, regulated, and in some cases, abolished.

Ilan Peleg is Charles A. Dana Professor of Government and Law at Lafayette College. He is the author or editor of numerous publications on a variety of political and military topics, including *Begin's Foreign Policy, 1977–1983: Israel's Move to the Right* (1987) and *Emergence of a Binational Israel: The Second Republic in the Making* (co-edited with Ofira Seliktar) (Westview, 1989).

About the Contributors

Anonymous. Born in the 1940s, the author of the chapter on the censorship situation in the Arab world has resided and attended academic institutions in both the West and Middle East. She/he currently resides outside the region depicted in the chapter.

J. M. Balkin is Charles Tilford McCormick Professor of Law at the University of Texas at Austin. He has written widely on American constitutional theory, including free-speech issues, and on the intersections of law with literary and interpretive theory, semiotics, and deconstruction.

Jan K. Dargel is a professor and lawyer with a J.D. from ITT/Chicago-Kent College of Law. She has studied and worked in four countries and has successfully argued before state supreme courts, including making a constitutional challenge on behalf of a death row inmate. She is currently an associate professor at the University of Tampa, concentrating on U.S. and European comparative and constitutional law.

Scot A. Duvall is an associate with the law firm of Stites & Harbison in the firm's Louisville, Kentucky, office. A graduate of the Department of Government and Law at Lafayette College, he received his J.D., cum laude, from the Washington and Lee University School of Law, where he served as a Burks Teaching Fellow. He is also the author of "A Call for Obscenity Law Reform" in the inaugural issue of *The William & Mary Bill of Rights Journal* (March 1992).

Gary J. Jacobsohn is Woodrow Wilson Professor of Government in the Department of Political Science at Williams College. He received his Ph.D. from Cornell University and has published *Pragmatism, Statesmanship, and the Supreme Court* (1977); *The Supreme Court and the Decline of Constitutional Aspiration* (1986); *Apple of Gold: Constitutionalism in Israel and the United States* (January 1993); as well as several articles and reviews. His research interests include constitutional law and comparative constitutionalism.

Sue Curry Jansen is associate professor and head of the Communication Studies Department at Muhlenberg College, Allentown, Pennsylvania. Her publications include *Censorship: The Knot That Binds Power and Knowledge* (1988) as well as studies in news analysis, critical theory, gender and technology, and the rhetoric of science.

Gábor Mihályi studied at the Eötvös Lóránd University in Budapest. He received his Ph.D. in 1961. Editor of the English column of the monthly for world literature, *Nagyvilág* (1961–1991), since 1991 he has served as the editor of the Hungarian version of the quarterly *Lettre Internationale*. His books include *Mollièr* (1954); *Roger Martin du Gard* (1961); *Endgame: European and*

American Drama Between 1945 and 1970 (1971); *Theatre Disputes* (1978); *The Writer of Life-Fiascos: The Life and Work of Roger Martin du Gard* (1981); *The Kaposvár Syndrome: The Making of a Theatre* (1984); and *Classical Greek Drama Between the Past and Present* (1987).

Ilan Peleg is Charles A. Dana Professor of Government and Law at Lafayette College. He is the author or editor of numerous publications, including *Begin's Foreign Policy, 1977–1983: Israel's Move to the Right* (Greenwood, 1987); *The Emergence of a Binational Israel: The Second Republic in the Making* (coedited with Ofira Seliktar and published by Westview in 1989); and numerous articles on Middle Eastern politics, nuclear and conventional weapons, and ethnic politics.

Roger Reed is a journalist at the United Nations in Geneva, Switzerland. He graduated Phi Beta Kappa from Stanford University. After earning his law degree from Duke University, he was a deputy district attorney in Los Angeles. He has a doctorate in political science from the University of Geneva. His latest book is *The Cultural Revolution in Cuba*.

Richard E. Sharpless is an associate professor of history at Lafayette College. He is the author of *Gaitan of Columbia* (1978) and *The Kingdom of Coal* (1985). He has written numerous book chapters and articles on Latin American and nineteenth-century American history and politics.

Vladimir Wozniuk is associate professor at Western New England College. He is the author of *From Crisis to Crisis: Soviet-Polish Relations in the 1970s* (1987) and a number of articles and reviews appearing in various scholarly journals, including *Comparative Strategy, Conflict, East European Quarterly, Journal of Church and State, Journal of Politics*, and *Soviet Studies*. He has also contributed op-ed pieces to newspapers such as *The Christian Science Monitor, The Chicago Tribune*, and *The Atlanta Journal-Constitution*.

Index